The Essence of
Business Taxation

The Essence of Management Series

The Essence of Business Taxation

Helen G. Nellis

Lecturer
University of Buckingham

David Parker

Senior Lecturer
Cranfield School of Management

Prentice Hall

New York   London   Toronto   Sydney   Tokyo   Singapore

First published 1992 by
Prentice Hall International (UK) Ltd
Campus 400, Maylands Avenue
Hemel Hempstead, Hertfordshire, HP2 7EZ
A division of
Simon & Schuster International Group

Typeset in 10/12pt Palatino by
Keyset Composition, Colchester
Printed and bound in Great Britain by
BPCC Wheatons Ltd, Exeter

Library of Congress Cataloging-in-Publication Data

Nellis, Helen G., 1959–
    The essence of business taxation / Helen G. Nellis
and David Parker.
      p.   cm. — (The Essence of management series)
    Includes index.
    ISBN 0-13-285099-0
    1. Business enterprises — Taxation — Great Britain.
I. Parker, David, 1949– . II. Title. III. Series.
KD5501.N45 1992
343.4206'8 — dc20
[344.20368]   91-29440
                                         CIP

British Library Cataloguing in Publication Data

Nellis, Helen
    The essence of business taxation.
    — (Essence of management)
    I. Title II. Parker, David III. Series
    336.20941

    ISBN 0-13-285099-0

---

1 2 3 4 5 96 95 94 93 92

Disclaimer
While the contents of this book are sincerely believed to be
accurate, neither the authors nor the publishers can
accept any responsibility for actions taken, or not taken,
on the basis of them. The complex nature of the tax affairs
of most businesses, makes it impossible for a book of this
nature to cover all eventualities.

To Joe, Gareth and Daniel
Megan, Michael and Matthew

'To tax and to please, no more than to love and be wise, is not given to men.'

(Edmund Burke, 1774)

'The art of taxation consists in so plucking the goose as to obtain the largest possible amount of feathers, with the smallest possible amount of hissing.'

(Jean Baptiste Colbert, 1619–83)

Contents

Contents

xi

Contents

Preface

The mention of taxation is often met with apprehension and a belief that it is quite impossible to get to grips with the jargon and numerous regulations which are associated with the subject. Although managers realize that taxation can have a profound effect on their businesses, they feel forced to leave the subject to the specialist. UK taxation is an intimidating subject and this explains why so few study it and even fewer master it. The collected statutes amount to over 1,700 closely printed pages and each annual Finance Act adds further volume and complexity. In addition there are now over 3,000 reported tax cases and the courts hear a further fifty or so new cases each year. As if this were not enough, the Inland Revenue grant *extra statutory concessions* to mitigate the impact of some rules, and issue *Statements of Practice* describing what they believe to be the meaning of others. In addition, the Customs and Excise issue a plethora of tax leaflets and other advice to study, which could keep the average manager occupied for much of his or her working life.

In this book a determined effort is made to cut through much of the excess material, which, although vital for the practitioner, tends to fog the basic principles thereby making tax a mystery to most managers. Of course, it is impossible to dispense with the language of taxation altogether, but we have endeavoured to explain the technical issues in a way that is readily understandable to those who encounter the challenges of taxation in the business world.

The book is aimed at practising managers, as well as students on business and management courses at both undergraduate and post-graduate levels. It should also prove useful to those beginning a more detailed study of UK tax law and practice on professional and tax programmes. The book provides a concise review of the major UK taxes with the overriding objective of making its readers 'tax literate'. We were motivated to write the book by our belief that, while managers should always seek professional advice in such a complex area as tax, nevertheless they should be able to communicate with their advisers on a more equal footing. Also, managers should be able to identify a potential tax problem before it arises so that the necessary action can be taken. Business decisions are made daily which have profound tax consequences. Unfortunately, managers too often become aware of these consequences only when it is too late to make amends.

We should like to thank Christine Williams and Valerie Cook for assisting in the preparation of the final manuscript and the series editor, Professor Adrian Buckley, for his support. Our thanks also go to past students at the Cranfield School of Management and the University of Buckingham. Teaching them has improved our understanding of taxation immeasurably! Last, but far from least, we are indebted to our families and close friends for their support during the writing of this book.

We would like to acknowledge with thanks the permission of HMSO, Inland Revenue and HM Customs and Excise to reproduce official forms.

Helen Nellis, University of Buckingham
David Parker, Cranfield School of Management

1

How businesses are taxed

None of us likes taxation, but most of us have to pay it. Despite government by an administration which in three General Elections between 1979 and 1987 was mandated to cut the burden of taxation, taxation still accounts for around 43% of national income and impinges on most business activities. Decisions, for example, on pricing, investment, takeovers and mergers, and employment all have tax implications, and these tax implications may make the difference between success or failure. Nevertheless, tax is rarely covered adequately in management and business-related courses and generations of students leave our education system with no exposure to the subject of tax whatsoever. Even where tax is of profound importance, examination questions often carry the rubric, 'ignore taxation', as if somehow in the real world we are able to do this! Each year the Budget is watched by millions on television, but only a handful really understand the meaning of fiscal changes. Little wonder, therefore, that after the Budget statement, the media focus on the effects on the individual resulting from changes in the duty on 'beer and cigarettes'.

The good manager today is a generalist, with a broad appreciation of all those factors which affect his business. But there is a scarcity of tax awareness or 'tax literacy' in management ranks. Too often, managers, who spend hours poring over investment decisions, management strategies, human resource programmes and the like, seem content to leave tax decisions to the experts. In consequence, apparently sound management policies turn disastrously wrong when the tax bill rolls in. Often, the first indication that there is a problem arises over twelve months later, when the auditors investigate, or the Inland Revenue or Customs and Excise pounce.

Deliberately omitting income from Tax Returns – tax evasion – is illegal, but ordering one's affairs within the law to minimize tax payments – tax avoidance – is quite sensible and requires making the most of all tax planning opportunities. This in turn requires a sound knowledge of tax law and practice. The purpose of this book is to provide managers and people involved in business with a clear, but concise, guide to UK taxation so that, at the very least, managers will be able to recognize a potential tax problem and seek the necessary advice.

The book comprises eleven chapters covering all of the major taxes which affect the business world. Although each of the chapters may be studied independently, where situations arise where more than one tax may be applicable, cross-referencing is used. The book takes into consideration the realities of the many businesses which currently operate not only in the 'home' market, but which also have considerable interests abroad. The concluding chapter brings together the principles outlined in the text by looking at the payment of tax. It includes a discussion of the difference between tax evasion and tax avoidance and the significance of pensions in tax planning. Throughout, emphasis is placed on the underlying principles of British taxation and the associated legal issues rather than detailed tax computations.

In this opening chapter we lay the scene for the more detailed discussion in later chapters by providing an outline of the taxes which are applicable to business. The chapter gives a brief introduction to each of the main taxes which are paid by businesses and explains, in broad terms, the differences between the tax treatment of sole traders, partnerships and companies and their employees. The chapter also provides an insight into the tax administration within the UK and includes an introduction to the rules on residence and domicile which are important in determining the precise liability to UK tax.

The organization of business

There are three main ways in which business is carried on within the UK. These are: as a *partnership*, as a *sole trader* and as a *company*. There are also other types of business structure, for example cooperative organizations, trusts or limited partnerships, but they are relatively uncommon in comparison to the initial three. Statistics show that in 1991 there were 3 million unincorporated (non-company) businesses which demonstrates the significance of this form of business structure.

Partnerships

A partnership describes the relationship which exists between two or more people carrying on a business in common with a view of profit. The way in which partnerships should conduct their business is primarily laid down in the Partnership Act 1890. The Act specifies how partners must behave in relation both to the other partners in the firm, and in relation to parties with whom they carry out their business.

Unlike a company, a partnership is not considered to be a separate entity distinct from the partners. This means that it is the partners themselves who bear the full liability for the debts of their business. There are far fewer rules relating to the establishment and operation of a partnership as opposed to a company, with the result that the existence of a partnership may often be questionable. Basic indicators of the existence of a partnership include people sharing profits and losses of the firm and having the ability to bind the partnership in relation to business decisions.

The Inland Revenue examine the exact status of a relationship in order to establish whether a business is being carried on in partnership.

Sole trader

As the title would suggest, a sole trader is a person who carries on his or her own trade. There is no one Act of Parliament which regulates the manner in which the trader establishes or conducts his or her business. Quite often the property used for the business will overlap with the property the trader makes use of privately (a car might be an example) and this has tax implications. The sole trader has no protection of 'limited liability' which means that it is he or she who must satisfy any debts in respect of his or her business creditors.

Although the sole trader is not regulated in the same way as a company or a partnership, he must maintain records for tax purposes. These must demonstrate both the profits he or she has made and provide a system of tax recording and invoicing if the trader is registered for VAT. However, sole traders (and partnerships) are not required to undergo an independent audit, nor are they required to file accounts for public scrutiny.

Company

A company is in law a separate entity as distinct from its members. This means that it can sue and be sued in its own name, as well as being capable of entering into contracts and holding property. The vast majority of companies in existence today are known as 'limited liability companies' which means that the shareholders are only liable for the company's debts up to the value of their shares. Because this form of trading provides immense protection for the members of a company, there is a large amount of statutory regulation to be found in the Companies Act 1985 and 1989 and the Insolvency Act 1985, which govern the way in which a company must be established and run. For example, strict standards are imposed with regard to the keeping of accounts and it is obligatory for an annual audit to be carried out by qualified accountants and filed with the Registrar of Companies.

In order for a company to come into existence, it is necessary for the Registrar to issue a certificate of incorporation. This will only occur when he is in receipt of a number of documents which basically set out the trading purposes of the company, the manner in which the company will be regulated internally and a dossier containing particulars of the directors and main officers of the company.

There are undoubted benefits in being incorporated. Because the company is separate from the shareholders, there is a continuity of business which cannot be provided by other mediums. If the shareholders change this will not affect the company, and there will always be continuity of management by the directors. Another possible advantage results from the management of the company being divorced from the provision of capital.

However, there are disadvantages which must be weighed against the advantages. These concern the numerous rules laid down in the legislation which are complex and can be costly to administer. Further, a good deal of privacy is surrendered in respect of the financial condition of the company as a result of having to file annual accounts. As far as the shareholders are concerned, they obviously have rights in the company. If they are able to come to an agreement, acting together they may be able to direct the company's affairs. However, because the company is deemed a separate legal entity, the shareholders are not the owners of the company assets and therefore they do not have the power to withdraw these assets at will.

Outline of the taxes payable by businesses

In this section the taxes which are applicable to UK businesses are outlined to provide an overview of how they affect business transactions. The main taxes are then examined in greater detail in later chapters. The taxes discussed in the overview are Income Tax, Capital Gains Tax, Corporation Tax, Inheritance Tax, Petroleum Revenue Tax and Stamp Duty – which are administered by the Inland Revenue – and VAT and Customs and Excise Duties – administered by the Customs and Excise department. There is also a brief note on national insurance contributions.

Income Tax

Generally, Income Tax is payable by any individual who is either resident in, or who is deriving income from, the UK. Income Tax is not paid by companies and in terms of business organizations it is applicable to sole traders and partnerships. The time period for which Income Tax is measured is known as the 'fiscal year' which runs from 6 April to 5 April. The fiscal year is labelled with the two calendar years to which it relates. For example, the fiscal year 1991/2 relates to the year beginning on 6 April 1991 and ending on 5 April 1992.

Income Tax is charged in accordance with the Income and Corporation Taxes Act 1988 (more commonly referred to as the Taxes Act) as amended by subsequent Finance Acts. The 1988 Act consolidated earlier legislation and classifies the various type of income into a series of Schedules and Cases (see Table 1.1). Tax assessments are issued separately under each Schedule and Case (except for Cases I and II of Schedule D). Therefore, a person may receive more than one Income Tax assessment each year. Nevertheless, the rules require that annually all the taxable income received by an individual is totalled up. Deductions are then allowed in respect of that total; the most important are personal allowances and mortgage interest relief. Claims for allowances and reliefs are normally made when completing a Tax Return.

For example, the 1991/2 Tax Return requires a return of income and capital gains for the previous year and a claim for allowances and reliefs for 1991/2. At any other time, however, a taxpayer may make a claim for allowances and reliefs going back over a six-year period dating from the end of the current tax year. For instance, provided a claim is made before 5 April 1992, reliefs may be claimed back to the

Table 1.1   A summary of the Income Tax Schedules

Schedule and Case	Assessable income
A	Rents and other income from landed property in the UK less allowable expenses
C	Interest on UK government securities plus interest on overseas government securities if paid through a UK paying agent. No deductions allowable
D Case I	Income of a trade or business less allowable expenses
D Case II	Income of a profession or vocation less allowable expenses
D Case III	Interest not taxed at source*
D Case IV	Income from foreign securities
D Case V	Income from foreign possessions
D Case VI	Annual profits and gains not covered under another Schedule or Case
E	Income from employment
F	Dividends paid by UK companies

Note: Schedule B tax, which related to income from woodlands has been abolished.
*Other incomes covered by the rules of Case I include annual payments such as patent royalty income under deeds of covenant and maintenance payments.

year 1985/6. The balance which remains is the taxable income for the year, and therefore the amount on which Income Tax is due.

The rate of Income Tax is announced by the Chancellor of the Exchequer on a yearly basis, at which time he also declares the personal reliefs which will be available to mitigate the amount of tax payable. In 1991/2 there were two rates of tax – a 'basic rate' at 25% and a 'higher rate' at 40% on taxable incomes of over £23,700. Since April 1990 married couples have been taxed separately.

Schedule E

In the case of an employee, earnings are taxable under Schedule E. This form of income usually suffers deduction of tax at source, which means that the employer deducts the amount of tax owed before the employee receives his wages. This is known as the 'Pay as you earn' system (PAYE) and is discussed in detail in Chapter 4.

Cases I and II Schedule D

Self-employed individuals and partnerships are taxed under Schedule D Cases I or II on the profits of their business. The assessment is normally made on the basis of a Tax Return with supporting accounts. Case I covers profits which derive from a trade and Case II relates to profits from a profession or vocation.

The Taxes Act also specifies the 'basis of assessment'. Income may be assessable during the tax year in which it actually arose (the 'actual basis' of assessment), or it may be a particular type of income which is assessed on a 'preceding year basis'. The taxable profits of a sole trader and partnership are usually assessed to Income Tax on this basis so that the assessment for the tax year will be based on the profits of the accounting period which ended in the previous tax year. Special rules provide for the calculation of tax on the commencement and cessation of trading.

A variety of allowances are available under the Income Tax regulations but business expenses are subject to the general rule that they must be incurred 'wholly and exclusively' for the purposes of the business. Some of the more common expenses normally allowed include: accountancy and audit fees, bank charges, heating and lighting, insurance premiums, employees' national insurance contributions and wages, telephone charges and the purchase of trading stock.

Capital expenditure is generally not tax deductible. However, there are special provisions which exist to allow the cost of capital purchases in the form of 'capital allowances'. Capital allowances are available only for the types of capital expenditure specified in the legislation. These include plant and machinery, industrial buildings, agricultural land and buildings, certain specialized allowances and research costs.

Where the business is making a loss two main possibilities arise. The first is to carry the loss forward to offset it against future profits in the same trade. The second is to set it against other taxable income which arises in the same tax year or in the following tax year. There is a concession to new businesses which enables a loss incurred in the early years of trading to be carried back for three years. This could result in the taxpayer obtaining a refund of tax paid in years prior to the existence of the business.

7

Income from business property

Income derived from business property consists mainly of three types: interest on loans and savings, dividends from UK companies, and rents from properties. Interest is taxed under Schedule D Case III, dividends under Schedule F and income from land or property under Schedule A, or in the case of furnished lettings, Schedule D Case VI. Each of the Schedules provides rules relating to the basis of assessment, the allowable expenses and the treatment of losses.

Capital Gains Tax

The main legislation on capital gains is the Capital Gains Tax Act 1979 which states that the Capital Gains Tax will arise in any given year whenever a chargeable gain accrues to a taxpayer on the disposal of a chargeable asset. The computation of Capital Gains Tax requires four stages of analysis. The first stage is to decide whether or not there has been a disposal. This is not as straightforward as one might think. As well as the everyday meaning of the word, the law also deems various events to be disposals. For example, if a person loses an asset and receives compensation for it, and then he keeps the money rather than replacing the asset, he may be deemed to have made a disposal.

The second stage is to decide whether the asset disposed of was a chargeable asset'. This concept is widely defined and includes 'any right that can be turned to account'. This means that the more obvious forms of property such as buildings are included, as are more obscure assets such as options and debts. There is a list of exemptions which precludes the charging of Capital Gains Tax on various items. Some examples of these are: a person's principal private residence, private motor cars and UK Government Stocks.

The third stage is to assess whether a chargeable gain arises. The rules of computation can be tricky as they encompass a network of reliefs, the most notable of which is indexation, which exists to offset the effects of inflation.

The fourth and final stage is to analyse whether tax on the computed gain has to be paid immediately, or whether it is possible to delay the payment until the asset is disposed of on the next occasion, or indeed to postpone the payment of the gain indefinitely. In this regard there are two reliefs of particular significance to businesses and these are 'roll-over relief' and 'retirement relief'. As will be established later on, many of the rules relating to the assessment of chargeable gains are equally applicable where companies are concerned. However, although companies make use of these rules, their chargeable gains are subject to Corporation Tax not Capital Gains Tax.

Capital Gains Tax only produces a very small amount of revenue for the government (see Figure 1.1) which is an indication of the availability of the many reliefs and exemptions which are available to reduce the tax bill.

Corporation Tax

Companies are liable to pay Corporation Tax on their profits as are certain unincorporated associations, such as working men's clubs. Profits include both income and chargeable gains and the rate of tax is announced annually. Statistics from the 1991 Budget speech show that around 50,000 companies pay Corporation Tax at the full rate. Many

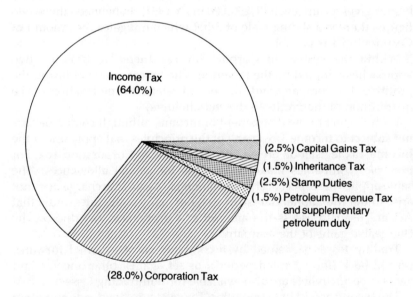

Note: The shares for Capital Gains Tax and Inheritance Tax also include small amounts of revenue from capital taxes now abolished.

Figure 1.1   Sources of tax revenues: the Inland Revenue 1989/90
(Source: Inland Revenue Statistics 1990, HMSO, p. 13)

more pay the tax at a lower rate. A company is defined as being 'any body corporate or unincorporated association'. The definition excludes, however, partnerships, local authorities and local authority associations.

The tax is charged on the amount of profit made in the company's 'accounting period' and at the tax rate of the appropriate financial year into which the accounting period falls. Where these two periods do not coincide, the profits are apportioned between financial years and are charged at the rate of tax applicable to each year. Corporation Tax is generally payable nine months after the end of the accounting period. The financial year for Corporation Tax runs from 1 April to 31 March and is known by the year in which it commences. Thus 'FY 1990' runs from 1 April 1990 to 31 March 1991.

The law differentiates between companies on the basis of the level of profits they achieve in their accounting period. If a company's profits do not exceed a lower given profit level (which for FY 1991 is £250,000) it will pay the 'small companies rate' (25% in FY 1991). The full rate of tax (FY 1990 = 34%, FY 1991 = 33%) is paid when profits exceed a higher given profit level (£1,250,000 in FY 1991). In between those two figures there is a sliding scale of relief which mitigates the amount of Corporation Tax payable.

Within the system of Corporation Tax there are basically two approaches adopted by the Revenue. The first is aimed at taxing the profits of the company and the second relates to the taxation of the distribution of the profits to the shareholders.

With respect to the assessment of income, although companies are not subject to Income Tax, many of the principles that apply under the Income Tax legislation are equally applicable to Corporation Tax. For example, companies make deductions for capital allowances. The same applies in respect of chargeable gains. Again, the charge does not arise under the Capital Gains Tax Act, but many of the rules under that Act are used to assess the amount of Corporation Tax due on the chargeable gains of the company.

Trading losses sustained by a company can be carried forward, carried back (for a limited period), or set against other income and gains. Specific reliefs are also available for non-trading losses.

The second aspect of Corporation Tax relates to dividends and other distributions, and what is known as the 'imputation system'. The system means that every time a company makes a distribution, it makes a payment to the Revenue equal to the basic rate of Income Tax on the gross amount of the distribution. This payment is called 'Advance Corporation Tax' (ACT). ACT is calculated as a percentage of the distribution and is equivalent to the basic rate of Income Tax. The person who is the recipient of the dividend is likely to be liable to pay Income Tax on the income. However, because the distribution has a 'tax credit' attached to it, which is equal to the amount of Advance Corporation Tax paid, this satisfies the shareholder's liability to basic rate tax. The payment of dividends therefore involves taxation at source – the Revenue's favourite method of collecting taxes! ACT is a vital link in the taxation of distributions and profits because, as well as providing a tax credit for the recipients of distributions, it can be set off by the company which makes the distribution against its Corporation Tax liability.

Companies receiving distributions are not liable to pay Corporation Tax on them if received from other UK companies. The tax credit on the distributions received can be used by the receiving company to reduce the amount of ACT they pay in respect of their own distributions. The ways in which companies and groups of companies make use of these rules are discussed in detail in Chapter 8.

Recently, a new system for payment of Corporation Tax was announced by the government and is due to be implemented in or after 1993. The procedure is called 'Pay and File'. It will mean that the company itself will have to make an assessment of its tax position, and Corporation Tax will be payable nine months after the end of the company's accounting period, whether or not it is then able to submit final accounts to the Revenue. If the company fails to pay at the appropriate time, interest on the outstanding tax will begin to accrue from the date the payment was due. If subsequently it is discovered that tax has been overpaid (which is perfectly possible) the excess will be repaid to the company with interest.

Inheritance Tax

The main legislation is contained in the Inheritance Tax Act 1984. Inheritance Tax is payable on large gifts or transfers which are not at market value and which occur either on the death of an individual, or within seven years of his or her death. Tax is also payable at other times when transfers are made in and out of certain settlements or trusts. In general, Inheritance Tax is not paid by companies.

The assessment to Inheritance Tax is made on the basis of a cumulation of all the relevant transfers which are made by the transferor within seven years of death and at death. When the total of the transfers exceeds the prescribed limit (1991/2 £140,000) a liability to Inheritance Tax will arise on the balance at the rate set for that year (a flat rate of 40% in 1991/2).

Inheritance Tax which arises on lifetime gifts is usually paid by the donor but can be paid by the donee and possibly in instalments. When it occurs on death, it is usually the personal representatives who pay the tax. When Inheritance Tax arises as a result of transfers in and out of a settlement or trust, it is the trustees who will have the responsibility to pay the tax. In some senses there is an overlap between Capital Gains Tax and Inheritance Tax. But the basic principle is that each of the taxes operates independently from the other and the overlap is minimized because Capital Gains Tax is not charged at death. There are many exemptions which apply to Inheritance Tax, but where a transfer is exempt, it may still be taxable as a disposal of assets for the purposes of Capital Gains Tax. Also, where Capital Gains Tax is charged on the disposal of an asset which also is a chargeable transfer, the amount of Capital Gains Tax borne is credited against the amount of Inheritance Tax due.

There are several reliefs available under Inheritance Tax which are particularly relevant to business. For example, if there is a transfer of a business, or a business interest, a relief of up to 50% is available against the value of the property transferred. Relief may also be given to a varying degrees where particular share holdings or agricultural interests are transferred.

Settlements, or trusts, are a way in which tax may be minimized. They consist of three types. The first is a 'discretionary trust', where property is held for the benefit of named people (the beneficiaries) but the trustees have the power to decide when and to what extent those people benefit. The second is where an 'interest in possession' exists. Usually in these cases the beneficiaries receive income only from the trust, with the trustees retaining the discretion to advance capital. The third class is the 'accumulation and maintenance' trust which is a tax-efficient way of protecting money for children until they attain the maximum age of 25.

Petroleum Revenue Tax

A special tax regime exists for the North Sea oilfields, but it will only be briefly outlined here since it is unlikely to impact on many managers. A royalty is payable to the government by oil companies, currently at 12.5%, on the value of oil extracted. Also, Petroleum Revenue Tax

(PRT) is charged at 75% on the net revenue obtained from selling North Sea oil (sales receipts less costs of exploration and extraction). The tax is levied on each oilfield and there are generous provisions for writing off capital expenditure. Oil companies may also pay UK Corporation Tax on their profits, but a 'ring fence' is drawn around the North Sea to prevent tax losses and double taxation relief from other activities being used against North Sea profits. In addition to PRT, since 1980 a Supplementary Petroleum Duty (SPD), has been levied at broadly 20% of gross revenues achieved on oil outputs above a given level. In 1982 its name was changed to Advanced Petroleum Revenue Tax and it is offset against future PRT payments. Finally, a Gas Levy is applied to divert to the Treasury some of the profits from North Sea gas.

Stamp Duty

Stamp Duty is a tax on documents relating to property transactions. A percentage rate is imposed on various transactions, the most usual examples of which have been the duty on share transactions and the duty on the purchase of land and buildings. Where a Stamp Duty liability arises, it must be paid at the Stamping Office of the Revenue within thirty days of executing the document. Penalties are levied where payment is made late.

In the near future Stamp Duty is to be abolished on all forms of property transaction except for the following:

1. A 1% duty on land and buildings and the associated fixed charges.
2. The charge on the premium and rent of new leases, known as lease duty.

This means that the duty on share transactions will disappear.

Value Added Tax (VAT)

VAT is a tax on the supply of goods and services made by a business in the UK. It is not, therefore, a direct tax on income or profits, but a tax on the goods and services businesses sell. It is the main 'sales tax'. Its other feature is that it is also payable on imports of some goods and services into the UK. It differs from other taxes in that it is an *indirect tax*, which means that it is collected by businesses at all stages in the production chain, but is paid ultimately by the consumer in higher prices and by firms through reduced profit margins.

There are two rates of VAT: a standard rate (1991/2 17.5%) and a zero rate. At the same time, some goods and services are outside the VAT system and are known as 'exempt supplies'. It is obligatory for businesses which have an estimated turnover of taxable supplies in excess of a given limit (1991/2 – £35,000) to register with the Customs and Excise and charge VAT on their outputs. In addition, businesses with turnovers below this level may register voluntarily.

The VAT system revolves around the concept of 'input tax' and 'output tax'. Whenever a taxable supply of goods or services is made, VAT must be added to the bill and collected by the supplier. This tax is called the output tax. Whenever a supplier pays a bill for goods or services which are taxable supplies, he will pay VAT on that transaction. This VAT is called the input tax. Traders usually quarterly pay the net difference between their output tax and their input tax over to the Customs and Excise. Where the input tax total exceeds that for output tax, they claim back the difference from Customs and Excise.

Customs and Excise Duties

For completeness it is necessary to mention that duties are levied on alcohol, tobacco and hydrocarbon oils in the UK. The rates of tax vary. Certain imports, gaming and cars are also subject to duties administered by the Department of Customs and Excise, though as Figure 1.2 illustrates the revenue from VAT dwarfs the other tax revenues. Further information is given in Chapter 9.

National insurance contributions (NIC)

National insurance contributions are administered, in the main, by the Department of Social Security. Individuals in the UK pay NIC in return for entitlement to state pensions and certain other welfare benefits. Although called a 'contribution', in recognition of their origin as part of a national insurance scheme, today NIC are essentially a tax. Employees pay Class I contributions which are related to earnings and whether the employee is 'contracted in' or 'contracted out' of the state earnings-related pension scheme. The self-employed pay Class II contributions at a fixed rate above a minimum earnings level, and Class IV contributions which are related to profits. Finally, Class III

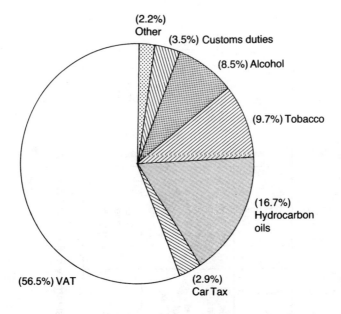

Figure 1.2 Sources of tax revenues: the Customs and Excise 1989/90
(Source: HM Customs and Excise)

contributions are made by those who do not fall into the employed or self-employed categories, yet wish to preserve their rights to state benefits. More information on NIC is provided in chapters 2 and 4.

Figure 1.3 provides a summary of the main taxes which affect business.

The international influence

Although the UK is an island, its tax system does not operate in isolation. Because of the nature of the business world today it is constantly subject to the influence of foreign jurisdictions. This influence may occur either because the business may have interests abroad, or because the owners of the business reside or spend much of their time outside the UK. British tax law covers the UK and its territorial waters. The Channel Islands and the Isle of Man are generally not included.

WHICH TAX	INCOME TAX	CORPORATION TAX	CAPITAL GAINS TAX	VALUE ADDED TAX	INHERITANCE TAX
WHO PAYS IT	Individuals, partnerships, trusts	Mainly companies	Individuals, partnerships, trusts, companies (in form of Corporation Tax)	Any form of business involved with the supply of goods or services	Individuals, partners, trusts
MAIN LEGAL SOURCE	Income and Corporation Taxes Act 1988	Income and Corporation Taxes Act 1988	Capital Gains Tax Act 1979	Value Added Tax Act 1983	Inheritance Tax Act 1984

Figure 1.3 How businesses are taxed: a summary of the main taxes

The principal difficulties which arise are those relating to where the potential taxpayer lives. The basic rules relating to a person's liability to tax are broadly as follows:

1. A person who is not resident in the UK only has to pay Income Tax on income which arises from a trade or employment in the UK or from property situated in the UK.

2. A person who is not resident or ordinarily resident in the UK only has to pay Capital Gains Tax if he or she is carrying on a trade through a branch or agency in the UK.

3. A person who is resident and ordinarily resident in the UK must pay Income Tax on his or her income wherever it arises.

4. A person who is resident or ordinarily resident in the UK must pay Capital Gains Tax on capital gains arising in the UK.

5. A person who is also domiciled in the UK must pay tax on his or her foreign income or capital gains.

6. A person who is not domiciled in the UK will only pay tax on foreign income or capital gains which are remitted to the UK.

7. A person who is UK-domiciled is subject to Inheritance Tax on capital no matter where it is situated. If he is not UK-domiciled, the charge arises only if the assets are located in the UK.

The terms 'residence', 'ordinary residence' and 'domicile' are explained in detail in Chapter 7, alongside a discussion of 'double taxation relief' (DTR). DTR credits against the tax liability in one country the tax already paid on the same source in another.

The administration of the tax system

In this section the way in which the tax system is administered is explained. The direct taxes are administered by the Inland Revenue, under the provisions of the Taxes Management Act 1970 as amended by subsequent Finance Acts. The Act establishes a structure by which taxes are assessed and collected.

At the head of the Revenue is the Board of Inland Revenue (also called the Commissioners of the Inland Revenue) which is made up of a group of civil servants within the Treasury. The UK is divided into regions with each region having a controller at its head. The regions are subdivided into tax districts and collection offices headed by Tax Inspectors and Tax Collectors.

Her Majesty's Tax Inspectors are the people with whom the businessman will have most contact. His or her office is responsible for the issue of Tax Returns, the preparation of assessments, dealing with the initial stages of tax appeals, agreeing tax repayments and appearing on behalf of the Inland Revenue when appeals go before independent tribunals known as the General or Special Commissioners (see Figure 1.4). If the Inspector either does not receive a completed Tax Return or is not satisfied that it is correct, he is empowered to raise an estimated assessment of the tax payable. The taxpayer can then appeal in writing within thirty days against the assessment and ask for the collection of the tax in contention to be postponed. If the taxpayer and the Inspector are unable to agree a settlement, the appeal is taken at first instance to the General or Special Commissioners. Appeals made after the thirty-day limit has expired will only be allowed provided that the taxpayer can satisfy the Inspector that there was a reasonable excuse for the delay, and that the application for a late appeal was made without undue delay.

Within the office of the Tax Inspector there are officers who are engaged in tracing 'moonlighters' or 'ghosts' (people who are unknown to the tax authorities). They spend their days following up anonymous leads, scanning local newspaper reports, looking in telephone and trade directories, and so on.

In addition to the District Offices there are 'Special Offices' and the Enquiry Branch of the Revenue, which are engaged in investigating larger-scale tax evasion cases and may instigate criminal prosecutions. Enquiry Branch is also likely to become involved if the integrity or competence of accountants is called into question. Inheritance Tax, taxes on the North Sea oilfields, and Stamp Duty are administered by specialist sections of the Revenue.

The Collector of Taxes, as the name suggests, is responsible for collecting the tax which has been assessed by the Tax Inspector. This office is entirely separate from that of the Inspectorate. If payment has not been forthcoming, the Collector has the power to distrain the goods and chattels of the taxpayer. This is not usually the method first adopted by the Collector, who will instead seek a Court Order to ensure payment of the debt. Integrated into this department is the specialist unit, PAYE Audit, whose primary role is to check compliance with the PAYE regulations. Members of the unit systematically visit business premises and inspect the books and records.

Special Commissioners and the General Commissioners also exist

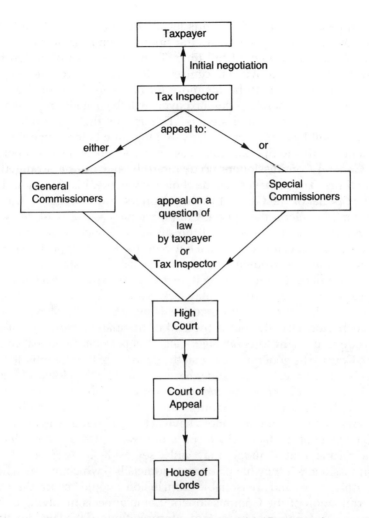

Note: Applies to taxes administered by the Inland Revenue only.

Figure 1.4 Tax appeals

within the tax structure (they have no connection with the Commissioners of the Inland Revenue, the Revenue Board). Their function is to act as independent tribunals which hear disputes between taxpayers and the Revenue. The General Commissioners are not specialized in tax law, but rather are experienced business men and women with a local knowledge of trading and business practice. They sit locally to hear appeals with a clerk, who is legally qualified and who advises them on tax law. By contrast, the Special Commissioners are tax experts and are appointed full time. They are based in London but hold hearings in provincial centres. Hearings before the Special Commissioners tend to be far more formal than those of their lay counterparts. Generally, the taxpayer will be legally represented before the Special Commissioners. This means that quite often the taxpayer will have to wait a relatively long time before obtaining an audience with the Special Commissioners, whereas hearings before the General Commissioners occur monthly and can be arranged at other times. The taxpayer has the choice of whether his case should go to the Special or the General Commissioners, but where it is evident that a person elects the Special Commissioners as a way of delaying payment of tax, he or she will be disallowed such a hearing. For 'genuine' appeals it is the choice between having an appeal heard by business men or women who have a local understanding of the difficulties of trading, or having it heard by tax experts who know the intricacies of the law but who may lack sympathetic local knowledge.

The decision of the Commissioners is binding on the taxpayer and the Inspector. Usually that is the end of the matter. However, if the decision is thought to be *wrong in law*, it is possible to appeal to the High Court. The general rule is that the decision of the Commissioners on a question of fact is final and it has been held by the House of Lords in the case of *Edwards* v. *Bairstow and Harrison* (1956) that a determination of the facts by the Commissioners can only be set aside if 'it appears that the Commissioners have acted without any evidence or upon a view of the facts which could not reasonably be entertained'. This means that a judge may only set aside a decision of the Commissioners if they have not acted judicially – which means where the only true and reasonable conclusion would contradict the determination of the Commissioners. Some appeals involving either huge sums of money or important interpretations of the law may then go to the Court of Appeal and finally to the House of Lords. The appeal procedure is summarized in Figure 1.4.

When an excessively large assessment is made because of some error or mistake in the taxpayer's return, the taxpayer is able to claim relief within six years of the relevant tax year and have the assessment revised. The law envisages errors of omission, arithmetical errors and mistakes arising from a failure to understand the law. The relief does not extend to appeals against an assessment on other grounds.

In addition to the specialist units mentioned above, the Revenue has a number of smaller investigative bodies which work either independently, or in conjunction with the tax offices. An example is the Special

Trades Investigation Unit, which was established in 1986 to fight against the losses which arose as a result of the closure of textile companies owing large amounts of back tax. The directors of these companies would then move on and set up new companies undertaking the same trade but freed from tax debt (a tax dodge known as 'phoenixation').

Another example is the Investigation Office, which focuses on suspected cases of fraudulent claims, often involving personal allowances against tax. Criminal prosecutions result from 90% of the investigations carried out by this office.

The administration of VAT

The system which has been described thus far is that relating to the assessment and collection of direct tax. As was mentioned earlier in the chapter, VAT is a form of indirect tax so it has a different system of administration. The tax is administered by the Customs and Excise department, which is divided into regional and local VAT offices. VAT returns are submitted to the central unit at Southend, but it is local officers with whom the business man or woman will have most personal contact. The responsibility for submitting a correct assessment of VAT rests on the business. The basis on which these returns are prepared, and therefore their reliability, is periodically checked by Customs and Excise officers through a series of *control visits*. VAT officers have statutory powers which enable them to enter business premises at any reasonable time and they may require information to be given regarding the supply of goods and services with which the business is involved. Where there is a dispute between the taxpayer and the Customs and Excise department, it is possible to appeal to a VAT tribunal. The decision made by the tribunal is final on a question of fact. However, as with the appeals system for direct taxes, if there is a question of law in dispute, appeal can be made to the High Court, then to the Court of Appeal and finally to the House of Lords (see Figure 1.5).

Creating tax legislation

The major source of tax law is that created by Parliament under statute. However, the courts play an important role in terms of interpreting the meaning and scope of the taxing statutes and the decisions which they

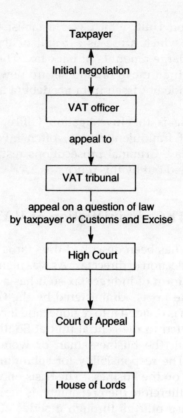

Figure 1.5 VAT appeals

arrive at are an essential part of the law. These two sources are supported by regulations under statutory instruments, 'extra statutory concessions', and the Revenue's own interpretation of the law as set out in various press releases and statements of practice.

The primary law is to be found in a series of Finance Acts, which from time to time are codified into a Consolidating Act. The method by which a Finance Act comes into being starts with the delivery of a great British institution, the Budget speech, normally in mid-March. On this occasion, the Chancellor of the Exchequer puts the government's proposed tax changes for the coming fiscal year before Parliament. The House of Commons then discusses the proposals arriving at a series of Budget resolutions which are published about one month later in the form of the Budget Bill. After further parliamentary debate and amendment, the Bill receives the Royal Assent and the contents are

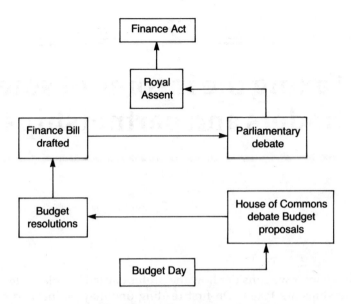

Figure 1.6 Creating tax legislation

then enacted and become the Finance Act of that year (see Figure 1.6). This usually occurs in July. Prior to the Bill being passed, the new tax rates and changes to personal allowances and reliefs announced in the Budget speech have force of law under the Provisional Collection of Taxes Act 1968.

Concluding comment

This chapter has provided an outline of the UK tax system and its impact on business.

In the following chapter we turn to a detailed treatment of the taxation of the income of sole traders and partnerships.

2

Taxing the income of sole traders and partnerships

In this chapter we consider how the profits earned by sole traders and partnerships are taxed. On first reading one may be inclined to the view that taxation was designed by someone who set out to ensure that it could never be understood by anyone without a professional tax qualification! But it is worth persevering. In fact, the taxation of sole traders and partnerships has an internal (if sometimes tortuous) logic as we shall demonstrate. Once the basic principles are understood, then, hopefully, this logic will become apparent.

Fundamental to the taxation of the profits of sole traders and partnerships is what is known as the 'preceding year' (or PY) basis. That is, the profits earned in one year are assessed in the following financial year (6 April to 5 April). Exceptions to this rule include the following: profits earned when a business first starts trading (the commencement period); when a business ceases trading (the cessation period); and whenever there is a change in the date to which the accounts are drawn up. In his Budget statement on 19 March 1991 the Chancellor of the Exchequer announced that a consultative document would shortly be issued on simplifying the taxation of unincorporated businesses. It is widely expected that this will eventually lead to the demise of the PY basis of assessment. However, as PY is likely to remain with us for some years yet, it is explained in detail here.

Other issues discussed in this chapter include: the type of income (or trading receipt) which is taxable; which business expenses can be deducted from this income when computing taxable profits; the treatment of trading losses; and the allocation of taxable profit in a partnership. Although companies pay Corporation Tax and not

24

Income Tax on their profits, the law on what is a trading receipt and what is a deductible business expense, outlined in this chapter, applies equally to companies as it does to sole traders and partnerships.

Profits of trades, professions and vocations

The profits from trading of both sole traders and partnerships are assessable to Income Tax under Case I Schedule D, while the profits from professions or vocations fall under Case II Schedule D. Since Cases I and II are treated identically under tax law, there is rarely a need to distinguish between them. Therefore, throughout the book the term 'trading profits' is used to include the profits both of professions and vocations.

In computing trading profits an 'accruals' basis must normally apply. That is to say, business accounts must include not only the cash incoming and outgoings during the year but also debtors at the year end (sales made but not yet paid for) and outstanding liabilities (bills received but not yet paid). Accounts drawn up on this basis give a truer reflection of profits or losses made in the year and it is the normal basis adopted by accountants. In exceptional cases the Inland Revenue will accept accounts drawn up on a cash basis (excluding debtors and accrued liabilities) where it can be demonstrated that this is more appropriate to the nature of the business and the effect on the tax liability is unlikely to be material. The cash basis, however, is *always* accepted by the Revenue for barristers since, in law, they cannot sue for their fees and hence have no trade debtors.

The Income and Corporation Taxes Act 1988 (s.832) defines a trade as 'every trade, manufacture, adventure or concern in the nature of trade', therefore leaving more precise interpretation to the courts. Generally speaking, it has been held that a trade involves buying and selling or manufacturing of some kind, while a profession is likely to involve the provision of a service requiring intellectual skill. A vocation is a little more difficult to define, but the courts have held actors, tipsters and jockeys to be carrying on a vocation.

Over the last century or so the courts have considered numerous cases where there was disagreement over whether the profits earned resulted from a trade, profession or vocation. On the basis of these decisions, the Royal Commission on Taxation in 1955 derived six key indicators (sometimes called 'the badges of trade') which today guide tax practitioners and the Inland Revenue on what is a trading activity.

In particular, the courts have endeavoured to distinguish trading from investment. (It should be noted that capital gains on investment are subject to Capital Gains Tax not Income Tax. When Income Tax rates were much higher than Capital Gains Tax rates this was important. It is of much less significance now that capital gains are taxed at a rate equivalent to the taxpayer's highest marginal rate of Income Tax; see Chapter 6.)

The badges of trade

---

1. *Type of asset*. The nature of the item from which the profits are derived can be material. For example, a painting might be purchased for the enjoyment of a work of art, or as an investment. A taxpayer would find it easier in such a case to argue successfully that any profit on resale was not the receipt of a trade. For example, in the case of *Rutledge* v. *CIR* (1929), the taxpayer purchased and resold 1¼ million toilet rolls producing a profit of £10,000. This was held to be a trading profit even though it arose from an isolated transaction. The toilet rolls could not be classified as investment or something purchased for personal enjoyment (or use!). Similarly, the case of *Martin* v. *Lowry* (1927) involved the purchase and resale at a profit of 44 million yards of aircraft linen. Again, the subject matter of the transaction implied a trade.

   It is worth noting that unless someone is a full-time dealer in shares, it is difficult to convince the courts that share transactions amount to trading. This means that losses through speculating in shares and similar investments cannot be used to claim a repayment of tax on other income under the loss relief provisions detailed later in this chapter (*Salt* v. *Chamberlain* 1979). The same applies to gambling losses!

2. *Interval between purchase and sale*. Quickly reselling an item after purchase lends support to the view that the transaction amounts to trading. For example, where a taxpayer contracted to resell land eight days before he purchased it this was held to be a trading venture (*Johnston* v. *Heath* 1970). The length of ownership, however, is not decisive and it would be wrong to infer that postponing resale will necessarily reduce the chances of profits being taxed.

26

3. *Number of transactions.* The more often an activity is repeated, the more likely it is that the authorities will view the profits as arising from a trading activity. In *Pickford* v. *Quirke* (1927) the taxpayer made profits by buying mill-owning companies and then stripping out the assets. The court ruled that whereas an isolated activity of this kind would normally be treated as a capital transaction, when he embarked on the exercise for a fourth time he must be pursuing a trade in mill company asset-stripping.

4. *Modification of asset.* Undertaking repair or improvement work has been interpreted as indicative of a trading venture. For instance, the fact that effort went into blending a quantity of brandy which was then resold at a profit was an important reason for the court's decision that the activity was a trading venture (*Cape Brandy Syndicate* v. *CIR* 1921).

5. *Organization of sales.* Where there is investment in a sales force or marketing and advertising to boost sales this has been interpreted as evidence of a trading venture. Returning to the case of *Martin* v. *Lowry* and the purchase and resale of aircraft linen, the fact that the taxpayer set up an office, advertised the sale and appointed sales staff was judged important.

6. *Acquisition method.* If a person acquires something with no intention of disposing of it later at a profit (e.g. inheriting property), or the property is sold in such circumstances as to negate the presumption that it is in the course of a trade (e.g. to raise money in an emergency), then this would tell against the transaction being treated as in the nature of a trade. For example, a taxpayer bought a large mansion on impulse with the intention of making it his home. He quickly changed his mind and sold the property, but only after gaining planning permission for the site to be developed. The resulting profit was held not to be a trading receipt because at the time of purchase there had not been the intention to enhance the value of the property and resell (*Taylor* v. *Good* 1974). The same principle applied in the case of *Simmons* v. *CIR* (1980), where a property company was established to build up a portfolio of investment properties with a view eventually to going public, but later the properties were sold. The House of Lords concluded that the circumstances in which the company had acquired, developed and disposed of property all suggested that it had not been acquired as trading stock.

7. *Method of finance*. Where the method of financing the purchase of an asset requires that it be resold at a profit to repay the finance, this may indicate a trading venture.

8. *Existence of similar transactions*. Repeated transactions of a similar kind may turn what would otherwise be a non-trading receipt into a trading receipt. For example, between 1955 and 1959 a taxpayer started thirty driving schools, transferring them in turn to companies in return for cash and shares. He accepted a decision by the Special Commissioners that the consideration was a receipt of a trade, except for the sum received for the first transaction. His appeal was rejected. It was held that the Commissioners were entitled to take the subsequent twenty-nine transactions into account in determining the nature of the first sale (*Leach* v. *Pogson* 1962).

9. *Profit-seeking motive*. The courts have tended to place particular importance on the motive behind the transaction. Indeed, the other 'badges of trade' can be interpreted as indicators of motive. Where goods are acquired with a view to resale later at a profit, it would be much easier to argue that there was a trading venture than where they are acquired by gift or inheritance (though buying assets in the hope of reselling them later at a profit could amount to an 'investment'). In *Wisdom* v. *Chamberlain* (1969) the well-known comedian Norman Wisdom purchased as a hedge against a possible devaluation of the pound and later resold at a profit £20,000 worth of silver bullion. Although the motive for purchase was a hedge against losses on earnings resulting from a devaluation of the currency, the transaction was still held to be of a trading nature.

Quite clearly, whether a trading activity exists or not turns on the *facts* of the case. None of the 'badges of trade' (see Figure 2.1) is decisive in itself – they are merely intended as guidelines. However, if a coherent argument can be put forward to the Revenue based on the 'badges' to demonstrate that profits were not derived from a trade, there is a good chance (though no certainty) of success. It is also worth noting that illegal activities can still amount to trading, for example illegal bookmaking (*Southern* v. *A.B.* 1933).

Profit-seeking motive
Acquisition method
Number of transactions
Type of asset
Organization of sales
Modification of asset
Interval between purchase and sale
Method of finance
Existence of similar transactions

Figure 2.1   Badges of trade: what a PANTOMIME!

Transactions in land

In the cases of *Taylor* v. *Good* and *Simmons* v. *CIR* a claim that land and buildings had not been acquired with a view to resale at a profit proved effective in preventing the profits from being taxed as trading receipts. Moreover, in a further case, where property was acquired with a view to resale at a profit but in the meantime was rented out, it was treated as an investment and not as trading stock (*CIR* v. *Reinhold* 1953).

To close what the Revenue saw as a tax loophole, legislation was passed in 1969 to charge to Income Tax under Case VI Schedule D certain gains of a capital nature arising from the disposal of land. It applies where the following occurs:

- Land or buildings and other property deriving their value from land is acquired with the sole or main object of realizing a gain from its disposal (excluding the taxpayer's principal residence).
- Land is trading stock.
- Land is developed with the sole or main object of realizing a gain from disposing of land when developed.

Following this legislation it is more difficult to be involved in land transactions and escape Income Tax (in the case of companies, Corporation Tax) on the consequences. The legislation also extends to the disposal of property deriving its value from land, namely settled property including land, or a shareholding in a company or an interest in a partnership which owns land.

Business receipts which are taxable

All receipts from a trading activity (or profession or vocation) are generally taxable under Cases I and II of Schedule D provided that they are not of a capital nature. This includes, of course, normal day-to-day receipts, but can also include 'lump-sum' payments and *ex gratia* payments (it also includes payments under the government's enterprise allowance scheme designed to help the unemployed start in business, though these are technically assessed under Case VI of Schedule D in the year of receipt). At the same time, some income received by the trader will *not* be included in the profits of the trade. The three main types are as follows:

1. **Receipts of a capital nature**, i.e. from sales of fixed assets such as property, shares and plant and machinery – these will either be subject to Capital Gains Tax (see Chapter 6) or taken into account in calculating capital allowances (see Chapter 3). *Fixed capital* must be distinguished from *circulating capital*, which is capital not retained in the business but flows in and out of it in the course of trading – notably trading stock. The receipts from circulating capital are trading income and in determining the nature of the capital we need to consider the type of trade. For example, textile machinery will be fixed capital of a textile clothing business but circulating capital of the textile machinery manufacturer.

2. **Income specifically exempted from tax**, for example interest *paid* by the Inland Revenue on overpayments of tax (so-called 'repayment supplements' – see pp. 276–7 for details).

3. **Income taxed under one of the other Schedules of Income Tax** (see especially Chapter 5) – the most common examples which may be found in business accounts are dividends on shares, interest on bank deposits and other investments, and rental earnings on property (unless the rents relate to part of the business premises sublet, in which case the Revenue may permit the inclusion of the rental income in trading profits).

Voluntary payments and compensation receipts

A difficult area concerns the treatment of lump-sum payments relating to ending business relationships and terminating contracts.

Where the payment is made in recognition of a long-standing business relationship, but not in return for specific goods or services, then the payment may not be a trading receipt. For instance, in one case companies in a group did not renew the auditing contract with a firm of accountants whom they had used for a number of years. In recognition of the termination of the relationship, the companies paid the accountants an *ex gratia* and unsolicited sum of £2,567. It was held that this was not a trading receipt (even though it was calculated on the basis of one year's auditing work). There was no evidence that the payment was for specific services performed in the past, nor did it terminate an on-going trading contract (see below) and nor was there a contractual obligation to pay compensation (*Walker* v. *Carnaby, Harrower, Barham and Pykett* 1970).

The fact that the business connection had ceased and that, although in recognition of past services, services were not inadequately rewarded in the past, were both important considerations in this judgment. Where an additional payment is made for services considered to be underremunerated in the past, even where it is made voluntarily, the receipt is likely to be taxable as a receipt of the trade. In *McGowan* v. *Brown and Cousins* (1977) an *ex gratia* sum of £2,500 paid by developers to estate agents to compensate for work they did not receive was held to be taxable. Critical here was the fact that the estate agents had charged less for earlier work for the developers in the expectation of receiving further work. In the Walker case the receipt had been *deserved*, while in the McGowan case it had been *earned* – the taxpayer had undertaken work in the past for which he had not been fully paid.

Where a payment is made to restrict trading activities, if the payment is to be excluded from the trading receipts it must be in return for the restriction and not be an alternative form of remuneration for services. So when Sir Laurence Olivier agreed not to act in other films for eighteen months, in return for a payment from a company with whom he had recently made the film *Henry V*, this sum was not taxable as a receipt of his profession (*Higgs* v. *Olivier* 1952). The payment was for the restriction and was not judged to be further remuneration for his acting role in the film.

This case contrasts with that of *White* v. *G. & M. Davies* (1979) which involved a dairy farmer who was paid by the EEC to switch to beef production. This sum was held not to be a payment for giving up farming (a restriction of trade); instead it was judged to be an incentive to farm in an alternative way. It replaced income that the farmer would have received for his milk and was therefore taxable.

From other cases we can ascertain that where a restriction is substantial, *affecting the whole profit-making activity*, it may be excluded as a trading receipt. This is borne out by the early and celebrated case of *Glenboig Union Fireclay Co. Ltd* v. *CIR* (1922). Here a company that mined fireclay received compensation from a railway company whose line was threatened by the mining in return for leaving the fireclay unworked. The House of Lords ruled that the receipt was a capital receipt because 'a capital asset of the company . . . [had] been sterilised or destroyed'. However, if the compensation relates to trading stock it is likely to be treated as a trading receipt. For example, when part of a stock of rum of a brewery company was compulsorily acquired by the Admiralty, the compensation was judged to be a taxable receipt of the trade (*CIR* v. *Scottish and Newcastle Breweries Ltd* 1927).

A similar principle holds with regard to compensation payments (or damages) for terminating, changing or breaching a contract. The crucial issue is the nature of the contract. It was determined in the case of *Van den Berghs Ltd* v. *Clark* (1935) that payments relating to contracts which affect 'the whole structure of the recipient's profit-making apparatus' are capital receipts. In this case an English margarine manufacturer received a substantial sum from a Dutch company with whom it had a contract which restricted competition and shared profits between the companies. The payment was compensation for terminating the contract which still had thirteen years to run. As the contract affected the whole profit-making activity of the business, the payment was judged to be a capital receipt.

On the other hand, when normal trading contracts are terminated or altered and a compensation payment is received, this will be a trading receipt. The loss of such a contract is part of the normal risks of business and cannot be said to alter radically the *structure* of the trade (*Kelsall Parsons & Co.* v. *CIR* 1938). Often the payment will clearly be designed to fill a hole in the trading income left by the cancellation of the contract. Since the trading income would have been taxable, it follows logically that the compensation payment should enter into trading profits. The same principle applies to compensation payments relating to the loss of use of income-earning assets. In *Burmah Steam Ship Co. Ltd* v. *CIR* (1930) a sum of £3,000 paid by ship repairers to the company for late delivery of a ship was held to be a receipt of the trade. It was compensation for profits lost by the company because of the ship's late delivery.

A similar logic applies to insurance receipts. Insurance receipts relating to the loss of capital assets (e.g. the cost of a factory building lost in a fire) are not trading receipts (they may, however, enter into capital allowance computations – see the next chapter). Insurance payments which compensate for trading stock lost, or loss of profits because the factory is not producing, *are* treated as receipts of the trade.

Business expenses which are deductible

Since Income Tax on trades, professions or vocations is assessed on profits, it follows that not only must we be clear about what is a trading receipt, we must be familiar with what expenses can and cannot be deducted from these receipts when calculating profits.

The starting-point will usually be the business trading and profit and loss account. There is an example below of a typical account for a small grocery business owned by a Tom Dickens.

EXAMPLE

Tom Dickens: Trading as 'Tom's Corner Shop'

Trading and profit & loss accounts year ending 31 December 1991

	£		£
Opening stock	12,000	Sales	102,000
Purchases	63,200	Closing stock	10,500
Gross profit	37,300		
	112,500		112,500
		Gross profit	37,300
Heat and lighting	800		
Telephone	600		
Wages	23,000		
Lease rent	800		
Rates	500		
New refrigerator	800		
Depreciation	2,000		
Repairs	3,000		
Net profit	5,800		
	37,300		37,300

In deciding whether an expenditure can be deducted when calculating business profits for tax purposes, we must turn first to the Income and Corporation Taxes Act 1988 (s.74). This states that expenditure may *not* be deducted if it is of a capital nature and it must be 'wholly and exclusively laid out and expended for the purposes of the trade, profession or vocation'. Note that there are three parts to this rule as follows:

- The expenditure must not be of a capital nature.

- The expenditure must be *wholly and exclusively* for business purposes; hence, expenditure which has a dual purpose (incurred partly for business and partly for private purposes) is not deductible unless the non-business purpose can be separately identified.

- The expenditure must have been incurred *for the purposes* of the trade, profession or vocation.

This general rule has been interpreted by the courts over the years in numerous hard-fought cases. In addition, certain statutory provisions have been introduced which modify the rule specifically to allow or disallow certain kinds of expenditure.

We can rehearse the implications of the basic rule on allowable business expenses by returning to Tom Dickens' trading and profit and loss account.

Purchases

Provided all of the purchases were wholly and exclusively for business purposes the full £63,200 will be deductible in calculating the taxable profits. One obvious area of difficulty is purchases which are taken by Tom Dickens and his family for their own consumption – presumably none too rare an event in a grocery trade. How should we account for the food and other items Tom and his family take for their own use (usually referred to as 'own goods')? As in other areas of tax, the treatment depends upon the facts and case law. There are two possibilities as follows:

- Own goods which *never* enter trading stock. This would include, for example, a bottle of Scotch which Tom bought for himself along with items intended for resale in his business while at the 'cash and carry'. Since the Scotch was never part of the trading stock it should never have entered the business books. In other words, the cost of the bottle of Scotch is excluded from purchases in the accounts.

- Own goods which *did* enter trading stock. This is somewhat more complex because the goods could be alternatively valued at *cost* or at the (higher) *price* at which the item was to be sold in the shop. For example, Tom might take from his shelves a can of soup for his lunch. Suppose the can cost Tom 30p at the cash and carry but is priced in his shop at 45p. The Courts have ruled that in this case the own goods should be valued at 45p. The seminal case of *Sharkey* v. *Wernher* (1955) involved a taxpayer who transferred five horses from her stud farm to a racing stables which she ran as a hobby. The House of Lords ruled that the stud farm accounts should be credited, not with the cost of rearing the horses as the taxpayer claimed, but with their market value.

This might seem harsh since it implies that Tom must pay the full price for the can of soup taken from stock, including his profit of 15p. Nevertheless, that is the law and it emphasizes a general point, brought out on many occasions throughout this book, that businesses need to be very careful how they conduct their affairs, for the tax consequences can vary dramatically. Tom could have saved himself the tax on 15p if at the 'cash and carry' he had bought the soup for his own use separately from his business purchases.

To return to Tom's account, in calculating taxable profits we must add back goods taken for private purposes (own use). Let us suppose that, valued on the principles set out above, this amounts to £3,000 during the year. Some business people pay cash for the goods they take from their shelves. That is to say in Tom's case he could have put 45p in the till when he took the soup. In which case no further adjustment is required when calculating taxable profits because the sales figure fully reflects the value of the own goods taken. It is worth noting, however, that Inland Revenue Inspectors tend to take a sceptical view of the argument that a trader *consistently* puts into his till the full price of goods taken. It may be better practice, therefore, when dealing with the Revenue, not to pay for goods when they are taken but instead to add an allowance for own goods to profits when submitting the tax computation. The amount, however, must be realistic and to avoid Revenue suspicion, what are clearly notional amounts (e.g. £520 = £10 per week) should be avoided.

We shall assume in Tom's case that the Revenue accepts an add-back for own goods of £3,000.

Opening and closing stock

The general rule is that stock should be valued at the *lower of cost or market value* (except when a trade ceases, in which case the unsold stock is brought in at its full market value on the date of cessation, unless the stock is sold to another trade subject to UK tax or the trade has ceased because of the death of the trader). Each item should be valued separately on this basis. Assuming this has been done correctly, no further adjustment is required for tax purposes.

The same rules broadly apply to work in progress by professionals such as surveyors and architects. A consistent method of valuation must be followed on the basis of cost, or cost plus overheads, or cost plus overheads and a profit contribution. However, authors and artists do not need to bring work in progress into account.

Heat and lighting

Provided that the expense in Tom's account of £800 relates *wholly and exclusively* to the shop or other business premises, it is fully allowable for tax purposes. Problems often arise where part of the bill relates to domestic accommodation (for instance, a flat above the shop which is not separately metered). In this case, a 'personal use' adjustment must be made based on an appropriate allowance for the domestic use. This will need to be agreed with the Inspector. A commonly accepted method is to split the bill according to the number of rooms (usually excluding the bathroom and kitchen). For example, a writer using one room wholly and exclusively as a study in a property with two other bedrooms and a lounge and dining room, might claim one-fifth of the heating and lighting bill. This is a broad brush approach, however, and the Inspector might insist upon an adjustment based upon square metres of business to domestic space in the house, or some other method which provides a more accurate reflection of the true business expense. It is important to recognize that if a room is not wholly and exclusively used for business purposes (the study doubles as a bedroom) technically *no* part of the heating and lighting for that room is tax deductible. Personal use adjustments can only be made where it is possible to distinguish the personal and business usage. In other cases, a *dual purpose* is sufficient to make an expense completely non-deductible.

Let us suppose that Tom lives above the shop, and in his case in calculating the taxable profits the Inspector agrees that one-fifth of the heating and lighting bill should be added back to reflect the domestic accommodation.

Telephone

An identical principle applies here. If there is both business and domestic use of the telephone an appropriate personal use adjustment must be agreed with the Inspector. Usually this is estimated, but a rigorous Inspector might insist that a record is kept of business and private calls so that the correct adjustment can be made. The way around this imposition is to have a separate business line installed. In our example, we shall assume Tom had a separate line installed two years ago and the telephone charge in his accounts relates solely to this line. Therefore, no further adjustment is required.

Wages

Wages, including pension and national insurance contributions for staff are allowable. Where wages are paid to members of the family, provided the amount paid is commensurate with the duties undertaken, it is also deductible (*Copeman* v. *William J Flood & Sons Ltd* 1941). The Inland Revenue treats with suspicion, however, cases where they believe payments are made to family members merely to minimize the tax paid. For example, Tom might pay his spouse, who has no other taxable earnings, £3,000 for 'keeping the business books'. The question arises whether this is a reasonable payment for the job. The Inspector would note with interest that the payment was covered by the spouse's personal allowance so that no tax was payable on the sum! Had Tom kept the income but paid it to his wife as 'housekeeping', £750 extra tax (£3,000 × 25%) would have been due on his additional profits; hence the Inland Revenue's constant vigilance. 'Wages' (more correctly referred to as *drawings*) by the trader are *never* deductible since they are appropriations from profit. The same applies to the trader's own national insurance contributions and pension payments (special relief applies, however, to pension contributions and this is considered later in the chapter). We shall assume that Tom was aware of this and recorded his drawings separately and that the £23,000 charged as 'wages' in the accounts is fully deductible.

Lease rent

If this is the rental on the shop it is fully deductible for tax purposes. Any portion that relates to domestic accommodation would be added back, based on an appropriate division. In Tom's case let us assume the domestic accommodation is separately leased and the rent is not charged in the business accounts, so that no adjustment needs to be made to his profits for tax purposes on this account. A deduction can also be claimed where the lessee pays a premium under the lease. This is discussed in Chapter 5.

Rates

For individuals rates were replaced by the community charge in Scotland from 1 April 1989 and in England and Wales from 1 April 1990, but businesses continued to pay rates. The rate now levied is a *Uniform Business Rate*, which is set by central government and distributed to local authorities as a *per capita* grant. Rate payments are a legitimate business expense and tax deductible.

Capital expenditure and other expenses

Standard accounting practice takes all capital expenditure to the balance sheet. Hence, capital items, such as a 'refrigerator', should never appear in the trading and profit and loss account. Perhaps Tom drew up this account himself or employed an unqualified bookkeeper (in which case the Inland Revenue might take a special interest in the reliability of the remainder of Tom's accounts!). There is no legal requirement for sole traders and partnerships to have their accounts audited by a qualified accountant as exists for companies. But in any case, the Income and Corporation Taxes Act 1988 (s.74) states that capital expenditure, including an allowance for the depreciation of capital assets, is not deductible when calculating taxable profits (certain capital expenditure benefits from 'capital allowances' instead and this is discussed at length in the next chapter). Equally, neither profits nor losses on the sale or destruction of capital assets are taken into consideration when calculating trading profits.

More problematic is the treatment of 'repairs', including expenditure on renovations and renewals and improvements. The general rule is that the *restoration* of an asset (e.g. replacing a subsidiary part of it) is treated as an allowable expense; but the *replacement* of the entire asset is capital expenditure and not allowable. A grey area relates to the definition of an 'entire asset'. In the case of *Samuel Jones & Co. (Devondale) Ltd* v. *CIR* (1951) expenditure on replacing a new factory chimney was found to be deductible because the chimney was a subsidiary part of the factory. On the other hand, the replacement of a spectator's stand in a football ground was held not to be a 'repair' since the stand was held to be a distinct and separate part of the stadium (*Brown* v. *Burnley Football & Athletic Co. Ltd* 1980). Hence, we can state that replacing the motor of a refrigerator would be treated as a repair and deductible, but the replacement of the refrigerator would be capital expenditure and not deductible. The improvement of an asset will be treated as capital expenditure unless the improvement is incidental to the repair (the new refrigerator motor is more reliable than the old one).

A particularly contentious issue is the repair or renovation of an asset following its acquisition. The rule here is that expenditure on initial repairs to improve an asset recently acquired will be disallowed – for instance, making a newly purchased ship seaworthy as in the celebrated case of *Law Shipping Co. Ltd* v. *CIR* (1923). By contrast, repairs where the asset purchased is usable when bought, but repaired later, may be allowable (*Odeon Associated Theatres Ltd* v. *Jones* 1971). Moreover, where charging the expenditure on repairs to the profit and loss account accords with normal accounting practice, the courts have suggested that there will be a strong presumption in favour of allowing the expenditure. We shall assume that two-thirds of the repairs charged in Tom's accounts are deductible and therefore £1,000 needs to be added back when calculating his taxable profits.

On the basis of the above discussion, we are now able to determine Tom's profits for tax purposes. Whereas the accounts showed a net profit of £5,800, the taxable profit is £12,760 and is calculated as in Table 2.1.

There are some other items of expenditure as follows which are normally disallowed for tax purposes but which we did not come across in Tom's accounts:

- *Legal and accountancy expenses.* Legal expenses relating to non-trading items are not allowable and the same applies to expenditure on the *acquisition* of an asset (e.g. acquiring a lease or property or drawing up a partnership agreement). This is treated as capital expenditure. Similarly, fines and penalties (e.g. the trader's parking fines) cannot be deducted. Legal expenses incurred in

Table 2.1 Tom Dickens' taxable profit computation

		£
Profit per accounts		5,800
Add disallowed items		
Own goods	3,000	
1/5 heating and lighting	160	
Refrigerator	800	
Depreciation	2,000	
Repairs	1,000	6,960
Taxable profit		12,760

renewing a lease, however, are allowable provided the renewal period is less than fifty years. The renewal of a lease is akin to preserving or defending the *existence* of a capital asset. Expenditure incurred in defending the integrity of an asset is usually allowable; it is similar to repairing and thereby preserving an asset. Similarly, legal costs incurred in defending a breach of a trading or employment contract are normally deductible. Also, the cost of meeting employees' parking fines incurred while on the employer's business is normally allowable.

Legal and accountancy costs incurred by a trader in disputing a tax assessment, however, are strictly not deductible (*Smith's Potato Estates Ltd* v. *Bolland* 1940). This follows since the tax assessment is on the individual not the business. In practice, the Inland Revenue will usually allow the costs except in cases of serious tax evasion. Interest and penalties levied by the Revenue for a tax offence are also not deductible, whereas the cost of the annual accounting audit, the preparation of the accounts and the cost of preparing the tax computation are allowed.

Incidental costs of obtaining *loan* finance, for instance commissions, advertising and publicity costs, are treated as a trading expense. However, in the case of companies, costs in connection with raising share capital are treated as capital spending and hence are not deductible (instead, they may be deducted when computing any Capital Gains Tax liability on the shares at a later disposal, see Chapter 6). From April 1991, tax relief has been extended to the costs of setting up approved employee share schemes and ESOPs (see pp. 114–6 for details of these schemes).

- *Provisions and reserves.* General provisions and reserves to meet unspecific contingencies are not allowable. If they were, it would be an easy matter for a trader to reduce his or her tax liability by making larger provisions. By contrast, a *specific* reserve against a bad debt is allowed. The Inspector may require to know the name of the debtor(s) so that it is possible, if desired, to verify that the provision is legitimate. Provision against unspecified bad debts (e.g. based on 'normally 5% of our debts turn out to be bad') is a *general reserve* and not deductible.

- *Debt write-offs.* An allowance can be made for trade debts written off, but not for a loan written off, unless the nature of the business is making loans.

- *Payments made under deduction of tax.* These are known in taxation as 'charges' and involve the payer deducting basic rate Income Tax on the payment; an example is payments to a charity under a deed of covenant. To ensure that the tax withheld is paid over to the Revenue, charges are never deductible in calculating taxable profits.

- *Entertainment and gifts.* Entertainment and gifts to employees, unless excessive, are normally deductible (the Inland Revenue has its own non-statutory working rules on what is 'excessive'). Hence, costs of the staff Christmas party and reasonable expenditure on a wedding present to a member of staff would usually be allowed. Under specific legislation, other forms of entertainment expenses are normally not deductible. This now applies to the entertaining of non-resident customers where a deduction used to be permitted prior to 15 March 1988. There is also a restriction on a trader deducting the cost of his own subsistence. In the case of *Caillebotte* v. *Quinn* (1975) a self-employed carpenter's claim for 30p per day as expenses to cover the extra cost of eating lunch away from home was rejected under the 'dual purpose' rule referred to earlier. The lunch served at least in part a personal purpose ('to feed the inner man') and this proved fatal to the claim that the expenditure was 'wholly and exclusively' for business purposes. Expenditures on gifts to customers costing not more than £10 per recipient per annum are allowable, but only if the gifts carry a conspicuous advertisement for the business and are *not* food, drink, tobacco or exchangeable vouchers.
  From 18 March 1991, gifts of equipment to educational establish-

ments are eligible for tax relief if the equipment is either manufactured, sold, or used in the course of the trade.

- *Gifts and staff secondments to charities*. There are restrictions on the deduction of donations to charities unless the business or staff benefit. A gift to a local hospital is an example of a case where such a benefit might arise. Also, since 1 October 1990 *companies* may make gifts to charities of £600 or more and deduct the cost as a business expense. The salary of an employee seconded to a charity is also deductible.

- *Clothing*. Expenditure on special protective clothing usually meets the requirements of the wholly and exclusively rule and is allowable. However, the Revenue, backed by the courts, has been most reluctant to extend the deduction to other clothing.

  The case of *Mallalieu* v. *Drummond* (1983) attracted much media interest, even in the tabloid press. It involved a lady barrister who claimed the cost of replacing and cleaning the black and white clothing she was required to wear in court. She argued that this clothing was never worn outside the court, therefore the expenditure met the wholly and exclusively requirement. After differing judgments in the lower courts, the House of Lords ruled against her claim on the grounds that part of the reason for wearing the clothing was warmth and decency. There was a *dual purpose* to the expenditure.

- *Defalcations* (fraud, thefts, etc.). Misappropriations of funds by the trader (or in companies, a director) are normally not deductible – otherwise the trader could steal from his own business and reduce his tax bill. But losses by staff are treated as an incident of the trading activities and are allowable.

- *Subscriptions and donations*. These are usually disallowed unless the expenditure is for the purposes of the business. This means that trade subscriptions (to a trade or professional association, for instance, an accountant's professional body) are generally deductible. Political donations and the like are usually not allowable unless it can be shown that the expenditure was incurred to ensure the survival of the business. This will be very rare. It was argued successfully, however, in the case of *Morgan* v. *Tate and Lyle* (1954) when the company mounted an expensive political campaign against the nationalization of their sugar business.

- *Interest charges.* Interest incurred on business loans, hire-purchase and overdrafts or business credit cards is deductible. Interest relating to personal expenditure is, of course, disallowed. Problems can arise where the business operates through a bank account which is also used for personal expenditures. In this case it has been known for the Inland Revenue to disallow some or all of the interest charged under the dual purpose rule, especially where the Revenue can maintain that an account is overdrawn because of excessive personal rather than business expenditures. The moral is, keep separate business and personal bank accounts. In any event, banks usually insist on separate accounts and it makes sense in terms of keeping track of business incomings and outgoings.

  Where *deep discounted stock* is issued, the yield to maturity is calculated and the borrower obtains tax relief for the discount year by year as it accrues. Deep discounted stock is stock issued by a company at a discount to its redemption price, where the discount is either greater than 15% or greater than 0.5% per annum for each complete year from the issue date to the date of redemption.

- *Travel overseas.* Provided an individual is UK-domiciled and carries on a trade wholly outside the UK, the costs of travelling to and from the UK and the costs of board and lodging at the overseas location are allowable (s.80 Income and Corporation Taxes Act 1988). The only other provision is that the taxpayer is abroad wholly and exclusively for the purposes of his trade. The cost of a solicitor attending a conference in America was disallowed because his trip also included a planned holiday (*Bowden* v. *Russell & Russell* 1965). If the taxpayer is absent for a continuous period of sixty days or more, the cost of up to two visits in any year of assessment by the spouse or child are also deductible.

- *Training and education.* Expenditure on staff training and education courses, provided they are wholly and exclusively for business purposes, is deductible. This also applies to courses attended by the trader.

- *Removal expenses.* By concession, the cost of removing the firm to another location and a reasonable allowance to finance staff moves are usually deductible even when they are strictly outside the normal expenditure rules.

- *Travelling expenses.* These are usually allowable if incurred during the course of business. However, the cost of travelling between home and the place of business is *not* allowable since such journeys are not for the 'purpose of the trade', they merely place a person in a *position* to trade (*Newsome* v. *Robertson* 1953). This may seem a fine point, but the Revenue police it rigorously. For example, the travel costs of a dentist who called at a dental laboratory between his surgery and home to deliver and collect work were disallowed under the dual purpose rule (*Sargent* v. *Barnes* 1978).

- *Redundancy pay and compensation for loss of office*. Statutory redundancy payments and voluntary redundancy payments equivalent to up to three times the statutory level are deductible (ss.90 and 579 Income and Corporation Taxes Act 1988).

- *Damages and compensation paid*. These can be deducted provided that they are not on capital account and are for the purposes of the trade. For example, payments to terminate employment contracts (*Mitchell* v. *B. W. Noble Ltd* 1927) or onerous trading contracts (*Anglo Persian Oil Co. Ltd* v. *Dale* 1932) are allowable.

- *Capital expenditure*. Capital expenditure is generally not deductible. This includes the purchase of tangible assets and also expenditure made 'with a view to bringing into existence an asset or advantage for the enduring benefit of the trade' (*British Insulated & Helsby Cables Ltd* v. *Atherton* 1926). Included are payments made to buy out and thereby eliminate a competitor (*Walker* v. *Joint Credit Card Co. Ltd* 1982).

It should be apparent from this lengthy discussion of business expenses that the profit shown in accounts is most unlikely to be the profit relevant for tax purposes. A number of items deducted in the accounts may be disallowed and will have to be added back in the tax computation, as in Tom's case. Also, there may be expenditure which has not appeared in the accounts (for example, business motoring expenses paid for out of the proprietor's own pocket) which needs to be deducted. Table 2.2 gives a summary of deductible expenses.

The basis of assessment

Once the taxable profit has been calculated, the next step is to determine how it will be taxed. An employee's earnings are taxed

Table 2.2 Summary of expenses in calculating taxable profits

Usually can be deducted	Usually cannot be deducted
Wages and employer's NIC and pension contributions	Capital expenditure including depreciation and losses on disposal of fixed assets (but see capital allowances, Chapter 3)
Legal expenses incurred preserving or defending assets or the business	Legal expenses relating to the acquisition of an asset
Repairs	Fines and penalties (except under certain circumstances for employees)
Defalcations (unless by the proprietor)	Entertaining (except reasonable expenditure on staff)
Education and training	Gifts (unless under £10 and carrying a conspicuous advertisement and not food, alcohol, tobacco or a voucher)
Removal expenses	Subscriptions and donations (unless for the purposes of the trade)
Travelling expenses (excluding home-to-work journeys)	General reserves against bad debts
Redundancy pay	
Damages paid (unless remote to the trade)	
Trading debts written off	
Specific reserves against bad debts	

when they are paid under the 'pay as you earn' (PAYE) system (see Chapter 4). This is not feasible, however, for the earnings of the self-employed since the taxable profit can only be calculated once the business accounts have been prepared bringing together all the year's receipts and expenses and this will be some time after the business year end. For example, a business which draws up its annual accounts to 31 December may not finalize these accounts until the following spring (or later). In the meantime the accountant is busy checking the books and records, reconciling the figures with bank statements, discussing the records with the proprietor and preparing the final accounts. For this reason, the profits of the self-employed are normally taxed on a *preceding year* (PY) basis (s.60 Income and Corporation Taxes Act 1988). That is to say, the profits in the accounting year ending in one tax year are taxed in, or are said to form *the basis of assessment*, for the following tax year. An illustration should clarify the meaning of this; we will stay with the accounts of Tom Dickens ('Tom's Corner Shop').

The normal basis of assessment and payment of the tax

As we saw earlier, Tom Dickens drew up his accounts to 31 December 1991 including all his business receipts and expenses in that year. After adjusting these figures to exclude expenses not permitted as deductions under tax legislation, we derived a taxable profit of £12,760. This taxable profit in the year to 31 December 1991 will be taxable because of the PY basis in the following fiscal year, i.e. 1992/3. Some other examples are shown in Table 2.3.

Table 2.3 Some examples of the basis of assessment

Annual accounts to	Accounts end in the tax year	Therefore, taxable in the tax year
6 June 1990	1990/1	1991/2
5 April 1991	1990/1	1991/2
6 April 1991	1991/2	1992/3

From these examples it is clear that by ending the accounts on 6 April rather than 5 April profits are taxed twelve months later. The tax is due and payable under Case I Schedule D in *two instalments*, on 1 January in the year of assessment and on the 1 July following. For instance, tax on the profits in the year to 5 April 1991 will be due and payable on 1 January 1992 and 1 July 1992. There is, therefore, clearly an advantage in terms of postponing the tax bill if accounts are drawn up to end in the early part of a tax year rather than at the end of a tax year.

When the normal basis of assessment is not applicable

The normal basis of assessment (the PY basis) applies to an on-going business, drawing up annual accounts and where the accounting date is not changed (i.e. the accounts end on the same date each year). The normal basis of assessment does not apply when a business commences or ceases, where non-annual accounts are prepared, or when the accounting date changes. There are also special provisions for 'averaging' the profits of certain trades especially subject to fluctuations in profit from year to year.

New businesses
For new businesses, the PY basis clearly could not apply because there is no preceding year's profits to tax. Hence, in the early period of

trading, profits are taxed as follows:

- In the first year of business, profits are allocated pro rata to the tax years in which they were earned and profits falling in the first tax year form the basis of assessment for that year (known as taxation on an 'actual profits' basis).
- The profits of the first full year of trading are then taxed *again* as the profits of the tax year in which the accounting period *ends*.
- The profits of the first full year of trading are taxed (yet again!) on the normal PY basis in the following tax year.

EXAMPLE

Suppose that Tom Dickens' annual accounts to 31 December 1991 were for his first year in business. They would be taxed as follows:

The year to 31 December 1991 falls in two tax years: 1990/1 (6 April 1990 to 5 April 1991) and 1991/2 (6 April 1991 to 5 April 1992). The tax assessments will be as follows:

- 1990/1 – $\frac{3}{12}$ × taxable profit year ending 31 December 1991 (i.e. three out of the twelve months fell in the 1990/91 tax year).
  Therefore, profit £12,760 × $\frac{3}{12}$ = taxable profit 1990/1: £3,190.
- 1991/2 – the full year's profits to 31 December are taxed in this year (even though this means that $\frac{3}{12}$ of the profits have now been taxed twice).
  Therefore, taxable profit 1991/2 = £12,760.
- 1992/3 – now the PY basis can apply since we have twelve months' accounts ending in the previous tax year to base the assessment on. The taxable profits in the year to 31 December 1991 are now taxed again.
  Therefore, taxable profit 1992/3 = £12,760.

The first year's accounts have formed the basis of the tax assessments for *three* tax years. Provided the business continues to trade and annual accounts are drawn up to 31 December the PY basis applies in future years.

In certain cases these 'commencement' rules could operate especially harshly. If in the second year of trading Tom Dickens had made much lower or even no profits he would still be liable to pay tax on the profits he made in his first year of trading. For example, suppose in the year to 31 December 1992 Tom's profits were a paltry £100, he would still be faced with a tax bill for 1992/3 based on profits of £12,760.

To avoid the obvious financial pressure that could result, the taxpayer can *elect* (s.62 Income and Corporation Taxes Act 1988) by writing to the Inland Revenue to be taxed in the second and third years of assessment according to the actual profits earned in those years. The election must be for *both* years and must be made within six years of the end of the third tax year; an election once made can be withdrawn within the same period. The election will be advantageous where profits *fell* in the second and third years of trading.

EXAMPLE

In the second and third years of trading, Tom Dickens' profits were £100 and £2,000 respectively. He elects to be taxed on an actual profits basis. The tax assessments will be calculated as follows:

1990/1 – $\frac{3}{12}$ × taxable profit year ending 31 December 1991 (as before) = £3,190.

1991/2 – $\frac{9}{12}$ × taxable profit year ending 31 December 1991 + $\frac{3}{12}$ × taxable profit year ending 31 December 1992 = ($\frac{9}{12}$ × £12,760) + ($\frac{3}{12}$ × £100) = £9,595.

1992/3 – $\frac{9}{12}$ × taxable profit year ending 31 December 1992 + $\frac{3}{12}$ × taxable profit year ending 31 December 1993 = ($\frac{9}{12}$ × £100) + ($\frac{3}{12}$ × £2,000) = £575.

1993/4 – taxable profit year ending 31 December 1992 = £100 (the normal PY basis of assessment).

1994/5 – taxable profit year ending 31 December 1993 = £2,000 (the normal PY basis of assessment).

The total profit taxed in the second and third years is £10,170. This compares with assessments for £25,520 (£12,760 + £12,760) on the normal commencement basis. The election is therefore clearly advantageous in Tom's case.

It should be noted that in the second and third years of assessment we took on a *pro rata* basis the annual taxable profits falling in each tax year. This is the method which must be adopted, even when the business records permit identification of the amount of the annual profit actually earned in each tax year.

EXAMPLE

Suppose in Tom Dickens' first year of trading to 31 December 1991 he suffered losses in the first three months, earning all his profit from April.

The fact that no profits were earned in the tax year 1990/1 is irrelevant, and $\frac{3}{12}$ of the annual profits will still be taxed in that year. One method of overcoming this rule is to draw up the first accounts for three months to 5 April 1991. There is nothing in tax law that prohibits accounts of less (or more) than twelve months, though if such accounts are prepared, the basis of assessment becomes more complicated because of the need to apportion accounts.

Table 2.4 gives a summary of the rules on taxing a new business.

Table 2.4   A summary of the rules on taxing a new business

Year of assessment	Normal rule	Trader's election
1st	Actual profits from date business starts trading to end of first tax year (i.e. 5 April)	–
2nd	Profits of the first 12 months of trading	The 2nd and 3rd years of assessment can be revised to an actual profits (6 April to 5 April) basis, i.e. profits in accounts are allocated on a pro-rata basis
3rd	Profits of the first 12 months of trading	
4th and subsequent years	Normal PY basis, i.e. annual profits for the accounting period which ended in the previous tax year	

A business ceases to trade

When a business stops trading the PY basis ceases to apply. For the tax year in which the trade ends the taxable profits based on the final accounts are allocated pro rata to that tax year. In addition, the Inland Revenue will put the penultimate *and* pre-penultimate years of assessment on to an 'actual' basis if this brings more profits into tax than leaving them on a PY basis (s.63 Income and Corporation Taxes Act 1988).

EXAMPLE

Suppose Tom Dickens had run an earlier business which ceased trading on 30 June 1988. His accounts had shown the following profits:

	£
Year to 31 December 1985	14,000
Year to 31 December 1986	20,000
Year to 31 December 1987	28,000
6 months (final account) to 30 June 1988	10,000

The tax assessments will be based on the following profits:

Accounts	Profits taxable on the normal basis of assessment	Form basis of the tax assessment for the tax year	Revision by the Inland Revenue onto an actual basis
Year ending 31.12.85	£14,000	1986/7	$\frac{9}{12} \times 20,000$
			$+ \frac{3}{12} \times 28,000 = £22,000$
Year ending 31.12.86	£20,000	1987/8	$\frac{9}{12} \times 28,000$
			$+ \frac{3}{6} \times 10,000 = £26,000$
6 April to 30 June 1988			
$\frac{3}{6} \times £10,000 =$	£5,000	1988/9	

In this particular case, the amount of profit charged to tax in 1986/7 and 1987/8 on the normal PY basis was £34,000. Once the trade ceases, however, the Inland Revenue will revise the tax assessments for these years onto an *actual* basis since this brings higher profits of £48,000 into tax. After cessation of trading, Tom Dickens will receive further tax assessments of £8,000 for 1986/7 and £6,000 for 1987/8.

This often provides a rude shock. It does, however, have a sound rationale, because if the penultimate and pre-penultimate years' assessments had not been so revised the taxable profit of £28,000 in the year to 31 December 1987 would have escaped tax altogether. Like many of the tortuous rules in tax, this one exists to close an obvious tax loophole. If the provision did not exist, whenever a trader had a bumper profits year there would be a tax incentive to cease trading in the following year! (It is important to realize, however, that *one* year's profits will still fall out of account, and that the Revenue's action merely affects which year. In the above example, the profits of the year to 31 December 1985 of £14,000 are now not taxed.)

By concession, the cessation rules need not apply on the death of a trader if the widow or widower takes over the business.

Table 2.5 gives a summary of the rules when a business ceases.

Non-annual accounts and changes of accounting date

Where accounts covering periods of more or less than twelve months are prepared, or the date to which the annual accounts are drawn up alters, there are provisions both to prevent profits escaping tax and unduly harsh tax assessments on the trader which could arise if the same profits were taxed twice. Broadly, the rules average the profits.

Short periods of trading

The first and last tax years have assessments based on the actual profits of those years. Also, a trader can elect to put the second and third years

Table 2.5 A summary of the rules when a business ceases

Year of assessment	Normal rule	Inland Revenue revision advantageous
Pre-penultimate	Profits of the annual accounts ending in the preceding tax year, i.e. normal PY basis	Inland Revenue will revise *both* of these tax years onto an actual profits (6 April to 5 April) basis if this brings more profit into tax
Penultimate year	Profits of the annual accounts ending in the preceding tax year, i.e. normal PY basis	
Final	Actual profits from 6 April to date trade ceases	

of assessment onto an actual profits basis if this is advantageous to him or her, and the Inland Revenue will put the pre-penultimate and penultimate years onto an actual basis if it is advantageous to them. It follows, therefore, that whenever a trader starts and ceases in less than five years, *all* tax assessments will be on an actual profits basis.

Averaging profits

The profits from farming and market gardening are especially subject to fluctuation and when profits are large the higher marginal tax rate may apply. To avoid hardship, the profits of two consecutive years may be averaged if the difference between them is at least 30%. There is a more restricted form of averaging where the lower profits are between 70 and 75% of the higher. There are also provisions to spread receipts from literary, musical and artistic works.

When does a business start or cease to trade for tax purposes?

The courts have ruled that this is a *question of fact*. The dates when someone says they started and ceased trading or from which and to which they draw up their accounts are not decisive. It is a matter of when trading *actually* began and ended. For example, a company which between June and October 1913 secured premises, employed staff and arranged contracts was not judged to have started trading until October because it was only then that it started production (*Birmingham & District Cattle By-products Co. Ltd* v. *CIR* 1919). Similarly, a firm of wine and spirit merchants who announced their decision to retire but continued selling their stock during the following year were held to have continued trading (*J. & R. O'Kane & Co.* v. *CIR* 1922).

Today there is much less need to argue with the tax authorities about the start and end of trading because of tax provisions which permit pre-trading expenses and which enable the Inland Revenue to tax receipts after trading ends.

* Expenditure which is incurred during the five years before the start of trading is treated as a *trading loss* incurred in the first year of trading (for companies it is treated as an expense of the first accounting period), provided it meets the usual rules on deductible trading expenses.

- Any income that arose from the trading activity but which was not included in the accounts before trading ceased is assessed to Income Tax (under Case VI of Schedule D) as a *post-cessation receipt*. This will apply, in particular, where accounts have been drawn up on a 'cash basis' since the final accounts will not have included receipts due from debtors.

It is also important to distinguish the extension of an existing trade from the start of a new trade because of the commencement provision under Cases I and II of Schedule D and because trading losses can only be carried forward and set off against profits of the *same* trade. In principle, a major change in the business implies a new trade. But there can be disagreement over the meaning of a 'major change'. For instance, a new activity of making food mixers was judged to be simply the extension of an existing trade of manufacturing cookers (*Cannon Industries* v. *Edwards* 1966). By contrast, a company that ceased brewing but continued to bottle and sell beer was considered to have embarked on a new trade (*Gordon and Blair Ltd* v. *CIR* 1962).

Taxing partnerships

Except in Scotland, a partnership is not a legal person in the UK. However, the Inland Revenue is empowered to raise tax assessments on partnerships rather than on the partners as individuals (s.111 Income and Corporation Taxes Act 1988). These assessments will be based on the trading profits of the partnership with any non-trading income (for example, interest and rent) assessed on the partners individually. As in the case of sole traders, partnership profits are assessed to Income Tax under Cases I and II of Schedule D.

The Partnership Act 1890 defines a partnership as 'the relations that subsist between persons carrying on business in common with a view of profit'. Whether a partnership exists or not is a matter of *fact*. If two or more people are acting together in such a way that they are effectively operating a partnership, they will be so treated for tax purposes. The existence or absence of a written partnership agreement is not conclusive in determining the existence of a partnership; though anyone contemplating a partnership is advised to obtain a written legal agreement to avoid later 'misunderstandings' (like marriages, partnerships too often end in tears)! In law, all partners, unless limited liability partners, are jointly liable for partnership debts. One partner can therefore be required to meet the debts run up by another partner. This applies equally to any outstanding tax liabilities on the partnership.

The amount of profit chargeable to tax is calculated in the usual way, but in order to calculate the liability the taxable profit has to be divided between the partners. The division is based on the profit-sharing agreement between the partners *applicable to the year of assessment*. Once the tax liability of each partner, after deducting personal allowances, has been calculated, the overall partnership assessment is simply the total of the partners' individual liabilities. The principal acting partner is required to make a tax return to the Inland Revenue showing the partnership profits and the way in which they are divided between the partners.

Although the method by which partnerships are assessed seems straightforward, in practice a number of complications can arise as follows:

- *Treatment of partnership salaries and interest on capital*. During the year the partners may have drawn salaries from the business and benefited from interest payments based on the amount of capital they have invested in the partnership. Such sums are *added back* when calculating the amount of tax due from the partnership.

- *The PY basis of assessment applies to partnerships as it does to sole traders* (the commencement and cessation provisions are identical too). This can cause problems. Suppose that the partnership profit-sharing ratio alters from one year to the next because the tax assessment is based on the profits of the *preceding year* but the profit-sharing ratio of the *current year*, there clearly can be anomalies. For instance, a new partner may be taxed on a share of profits earned in the previous year when he was *not* a partner. Similarly, a partner who took 60% of the profit last year, but is entitled this year to only 40%, will be taxed on only 40% of last year's profit. Moreover, if the profit-sharing ratio changes *during* a tax year (i.e. not on 6 April) the preceding year's profits, which form the basis of assessment, will have to be suitably apportioned and the former and the new profit-sharing ratios applied *pro rata*.

EXAMPLE

Sue and Carol have been in business as designers for a number of years. Until 30 September 1991 they shared profits equally. After 30 September Carol took less of a role in the business so her share fell to one-third. They draw up their accounts to 31 December and the taxable profits were as follows:

year ending 31 December 1990   profit £60,000
year ending 31 December 1991   profit £90,000

Remember that the profits to 31 December 1990 are taxed in 1991/2 and the profits to 31 December 1991 in 1992/3.

The partnership assessments will be split between Sue and Carol on the following basis:

	Sue	Carol	Total
1991/2:			
6.4.91–30.9.91	£15,000	£15,000	£30,000
1.10.91–5.4.92	£20,000	£10,000	£30,000
	£35,000	£25,000	£60,000
1992/3:			
6.4.92–5.4.93	£60,000	£30,000	£90,000

Note that the profit of each year of assessment has been apportioned between Sue and Carol in accordance with their profit-sharing agreement of the *year of assessment* and not the agreement that existed when the profits were *actually earned*.

- *Changes in partners.* A change in the composition of a partnership effectively creates a *new* trading venture. The rules on assessing profits to tax on the cessation and commencement of a trade, reviewed earlier in this chapter, then apply.

However, provided at least one person who was previously involved in the partnership continues to be involved, an *election* can be made for the partnership to be treated for tax purposes as operating on a continuing basis. The election for a continuation basis must be signed by all the old and new partners (or in the case of a partner's death, the personal representative) and made within two years of the date of the partnership change. It will be made where there are clear tax advantages in avoiding the imposition of the cessation and commencement rules. A good example is where the business profits are rising. The partners would presumably prefer to pay tax on the lower profits of the preceding year, postponing the higher tax liability.

Without this election the cessation and commencement rules apply. But because on cessation one year's profits escape tax, scope exists to engineer a partnership change to gain a tax advantage. The resulting advantages have been severely curtailed, however, since 19 March 1985. From that date, if a partnership change occurs where an election for a continuation basis *could* have been made but has *not* been made, the first *four* years of assessment of the new partnership will be taxed on an *actual* profits basis. The normal PY basis will apply only from the *fifth* year (although the partners can also elect to have the fifth and sixth years assessed on an actual basis). This provision, which modifies the normal rules for assessing the profits of a new business, applies only where there is a change in the composition of a partnership. It is not, therefore, applicable to the following cases where:

- A sole trader business becomes a partnership.
- A partnership is replaced by sole ownership.
- A brand-new partnership is created.

An election for *continuation basis* may be made by a sole trader who takes someone into partnership or where a partner retires leaving a sole trader. In this case neither the cessation provisions apply to the old business nor the commencement provisions to the new one. In effect, the change is ignored for tax purposes.

Where partnerships merge, both businesses are deemed to have ceased trading and a new business is deemed to have begun trading. An election for a continuation basis can be made only if the businesses carried on similar activities. Where a partnership splits, whether the trade continues is a question of fact to be agreed with the Revenue or decided by the courts.

Treatment of trading losses

Businesses are not always fortunate enough to make profits. How are trading losses treated for tax purposes? The rules relating to tax losses are especially formidable and here we deal only with Income Tax losses

– Corporation Tax losses (company losses) are discussed in Chapter 8. In essence the loss is treated as a zero profit for tax purposes with the amount of the loss relieved in a number of possible ways. The loss is calculated in exactly the same way as the taxable profit (deducting non-trading receipts and adding back expenses not permitted as deductions). It is important to know that a claim for loss relief cannot be restricted so as to leave sufficient profits to be covered by personal allowances.

EXAMPLE

Our old friend Tom Dickens made a trading loss for tax purposes in the year to 31 December 1993 of £10,000.

His tax assessment for 1994/5 (the accounts to 31 December 1993 form the basis of assessment for that year) will be on 'Profits Nil'.

This still leaves the loss of £10,000. There are broadly two ways in which the trading loss of an established and on-going business can be 'relieved': the loss can *either* be set against future trading profits or against other income to gain a tax repayment, as follows:

1. The trading loss is carried forward and set off against the *first* available profits of the *same* trade (note, it must be the same trade; hence if the trade changes the loss can no longer be carried forward). A claim must be made within six years of the year of the loss.

EXAMPLE

In the year to 31 December 1994 Tom makes a further trading loss of £6,000 but in the following year a profit of £20,000. The losses in 1993 and 1994, totalling £16,000, can be offset against the profit in 1995 of £20,000, leaving only £4,000 of that profit potentially chargeable to tax in 1996/7 (and all or part of this may be covered by personal allowances).

2. The set-off of trading losses against other income is a little more complex. The loss can be set off against the taxpayer's 'statutory total income' (defined as total income less 'charges') of the year *in which* the loss was suffered. In addition, where a balance of loss remains, it may be offset against the statutory total income of the

year *following* the year in which the loss was suffered. Any remaining loss still unrelieved can then be carried forward against future trading profits. From 6 April 1991, trading losses can also be set off against capital gains of a taxpayer made in the same or the following year.

Note that the loss arises in the year in which it is suffered, while profits are normally assessed on a PY basis. Hence, losses will be available to set off against the profits of the preceding year. Also, the relevant loss should strictly be the loss in the fiscal year, which means that unless accounts are drawn up to 5 April, the profits and losses in each accounting period will require apportioning to see if a loss in the tax year occurred.

EXAMPLE

Tom Dickens' loss of £10,000 in the year to 31 December 1993 followed profits of £12,000 in the previous year and £9,000 in the year to 31 December 1994.
The first step is to see whether a loss occurred in any tax year:

6.4.92–5.4.93 $9/12 \times$ profit £12,000 + $3/12 \times$ loss £10,000 = profit £6,500
6.4.93–5.4.94 $9/12 \times$ loss £10,000 + $3/12 \times$ profit £9,000 = loss £5,250

Therefore, £5,250 of losses can be relieved against other income. Assuming for simplicity that Tom has rental income of £4,000 in 1993/4, the loss relief is calculated as follows:

Tom's taxable income 1993/4	£
Profits of his trade (year ending 31.12.92)	£12,000
Rental income	4,000
Statutory total income	16,000
Less losses relieved	5,250
Taxable income	10,750

The balance of the loss, £4,750 (£10,000 − £5,250 relieved), can be carried forward against future trading profits.

There is, however, a *concessionary* basis for calculating losses available to established and on-going businesses (i.e. it cannot be claimed during the commencement and cessation periods) and this will sometimes be more advantageous than the strict basis described above. In this case, the loss in any tax year is the loss of the accounting year *ending* in that year. In Tom Dickens' case, on a concessionary basis he could claim the loss of £10,000 in the year to 31 December 1993 to be the loss for 1993/4. The loss is then set off against his statutory total income of that year in the usual way. In Tom's case the concessionary basis is clearly more advantageous because £10,000 of losses are available to set off against his income compared with £5,250 on the strict basis.

This loss relief must be claimed within two years of the end of the year of loss. Also, the relief can only be claimed if the 'business is carried on on a commercial basis with a view to the realization of profits'. In addition, it cannot be claimed for losses incurred in farming or market gardening if in *all* of the previous five tax years a loss was incurred (unless it can be demonstrated that there is now a reasonable expectation of profit). This provision is intended to prevent the operation of bogus, loss-making 'trades' set up to reclaim tax paid on other incomes.

Capital allowances in loss relief

Capital allowances are tax allowances given on certain kinds of capital spending by businesses. Full details are provided in the next chapter. They can be used to create or augment trading losses which are then relieved in exactly the same way as normal trading losses.

EXAMPLE

Suppose that for 1993/4 Tom was entitled to capital allowances of £3,000. The augmented loss, if calculated on the strict basis, would be the £5,250 trading loss + £3,000 = £8,250; or on the concessionary basis, £10,000 + £3,000 =£13,000.

Businesses transferred to limited companies

It is possible to carry forward trading losses incurred by a business to set against *income received* from a limited company to which the business is sold. This will be especially useful if a sole proprietor or partners wish to establish a company to run the trade, but would be inhibited in doing so if losses would otherwise be 'lost'. All unrelieved trading losses can be carried forward (though not unused capital allowances) and can be set off against the following:

- A salary derived from the company by the former business proprietor(s).
- Any interest and dividends earned by the former proprietor(s) from the company.

Note that the losses are *not* set against the company's profits.

For this relief to apply, the business must have been transferred to the company in return for consideration consisting of at least 80% shares in the company, which are then held by former proprietor(s) throughout the tax year in which the loss is relieved.

Trade charges and loss relief

Annual payments made by a trader under deduction of tax are referred to as *charges*; examples include patent royalties and donations to charities under a deed of covenant. The trader must then account for the tax to the Revenue and this is usually achieved by disallowing the payments when computing trading profits. When the trader makes a loss, however, the tax deducted cannot be accounted for in that way, hence the Revenue raises an assessment (known as an S.350 assessment) for the amount of the payment, thereby collecting the tax.

Where the charges in an S.350 assessment are *trade charges* (i.e. incurred wholly and exclusively for the purposes of the trade) they may be carried forward as if they were trading losses and set off against trading profits in future years.

Losses of new businesses

Any trading losses incurred in the first *three* years of a new trade (or *four* years if the taxpayer elects for the second and third years of assessment to be on an actual basis) are always calculated on the strict, tax year basis (i.e. the concessionary method outlined above does not apply. Any resulting loss can be carried forward against future profits of the trade or set against total statutory income in the way already outlined.

New businesses also have a third option – any trading losses incurred in the first *four* years of assessment can be set off against the proprietor's total income charged to tax in the *three* years preceding the year of loss, applying the loss to the earliest year first; i.e. a loss arising in 1993/4 will be set off first against income in 1990/1 (leading to a repayment of tax paid, perhaps on earnings from a previous employment) and then any balance of losses are available to set against income in 1991/2 and then in 1992/3. The loss can be augmented by capital allowances.

The trade must have been conducted with a view to profit and claims for this relief must be made within two years of the end of the year of assessment in which the loss was incurred. It should also be noted that *pre-trading expenditure* incurred in the five years before trading begins is treated as a loss of the year of assessment in which the business actually commences. The various loss reliefs then apply.

Losses when a business ceases trading ('terminal loss relief')

In the year the trade ceases any losses in the last *twelve months* of trading (augmented by unrelieved capital allowances and trade charges) can be set off against the trading profits, after capital allowances, of the *three* years prior to the year of cessation. Relief is available in later years first, i.e. a loss on cessation in 1995/6 would be set first against profits in 1994/5.

Relief for losses in unquoted trading companies

Relief is available for losses incurred in subscribing for shares in unquoted trading companies and in investment companies which subscribe for shares in qualifying trading companies. The loss can be set off against the taxpayer's statutory total income of the year in which the disposal occurs and/or the following year.

Partnership losses

Partnership losses are divided between the partners and each claims the same loss relief as available to sole proprietors. The loss is allocated between the partners on the same basis as a profit would have been allocated.

Maximizing income tax loss relief

To maximize the benefits of loss relief claims the following steps should be taken:

- Attempt to reduce taxable income in the year the income is subject to the higher rate of tax.
- If possible, preserve some income to be covered by personal allowances.
- Obtain the benefit of loss relief as soon as possible (this may weigh against simply carrying forward the loss).

National insurance contributions

The self-employed pay Class II national insurance contributions. The Social Security Act 1975 is the relevant legislation. These contributions provide entitlement to welfare benefits, notably the basic state pension and sickness and invalidity benefits, but *not* unemployment benefit and the earnings-related pension. Unlike employees, who broadly pay at a rate geared to their level of earnings, the self-employed pay contributions at a flat rate above a minimum level of business earnings (in 1991/2 £5.15 per week, with a small earnings exception limit of £2,900).

In addition, the self-employed suffer a further charge called Class IV national insurance contributions which are paid in two instalments alongside the Income Tax liability on their profits. Class IV contributions are based on the level of taxable profits after capital allowances, trade charges and trading losses brought forward (in 1991/2 at 6.3% on net profits between £5,900 and £20,280). One-half of the Class IV contribution paid is then deducted from the taxpayer's total income for that year in assessing the income to tax.

EXAMPLE

If Tom Dickens' profits in 1991/2 were £30,000, his Class IV contributions would be £905.94 (6.3% of £14,380 (£20,280 − £5,900)). One-half of this, £452.97, then reduces Tom's total income assessed to tax in that year.

Pensions

The self-employed must make their own arrangements for retirement. Just as employees receive tax relief on superannuation payments, so the self-employed benefit from concessions relating to pension premiums.

People up to the age of 35 may contribute up to 17.5% of their *net relevant earnings* up to a maximum earnings level (£71,400 in 1991/2) to a 'personal pension scheme' approved by the Revenue (for further details see pp. 271–3). Net relevant earnings are the taxable profits of the trade less capital allowances and loss relief. The premiums are then relieved at the individual's highest marginal rate of tax. For people over 35 the percentage that can be contributed rises with age, to a maximum of 40% for those aged 61 and over.

Relief is available in the year the premiums are paid or against income of the previous year (and where there were no relevant net earnings in that year, the year before that). Where the maximum premium is not paid, the shortfall can be carried forward for up to six years subject to certain conditions being met. It is permissible for the pension scheme to include both an element of life insurance and provision for a pension to a widow or other dependants.

Contractors and subcontractors

In order to overcome tax evasion in the construction industry, it is a legal requirement for contractors to deduct Income Tax at the basic rate when paying subcontractors unless the subcontractor has a valid exemption certificate. The contractor then pays over the tax to the Revenue.

To obtain an exemption certificate the subcontractor must fulfil the following conditions:

- Have a regular place of business.
- Keep proper records.
- Have a bank account which is used for business transactions.
- Be up to date with payments of tax and NIC.
- Have made full tax returns for at least three years.

- Have been either employed, or in business, or in full-time education or training, during the last three years (the period can include up to six months' unemployment).

There is a special scheme for new school leavers who do not have the employment record normally required.

Concluding comment

This chapter has been concerned with the taxation of the income of sole traders and partnerships, though the principles relating to what is a trading receipt and what is an allowable trading expense apply equally to companies subject to Corporation Tax.

In the next chapter we consider the reliefs which are available to businesses for capital expenditure.

3

The tax treatment of capital expenditure

We saw in the previous chapter that no deduction can be made for the costs of capital expenditure when a business computes its taxable profits. On normal accounting principles capital expenditure should be taken to the balance sheet and not the profit and loss account, and depreciation is not tax deductible because of the obvious scope for reducing taxable profits by accelerating its pace.

At the same time, governments have been anxious to promote business investment. The answer has been the introduction of special tax allowances called *capital allowances* for certain kinds of investment. These allowances can be claimed by both unincorporated businesses and companies and have the effect of reducing the amount of profit charged to tax. The types of expenditure, the appropriate rates of allowance and the method of calculation are summarized in Table 3.1. Subject to certain conditions, detailed in this chapter, they can be claimed against expenditure on the following:

- Plant and machinery (including thermal insulation of industrial buildings and safety expenditure at sports grounds).
- Industrial buildings and hotels.
- Patents, know-how and scientific research.
- Agricultural land and buildings.

Capital allowances are also available against expenditure on mines and oil wells, dredging and the provision of dwelling-houses for letting on assured tenancies. These allowances, however, are beyond the scope of this chapter.

Table 3.1   Capital allowances: a summary

Expenditure	Allowance and method of calculation
Commercial buildings in enterprise zones	100%
Scientific research	100%
Plant and machinery	25% p.a. reducing balance basis
Fire safety	25% p.a. reducing balance basis
Thermal insulation of industrial buildings	25% p.a. reducing balance basis
Safety at sports grounds	25% p.a. reducing balance basis
Patents	25% p.a. reducing balance basis
Know-how	25% p.a. reducing balance basis
Industrial buildings	4% straight-line basis
Hotels	4% straight-line basis
Agricultural buildings and works	4% straight-line basis

Expenditure and capital allowances

The purpose of capital allowances is to provide relief against tax for the depreciation in the value of qualifying assets. When an asset is sold, the capital allowances given over its life will be equal to the difference between the asset's acquisition cost and its sale or scrap price. This is achieved by giving *writing down allowances* each year (at rates which vary according to the type of expenditure), plus, in the year of disposal, a *balancing allowance* to reflect depreciation not accounted for in the capital allowances already granted, or, where the true depreciation is less than the capital allowances already given, the excess allowances are clawed back through a *balancing charge*.

Broadly, capital allowances are first given in the basis period in which the expenditure is incurred. Usually, expenditure is deemed to be incurred for capital allowance purposes on the date that the obligation to pay becomes unconditional (this need not necessarily be the date that payment is made), while capital expenditure incurred before the start of trading is regarded as having been incurred on the first day of trading. For the purposes of calculating capital allowances, the relevant expenditure includes the cost of the asset to the business plus any costs of transportation and installation. Excluded are interest charges on loans to finance the investment – interest charges will normally, however, be deductible as a revenue expense in computing the taxable profits (see Chapter 2). Where an asset is acquired through hire-purchase, it is treated as if it were purchased outright for cash and capital allowances can be claimed on the full price. The finance charge is treated as interest.

With the exception of regional development grants, where a business receives government aid towards investment costs, the subsidy must be deducted so that capital allowances are only allowed on the portion of the expenditure directly borne by the business.

In addition to businesses and companies, capital allowances may in certain circumstances be claimed by individuals to reduce the tax on their wages and salaries and against rental earnings (including the leasing of vehicles and industrial buildings). They can also be claimed by a tenant who is required under his lease to pay a capital sum for the use of the landlord's assets, e.g. lifts, and heating and ventilation plant.

Claiming capital allowances

Capital allowances are normally claimed when submitting the business or company tax computation. The Capital Allowances Act 1990 is the relevant legislation. A claim can be made for all or only part of the capital allowances entitlement for the year. Claiming part may in certain cases be advantageous; for example, a sole trader or partner may want to ensure that the profits after capital allowances are such that personal allowances are fully utilized, otherwise some or all of the personal allowances would be lost.

Capital allowances: basis periods

Businesses paying Income Tax
We have already noted that capital allowances relate to the basis period when the expenditure is incurred (or in the case of the industrial buildings allowance, the industrial building is brought into use). So, for example, in an on-going business drawing up its accounts to 31 December, any qualifying capital expenditure between 1 January 1991 and 31 December 1991 would be allowed against the business profits taxable in 1992/3. This follows since the profits in the year to 31 December 1991 are taxable in 1992/3.

A complication in calculating capital allowances arises where the period of accounts which forms the basis for charging profits to tax is less than twelve months (i.e. the 'basis period' is less than twelve months). For example, if XYZ Ltd drew up its accounts for six months to 30 September 1991, only $^6/_{12}$ths of the full capital allowances would be claimable.

Complications also arise during the commencement and cessation periods of a business or where there is a change of accounting date when the normal 'preceding year' (PY) basis of assessment does not apply. In these cases locating to which tax year capital allowances relate is far more complex. For example, in the opening years of a business the same profits will be taxed more than once. Whereas when the business ceases there will usually be a period of trading which escapes tax altogether (both situations are explained in Chapter 2). The following two questions arise:

1. How do we deal with capital expenditure which falls in a period which forms the basis of assessment for more than one tax year?
2. How do we treat capital expenditure which falls in a period which falls out of tax?

Without special provisions capital allowances might be given twice on the same expenditure in the former case, while no allowances would be given at all for expenditure in the latter period.

Rough equity is ensured by ruling as follows:

1. Where expenditure is incurred in a period which forms the basis of assessment for more than one tax year, capital allowances are given only in the first relevant year of assessment.

EXAMPLE

Bob began in business on 1 January 1990. His first accounts were made up to 31 December 1990 and in that year he had qualifying expenditure on which capital allowances could be claimed on 20 January, 10 April and 1 December.

The profits to 31 December will be taxed as follows (assuming Bob does not elect for the second and third years of assessment to be on an 'actual' profits basis):

Year of assessment	
1989/90	$^3/_{12}$ × Profit year ending 31 December 1990
1990/1	Profit year ending 31 December 1990
1991/2	Profit year ending 31 December 1990

The capital allowances will be related to the following years of assessment:

Expenditure	Claimed in year of assessment
20 January	1989/90
10 April	1990/1
1 December	1990/1

In other words, none of the expenditure falls in the 1991/2 year of assessment. The only capital allowances relating to that year will be writing down allowances based on the written down values brought forward from 1990/1 (how capital allowances are calculated on written down values is explained below).

2. Where a period falls out of account, the capital expenditure is treated as having been incurred in the following period, unless that period is the year the business ceases trading, in which case it is carried back and included in the previous period.

EXAMPLE

Doris ceased trading on 30 June 1991, having been in business a number of years. She purchased assets qualifying for capital allowances on 1 December 1988, 2 February 1990 and 1 March 1991. She has always drawn up annual accounts to 31 December.

The profits of the final years of trading will be taxed as follows (assuming the Revenue do not adjust the penultimate and pre-penultimate years onto an 'actual' profits basis):

Year of assessment	
1991/2	$\frac{3}{6}$ × Profit year ending 31 June 1991
1990/1	Profit year ending 31 December 1989
1989/90	Profit year ending 31 December 1988

The capital allowances will be related to the following years of assessment:

Expenditure	Claimed in year of assessment
2 February 1990	1990/1
1 March 1991	1990/1
1 December 1988	1989/90

In other words, capital expenditure for the period which falls out of account on cessation of trading, in this case 1 January 1990 to 5 April 1991, is treated as having been incurred in the previous period, year ending 31 December 1989. It cannot be added to the following period because that is the year the business ceased trading.

Where the taxpayer elects in the case of a new business for the second and third years of assessment to be on an actual basis, or in the case of a cessation the Revenue puts the pre-penultimate and penultimate years on an actual basis, a different year falls out of account. Nevertheless, the procedure for allocating the capital expenditure follows the rules set out above. These rules are only necessary because of the cumbersome way in which unincorporated businesses are assessed for Income Tax, namely the PY method.

For the sole proprietor and partnership businesses subject to Income Tax, capital allowances and balancing charges are shown separately in the tax assessment (i.e. the assessment will itemize the taxable profits, any balancing charges and any capital allowances).

Companies paying Corporation Tax

Companies can claim capital allowances in exactly the same way as unincorporated businesses. The rates of allowances are identical, as is the method of calculating the allowances and any balancing charges. However, since companies are not taxed on a PY basis but simply on the profits of their accounting period (see Chapter 8 for details) the complex rules (s.144 Capital Allowances Act 1990) relating to commencements and cessations of business do not apply. Also in the case of companies, balancing charges are added and capital allowances are deducted in *arriving at* the taxable profit rather than being separately itemized in the tax assessment. For example, capital allowances by a company in its accounting period to 31 March 1991 would be deducted in calculating its taxable profits for this period.

Just as capital allowances are restricted where businesses pay Income Tax on their profits for basis periods of less than twelve months, a similar restriction applies for company accounting periods of less than twelve months.

Capital allowances on plant and machinery

Qualifying expenditure

The starting-point must be, what is plant and machinery? Although there is no statutory definition, over the last hundred years or so there has been a large number of court cases concerned with whether a particular item of expenditure qualifies. From these cases it is clear that plant and machinery must be as follows:

- 'Apparatus . . . used by a businessman for carrying on his business – not his stock in trade which he buys or makes for sale; but all goods and chattels, fixed or moveable, live or dead, which he keeps for permanent employment in his business' (*Yarmouth* v. *France* 1887 – where it was decided that a horse could be plant!).

- *And* which is not part of the *fabric* of a building or the *place or setting* in which the business is carried on.

There is still, however, a degree of uncertainty about the meaning of the term 'setting'. For example, it has been judged that the canopy of a petrol station is not plant since it is the part of the setting in which petrol is dispensed (*Dixon* v. *Fitch's Garage* 1975). The same reasoning applied when the courts rejected as plant a ferry boat used as a floating restaurant (*Benson* v. *Yard Arm Club Ltd* 1978), prefabricated school buildings (*St John's School* v. *Ward* 1974) and a football stand (*Brown* v. *Burnley Football and Athletic Co. Ltd* 1980).

On the other hand, *moveable* office partitions (but *not* fixed partitions, which are considered to be part of the fabric of the building) qualify as plant (*Jarrold* v. *John Good and Sons Ltd* 1963). It has also been decided (in the case of *CIR* v. *Barclay Curle and Co Ltd* 1969) that a dry dock used by ship repairers was plant because it served the function of lifting boats out of the water. Similarly, a swimming-pool at a caravan site was considered to be plant because it was part of the means by which the holiday was provided (*Cooke* v. *Beach Station Caravans Ltd* 1974); as were light fittings, stags' heads, murals and metal sculptures in hotels and public houses because it was part of the company's trade to provide ambience to its customers (*CIR* v. *Scottish and Newcastle Breweries Ltd* 1982).

Therefore, in deciding whether an expenditure qualifies as plant and machinery we need to consider the precise role the asset plays in the business undertaken. It is possible for the premises to be plant, as in the above cases of the swimming-pool and the dry dock, if they are the apparatus by which the business is carried on rather than simply the place in which it is carried on. It is crucial to consider whether the item has a direct function in providing the business product or service or whether it is merely the setting in which the business is carried on (the *function* test). Where buildings are involved, careful planning at the design stage is needed to maximize the amount of qualifying expenditure.

Allowances available

Capital allowances are available against expenditure on providing new or second-hand plant and machinery used wholly and exclusively for the purposes of the trade. Plant and machinery not purchased but introduced into the business (for instance, the family car) will qualify for capital allowances from the date it is first used for business purposes based on its market value on the date it is so first used. This value will need to be agreed with the Inspector.

Expenditure on qualifying plant and machinery benefits from capital *writing down allowances* at the rate of 25% on a reducing balance basis.

EXAMPLE

Julie Smith, a newly self-employed veterinary surgeon, opened her first surgery spending £1,900 on equipment, £125 on an answerphone, £1,200 on replacement windows and £7,200 on a car which is 90% used in the business.

The replacement windows will not qualify as plant and machinery. Also, because new windows are capital expenditure the expense cannot be deducted in computing taxable profits and, since a surgery is neither an industrial building nor an hotel, no capital allowances are available under these headings (see below). It appears that Julie will receive no income tax allowances for this expenditure. This emphasizes the point that not all business expenditure is tax deductible. The other items, however, all qualify as plant and machinery. She can, therefore, obtain relief on total spending of £9,225 in the first year in which her profits are assessed to tax. Suppose this is the 1991/2 tax year then the allowance is calculated as follows:

		Plant and machinery pool £	Car £	Capital allowances £
Additions:	1,900		7,200	
	125	2,025		
Allowances @ 25%		507		507
			1,800 × 90%	= 1,620
Carried forward		1,518	6,400	

Julie is entitled to claim capital allowances against her profits of £507 + £1,620 = £2,127.

The tax treatment of capital expenditure

In the following year, 1992/3, Julie will benefit from capital allowances of 25% on the written down values carried forward, i.e. £1,518 and £6,400, provided the assets are still owned by her and used in her business. The allowances will again be calculated at a rate of 25%.

Year 2

	Pool	Car	Capital allowances
	£	£	£
Written down value brought forward	1,518	6,400	
Capital allowances @ 25%	380		380
		1,600 × 90%	= 1,440
Carried forward to third year	1,138	4,800	

This year Julie could claim capital allowances of £380 + £1,440 = £1,820.

With the exception of the car, all of the expenditure on plant and machinery was 'pooled'. It is a requirement to 'pool' or add together expenditure on plant and machinery when computing capital allowances. Cars form their own separate pool unless they either cost more than £8,000 or there is personal use (in which case they are not pooled but dealt with separately as in the example above). Also, an election exists to place in a separate pool assets with an expected life of five years or less (known as the 'short-life assets pool'). This will speed up the write-off of these assets for tax purposes. If they were placed in the main pool, their written down values would be carried forward long after the assets ceased to exist. This provision, however, does not apply to cars or to any assets which have an element of private use.

The capital allowances on the car were restricted to 90% of the maximum available. This reflects the fact that the vehicle is only used 90% for business purposes. Wherever there is non-business use of an asset by the *proprietor*, the capital allowances are restricted to reflect private use (this does not, however, apply to private use by *employees*, including directors, where capital allowances are allowed in full but the employee may be taxed on the 'benefit in kind'; see Chapter 4). This could equally have applied to the answerphone if it was also connected to a domestic line. In all cases personal use adjustments must be agreed with the Inspector and will be based on some equitable division. In the case of a car, it is helpful to keep a log of private and business mileages to support the submitted figure.

Additions and sales of plant and machinery

Qualifying assets benefit from capital allowances in the normal way from the date they are acquired. Most plant and machinery (excluding cars) are added to the *pool*. Whenever plant and machinery is disposed of, any sales receipts must be taken into account to calculate the true depreciation of the asset over its life. Where an asset is not sold but, for example, given away to a close friend or taken for personal use – this can often happen with motor vehicles – the market value must be added back. The Revenue also has powers to impose the market value in certain other cases where assets are transferred at less than their true value to gain a tax advantage, for example in sale and leaseback deals. If an asset is destroyed but there are insurance receipts, these receipts are treated as the sale values. In all cases, if a balancing charge is due it must not exceed the capital allowances granted.

Owing to the method of 'pooling', except for 'short life assets' or when cars are sold, balancing allowances and balancing charges are most commonly found when a business ceases trading. Where a business ceases trading or is sold, the disposal proceeds appropriate to each asset are deducted from the relevant written down values to determine the appropriate allowance or charge. Where a business is transferred to a 'connected person' (defined to include the spouse, relatives, business partners and certain others), an election can be made within two years to avoid the balancing allowance or charge. In this case, the new business inherits the written down values and its capital allowances are calculated on that basis.

EXAMPLE

Paul Rodgers has been in business for some years as a self-employed financial adviser. He draws up his accounts annually to 30 September. In the year to 30 September 1990 he traded in his existing car, a Vauxhall Cavalier, against a new Rover, receiving a part exchange allowance of £3,000. The new Rover cost £10,500. The Vauxhall's written down value for capital allowances was £2,000.

The profits based on the accounts to 30 September 1990 will be taxed in the year 1991/2 under the normal PY basis of assessment. Hence, the capital allowances we are concerned with are allowed in that year. Suppose the taxable profits are agreed to be £35,000 and there is no personal use of the vehicle. The tax assessment will read as follows:

	£
Profits	35,000
Plus balancing charge	1,000
	36,000
Less capital allowances	2,000
Taxable Schedule D Case 1	34,000

The net effect is to reduce by £1,000 the business profits charged to tax.
The capital allowances were calculated as follows:

	Vauxhall Cavalier £	Capital allowances £
Value brought forward	2,000	
Sale proceeds	3,000	
	1,000	
Balancing charge *Capital Allowance Clawback*	(1,000)	(1,000)
Carried forward to 1992/3	Nil	
	Rover	
Acquisition cost	10,500	
Capital allowances @ 25% (restricted)	2,000	2,000
Carried forward to 1992/3	8,500	

Notice in particular the following:

1. Because the disposal value of the Vauxhall was greater than its written down value for capital allowances, a balancing charge exists. This claws back some of the capital allowances given in earlier years. These allowances (which represent a notional depreciation rate) proved excessive, exceeding the true rate of depreciation.

2. The capital allowances on the new Rover have been restricted to £2,000 even though 25% of £10,500 is £2,625. Since 1979, capital allowances on cars costing over £8,000 have been limited to a maximum of £2,000 per annum. The rationale was to exclude large allowances for executive vehicles. Unfortunately, because successive Chancellors have been unwilling to raise the £8,000 limit as inflation eroded its value (the equivalent value today would be around £22,000), a basic family saloon is now caught by the restriction. The restriction does not apply, however, to other motor vehicles (vans, lorries, etc.) or to cars used for hire or in a taxi service.

Leasing or hiring cars

One obvious way to circumvent the £8,000 limit on the value of cars for capital allowances would be to lease or hire them. The taxpayer would then deduct the full lease charge as a business expense when computing profits. To prevent this, the charge is restricted by the following formula:

$$\text{actual rental} \times \frac{£8,000 + \tfrac{1}{2}(\text{cost} - £8,000)}{\text{cost}}$$

where 'cost' is the value of the vehicle when first leased.

For example, suppose a vehicle cost £20,000 and the annual rent was £6,720, the actual amount deductible for tax purposes would be limited to £4,704.

Companies which are in the business of leasing vehicles and other plant and machinery can claim capital allowances on the full expenditure.

Additional provisions

1. Expenditure on alterations to buildings during the installation of new plant and machinery, where necessary to enable the plant to

be used, is treated as if it were expenditure on plant and machinery. Therefore, the 25% allowance is due.

2. Expenditure on the following may also qualify for 25% capital allowance as plant and machinery:
    (a) thermal insulation of industrial buildings;
    (b) sports grounds to comply with the issue of a safety certificate;
    (c) fire safety.

3. If premises are leased, the landlord can claim capital allowances on contributions made towards the tenant's qualifying capital expenditure.

4. Where at the end of a hire-purchase or leasing agreement the ownership of plant and machinery belongs to the purchaser or lessee, the purchaser or lessee can claim capital allowances from the time the asset is used in the trade. In other cases, the lessor claims the capital allowances and reflects this in the leasing charge.

Industrial buildings allowance (IBA)

Capital allowances are available for the purchase of a new or existing industrial building or for extensions or improvements to such buildings (s.18 Capital Allowances Act 1990). The allowance extends to platforms, walls and walkways. In the case of existing structures, these must not be more than twenty-five years old. The amount of allowance varies between new and existing buildings.

What is an industrial building?

To be an industrial building for the purposes of capital allowances, the building must fall within one of the following categories:

1. Mills or factories used in a manufacturing trade or a trade in which goods and services are subject to a process.

2. Buildings used for the storage of raw materials for manufacture or future processing or to store finished goods manufactured by the occupier (this excludes most wholesale and retail warehouses).

3. Drawing-offices associated with an industrial activity (but not other office premises – though see below).

4. Canteens and other welfare buildings used by employees in one of the activities mentioned in (1).
5. Sports pavilions used by employees of any trade (not just qualifying trades).

Buildings used in connection with transport, docks, tunnels, bridges, agriculture, fisheries, mining and oil wells may also qualify. Activities which do not qualify (unless they are in enterprise zones – see below) are shops, restaurants, showrooms, places of entertainment and office blocks.

Offices

Although offices do not qualify for IBA, where they are used for personnel who are part of the manufacturing process they may qualify (i.e., a drawing-office, the offices used by shop floor supervisors and foremen). In the same way, where the offices are part of an industrial building, the whole cost of the building will qualify for relief provided that the non-industrial accommodation is not more than 25% of the total cost. If this limit is exceeded then the cost must be apportioned between the industrial and non-industrial parts and IBA will be given only on the former. It is normal to apportion on the basis of floor space where there is no separate costing of the non-industrial part.

Land

Expenditure on the land on which the industrial building stands does not qualify for IBA. A separate valuation must therefore be made of the land and this amount is subtracted from the overall purchase price for the building and land. However, expenditure on tunnelling, foundations, and the installation of approach roads to the industrial building qualifies for IBA.

New industrial buildings

A writing down allowance of 4% per annum based on the purchase price of the building, can be claimed on the purchase of a qualifying industrial building (for buildings new before 6 November 1962 the allowance was 2%). When the building is sold within twenty-five years from first use (fifty years for buildings first brought into use before 6 November 1962) a balancing allowance or charge is made, so that the depreciation in the value of the building between purchase and sale is covered by the capital allowances granted. Where, therefore, the building sells for more than its original cost, the balancing charge will recover all of the capital allowances given in past years. Once again, the balancing charge can never be more than the capital allowances claimed.

Extensions and improvements to existing industrial buildings (but not repairs, which are usually deductible in computing trading profits) are treated as if they were separate industrial buildings and receive IBA in the normal way.

EXAMPLE

Steve Williams, who has been in business as a toy manufacturer for some time, bought a new industrial building for £100,000 on 1 September 1990. He draws up his accounts to 30 September each year.

The industrial building was bought in the accounting year to 30 September 1990 and this forms the basis of the business tax assessment for 1991/2 (the usual PY basis). In calculating the tax liability on his profits for that year, he can claim IBA of £4,000 (£100,000 × 4%).

In the following tax year, provided the building is still used in his business as an industrial building, he can claim:

	£	Capital allowances
Cost of building	100,000	
IBA 1991/2	4,000	4,000
	96,000	
IBA 1992/3	4,000	4,000
Carried forward	92,000	

(handwritten annotation: "Straight Line Basis")

Note that the 4% continues to be calculated on the original cost – a straight-line basis – and not on written down values as used for plant and machinery.

Existing industrial buildings

The allowance that can be claimed by the new owner depends on the lower of the residue of expenditure after sale by the previous owner and the price paid by the new owner, as well as the amount of time from the date of the new purchase to twenty-five years after the building was first brought into use (whether or not it was used as an industrial building when first brought into use). For example, a building first brought into use on 1 January 1975 and then sold on 1 January 1980 and used as an industrial building would have a relevant time period for the new owner of twenty years.

EXAMPLE

Continuing our previous example: suppose that Steve sold the building on 1 September 1992 for £110,000, which is more than its original cost. The £8,000 IBA previously given would now be clawed back from him through a balancing charge for this amount in his 1993/4 assessment (the accounts to 30 September 1992 forming the basis of assessment for that year).

	£	£
Residue of expenditure before sale (written down value b/f)	92,000	92,000
Sale proceeds (restricted to original cost)	100,000	
Balancing charge 1993/4	(8,000)	8,000
Residue of expenditure after sale		100,000

The new owner could then claim an allowance calculated as follows:

£100,000/23 years* = £4,348 (to the nearest £)

*There are twenty-three years left to run from the date the building was first brought into use.

The new owner can claim IBA of £4,348 per annum for twenty-two years and a balance of £4,344 in the twenty-third year (giving total allowances of £100,000). Of course, should he sell the building in the meantime, then we would repeat the process with the allowance to the third owner calculated in a similar manner. After the end of the twenty-five years there are neither further capital allowances nor are there any balancing allowances or charges when the building is sold. In other words, the building ceases to have any significance as far as capital allowances are concerned.

Let us now change the example and consider what would have been the position if, instead of the building being sold for more than its original cost on 1 September 1992, it had been sold for say £90,000.

In this case the depreciation under Steve's ownership is £10,000 (£100,000 − £90,000) but he has only received IBA of £8,000. Therefore, he will now receive a balancing allowance of £2,000 in his 1993/4 tax assessment.

The new owner will be able to claim capital allowances as follows (assuming the building continues to be used as an industrial building):

£90,000/23 years = £3,914

For twenty-two years the allowance will be £3,914 with the residual amount of £3,892 claimable in the twenty-third year.

From the above two examples, it should be clear that the second-hand purchaser claimed relief based on the *lower* of the actual price paid and the price when new.

If a building ceases to be an industrial building, no further allowances are due until such time as the building reverts to being an industrial building. In the meantime, a *notional* IBA is calculated – notional because although it is not received by the taxpayer it is used in calculating the residual value of the building when sold. A notional IBA is also deducted from the cost of the building if initially it is not used as an industrial building.

EXAMPLE

Returning to our example, suppose Steve ceased to use the building as an industrial building on 1 September 1991, a year before selling it for £110,000. The capital allowances would now be calculated as follows:

	£	£
Cost of building	100,000	
Less claimed 1991/2	4,000	
	96,000	
Notional IBA 1992/3	4,000	
Residue of expenditure before sale	92,000	92,000
Sale proceeds (restricted to original cost)	100,000	
Balancing charge 1993/4	(4,000)*	4,000
Residue of expenditure after sale		96,000

*Note: Only the capital allowances actually given are clawed back.

The new owner could claim IBA over twenty-three years on the £96,000, i.e. £4,174 for twenty-two years and a balance of £4,172 in the final year.

The calculation becomes a little more complicated if a building is sold for less than its original cost following a period containing some non-industrial use.

EXAMPLE

Suppose the facts were as in the last example except that the building was sold for £80,000. Steve would receive a balancing allowance of £6,000, calculated as follows:

	£
Cost of building	100,000
Sale proceeds	80,000
Net cost	20,000
Less: net cost × (period of non-industrial use/total period from first use to sale) i.e. 20,000 × 1 year/2 years	10,000
Adjusted net cost	10,000
Allowances given	4,000
Balancing allowance 1933/4	6,000

The new owner can claim IBA over twenty-three years on the £80,000 he paid for the building provided the building continues to qualify as an industrial building. The £80,000 is taken since this is less than the depreciated value of the building for IBA purposes, i.e. £100,000 less the capital allowances (actual and notional given) £14,000. If the latter had been less, this figure would have been used, as in the previous illustration.

Note that, although IBA is lost if a building is turned to non-industrial use, if the building simply falls into temporary *disuse* there is no loss of allowance. In practice, 'temporary' is interpreted liberally so that any period of disuse normally qualifies.

Hotels, agricultural buildings and commercial buildings in enterprise zones

Hotels

There is specific legislation (s.7 Capital Allowances Act 1990) relating to hotels. Provided that the hotel has at least ten letting bedrooms available to the public – which are not in the same occupation for more than one month – provides meals and service in addition to accommodation, and is open for at least four months between 1 April and 31 October, a 4% writing down allowance may be claimed on the cost of constructing or extending it. The allowance is calculated on a similar basis to IBA.

Agricultural buildings

Expenditure on buildings or works on agricultural land qualifies for capital allowances (s.122 Capital Allowances Act 1990). Buildings include barns, farm cottages and up to one-third of the cost of a farmhouse. Ancillary structures such as fencing, roads and drainage also qualify. The allowance is on a straight-line basis at 4% of cost per annum. Where buildings and works are sold within twenty-five years, the new owner may claim the balance of the allowance.

Enterprise zones

Enterprise zones have been set up in recent years in an effort to rejuvenate areas of economic decline and are now found in over thirty-five areas of the country. Expenditure in these zones receives special tax advantages. Expenditure on commercial buildings, including offices, shops, and hotels, as well as industrial buildings attracts a 100% capital allowance in the year of expenditure. This means that the whole of the expenditure can be written off in the year in which it is incurred.

The treatment of buildings sold is exactly as in the case of industrial buildings outside enterprise zones, i.e. there is a balancing allowance or charge on the seller and allowances to the new owner are based on the number of years to run to the end of the twenty-five-year period following the building first being brought into use.

83

Patents, know-how and scientific research

Patents and know-how

Both capital costs incurred in acquiring a patent and expenditure on 'know-how' qualify for capital allowances (s.520 Income and Corporation Taxes Act 1988). 'Know-how' is defined as information and techniques likely to assist in the manufacturing or processing of goods or materials, or in connection with agricultural, forestry and fishing operations, or searching for or working mineral deposits. The allowance is at 25% and on a reducing balance basis (as for plant and machinery). When the patent expires there will be a balancing allowance based on the unrelieved amount of the expenditure. If the patent is sold there may be a balancing charge or allowance (the procedure is exactly the same as for disposals of plant and machinery).

Scientific research

There is a 100% allowance for expenditure on plant and buildings used for scientific research related to current or future trade. Day-to-day spending of a revenue nature, e.g. on staff and materials, will normally be deductible when calculating the taxable profits. By granting a 100% allowance both capital and revenue spending are effectively treated the same. Both can be completely written off in the year in which they are incurred.

Capital allowances and losses

Capital allowances can be used to create or augment trading losses which are then relieved as described for Income Tax in Chapter 2 and Corporation Tax in Chapter 8. For example, a business with a trading loss of £2,000 and capital allowances of £6,000, is in effect treated as having losses of £8,000. This occurs automatically for companies since capital allowances are deducted in *arriving at* the profit or loss.

However, in certain circumstances capital allowances are given 'by way of discharge or repayment of tax'; that is, they are set against the precise income to which they relate, for example against income from leasing plant and machinery or industrial buildings. In such cases, unused capital allowances are carried forward and relieved against income from *the same source* in future years.

Concluding comment

Capital expenditure is not allowable as a business expense when calculating taxable profits. However, as we have seen in this chapter, many items of capital expenditure do benefit from special capital allowances and thereby reduce the amount of income chargeable to tax.

In the following chapter we turn to consider the tax treatment of employees.

4

Taxing income from employment

It is essential that those running businesses understand how employees' earnings are taxed. UK tax legislation places a large onus on employers to ensure that so far as employees are concerned Income Tax collection is correctly operated.

Employees are taxed under Schedule E, which also extends to the emoluments of office holders. An 'office' denotes 'a subsisting, permanent, substantive position which has an existence independent of the person who fills it, and which is filled in succession by successive holders' (Rowlatt, J. in *Great Western Railway Co.* v. *Bater* 1920). Examples of office holders are trustees and executors, land charges registrars, National Health Service consultants and the directors of companies. Since the same tax treatment applies to the emoluments of offices and employments, the term 'employment' is used throughout this chapter to cover both categories.

The term 'emoluments' is defined widely in the relevant legislation (s.131 Income and Corporation Taxes Act 1988) to include 'all salaries, fees, wages, perquisites and profits whatsoever'. Pensions arising from a previous employment are also taxed under Schedule E. In addition, further legislation has been enacted over the years to bring into tax various *benefits in kind* (such as company cars, medical expenses and accommodation), certain social security payments, notably unemployment benefit, and certain kinds of 'golden handshake' which were not taxable under the normal charging provisions.

The chapter begins by considering how to distinguish employment from self-employment, before turning to how the emoluments of offices and employments are taxed, including the tax treatment of lump-sum payments, benefits in kind and employment expenses. While the kinds of incomes which can be charged to tax have been defined widely, as was stated in the case of *Lomax* v. *Newton* (1953), the rules on deducting expenses from the emoluments of an employment or office are 'notoriously rigid, narrow and restricted in their operation'. This chapter also reviews the 'pay as you earn' (PAYE) procedures, and concludes with a look at employees' national insurance contributions (NIC).

The meaning of employment

It is usually more tax advantageous to be categorized as self-employed than as an employee. The rules on allowable expenses are more generous for the self-employed. Also, the self-employed do not have tax deducted at source but instead settle their tax bills many months after the income is earned (as explained in Chapter 2). Therefore, it is not surprising that disagreements often arise with the Revenue as to whether someone is self-employed or an employee for tax purposes. Recently, for example, the Revenue has mounted a vigorous campaign to reclassify many entertainers as employees who were previously treated as self-employed.

Often it is quite clear whether someone is an employee. But there are a surprising number of grey areas. For instance, if a management consultant is taken on to advise on business plans, should he be paid under deduction of tax (the Schedule E treatment) or gross (the Schedule D treatment)? If someone manages a club or public house, should he treat the pianist and DJ as employees and what about casual bar staff? It is important that management get the answer right because it is the employer who is legally responsible for deducting the tax and national insurance under PAYE. Unless it can be shown that the employer took reasonable care to comply with the PAYE regulations, the Revenue can collect the tax and NIC from an employer even when he or she has failed to deduct the relevant sums from staff pay.

In Chapter 2 we considered the 'badges of trade' and how they can sometimes help in deciding whether someone is trading. Similarly, from numerous court cases over the years we are able to distil a number of indicators of employment. They are as follows:

1. *The nature of the contract.* The first question to be decided is whether the contract under which someone works is a *contract of service*

(which denotes employment) or a *contract for service* (associated with self-employment). Although employers have a legal obligation to provide written employment contracts, some fail to do so and we must fall back on the verbal or implied contract. But even where a written contract exists the courts will look through it if the facts suggest that the relationship is actually different. Therefore, it is not sufficient to get someone to sign a contract saying they are self-employed – if, in fact, they are not.

2. *Working time.* Is the time of work specified in the contract? Employees usually have stipulated hours of working, but this is not necessarily conclusive since a self-employed person may also be contracted to provide services in a given period.

3. *Location of the work.* Employees normally work at the firm's premises, though this is not always true and some self-employed people may also be based there.

4. *Provision of tools and equipment.* It is usual, though again not always the case, that employers provide their employees with the necessary equipment to undertake their duties, whereas the self-employed bring their own tools. In the case of *Nethermere (St Neots) Ltd* v. *Taverna* (1984) home workers using sewing machines provided by a firm and almost exclusively undertaking work for that firm were held to be its employees.

5. *The terms of payment.* Employees are usually paid each week or month whereas the self-employed are more likely to be paid at the end of the contract or through stage payments. Also, the self-employed are likely to quote a fixed rate for the job, though some may charge on a time basis.

6. *Risk-taking.* Self-employed people face risks of financial loss but also derive profits. This is not usually true of employees who receive agreed wages (though employee profit-sharing schemes exist).

7. *Freedom to subcontract.* Normally employees are not allowed to subcontract their work. This is sometimes, but not always, permitted for the self-employed.

8. *Entitlement to sick pay and paid holidays.* These are not usually provided to the self-employed.

9. *Frequency of engagements.* Where someone has a series of engagements and moves from one to another, then each engagement is likely to be treated as a mere engagement in practising a trade or profession. Employment implies the contemplation of obtaining a post and staying in it (*Davies* v. *Braithwaite,* 1931). At the same time, however, casual staff can be employees and in the case of *Fall* v. *Hitchen* (1973) a professional ballet dancer was held to be an employee of a particular company because the contract under which he was working appeared to be a contract of service.

What we have here is a list of 'guides', or *badges of employment,* as follows:

- Contract of service.
- Working time stipulated.
- Location at the employer's premises.
- Employer provides tools and equipment.
- Payment by wage or salary.
- No risk-taking.
- No freedom to subcontract.
- Entitled to sick pay and paid leave.
- Limited number of contracts.

None is in itself crucial. Instead, the facts in each case must be assessed on the basis of the guidelines. Overall, the question that has to be answered is the following: *is the person providing the services, performing them as a person in business on own account?* Where this is answered negatively, the person is an employee.

Taxing Schedule E income

The basis of assessment

From 6 April 1989 the rules for assessing Schedule E income were changed from assessing the earnings in a tax year to assessing the amounts received. A difference could arise, for example where a bonus or commission was earned in one tax year but not paid to the next. For the vast majority of taxpayers the change has had no effect because they receive their income shortly after it is earned. The new rule is important, however, for company directors, who regularly receive bonuses and other incomes which relate back to services given in earlier periods. They are now taxed on their income when it is received, which makes the administration simpler both for management and the Inland Revenue. Income when received no longer has to be apportioned to the tax years in which it was earned.

To avoid abuse, legislation has been passed to clarify when income is to be treated as received. The rule is that emoluments are to be treated as received at the *earliest* of the following times:

- The time when payment is made.

- The time when a person becomes entitled to a payment; it should be noted that when an emolument is credited to a director's account with his or her company – although there may be restrictions on freedom to draw on this account – for the purposes of Schedule E, including the operation of PAYE, the director is at that date treated as having become entitled to the payment.

- In the case of a director, where the amount of the emoluments for the period is determined only after the end of a period (e.g. the company's accounting year), the time when the amount is determined. But where the determination occurs before the end of the period, the relevant time is the end of the period.

The total amount taxed in any year will be the salary or wage plus any additional emoluments arising from the employment, such as bonuses and taxable benefits in kind. Where an employee's income tax is paid by the employer, he or she is treated as having received additional remuneration equal to the tax. The salary must therefore be grossed up and the Income Tax is calculated on this sum (with a basic rate of tax of 25%, the salary would be multiplied by 100/75).

An exception to the new receipts basis applies to 'golden handshakes'. These are still treated as being received at the date of the termination to which they relate. This provision exists to prevent the moving of payments to years where a lower tax rate applies.

The taxpayer is under a legal obligation to advise the Inland Revenue of all emoluments of the tax year when completing a Tax Return or, where the Inland Revenue has not requested a Return, within one year of the end of the tax year. Failure can lead to interest and penalty charges for evasion.

The cases of Schedule E

Schedule E is divided into the following three cases, which determine the precise emoluments charged to tax (s.19 Income and Corporation Taxes Act 1988):

1. *Case I.* This case applies to individuals who are resident and ordinarily resident in the UK. They are taxed on their emoluments no matter where they arise (whether in the UK or overseas). The terms residence and ordinary residence and the tax treatment of overseas earnings for those absent from the UK for a year or more, are discussed in detail in Chapter 7.

2. *Case II.* Those employees and office holders not resident or if resident not ordinarily resident in the UK are taxed under Case II. This case taxes only the emoluments from duties in the UK. In other words, overseas earnings for those not UK resident escape tax. However, those resident but not ordinarily resident may also suffer tax under Case III.

3. *Case III.* Case III taxes certain emoluments which would otherwise escape tax under Cases I and II. It applies to UK residents who have earnings from overseas duties, but only in so far as these earnings are remitted to the UK and not taxed under Case I. In other words, it falls on remitted earnings of employees who are resident but not ordinarily resident in the UK.

Lump-sum payments

Ex gratia payments

Over the years the courts have ruled that income is taxable under the rules of Schedule E if it is a reward for services arising from an employment. However, a payment will not be a reward for services where it 'is given by way of present or testimonial on grounds personal to the recipient' or where it is 'a gift to him as an individual . . . by reason of his personal needs . . . [or] by reason of his personal qualities or attainments' (Jenkins, L. J. in *Moorhouse* v. *Dooland* 1954). For example in the celebrated case of *Moore* v. *Griffiths* (1972), a bonus paid by the Football Association to the England team players following their 1966 World Cup success was held to be in recognition of a unique achievement and not a product of their normal services. Hence, the bonus was not taxable. Similarly, benefit-match gate money paid over to a professional cricketer towards the end of his career was judged not to be an emolument of his employment (*Seymour* v. *Reed* 1927).

In both of these cases, there was no *entitlement* to the payment under the employment contract and this was no doubt highly influential in the courts. However, the fact that there is no entitlement does not *necessarily* remove payments from tax. For example, in the case of *Laidler* v. *Perry* (1966) gifts by the employer of £10 vouchers to all staff at Christmas were held to be taxable. Nor does the payment have to be made by the employer. For example, in *Moorhouse* v. *Dooland*, a Lancashire League cricketer was entitled to have a hat passed around the ground whenever he scored 50 or took 6 for 30. The donations were held to be a reflection of the crowd's pleasure in his achievement as a cricketer. The donations were therefore taxable as emoluments of his employment. Equally important in this case was the fact that recurrent payments occurred. The cricketer received eleven collections in one season. This contrasts with the payment in *Moore* v. *Griffiths* where, as the judge aptly observed, the English World Cup success 'had no foreseeable element of recurrence'! At the same time, however, there does not *have* to be repetition for one-off payments to be taxable. A waiter who is tipped for good service only once, is still liable to be taxed on that tip!

Golden hellos

A related set of principles operates with regards to payments made to attract a person to a new employment. In the case of *Jarrold* v. *Boustead* (1964), an amateur rugby player turned professional and received a £3,000 signing-on fee. This escaped tax. The courts ruled that the payment was not related to services to be performed as a professional player but to compensate him for giving up his amateur status. The same principle applied where an accountant was given £7,000 in shares as an inducement to become managing director of a company (*Pritchard* v. *Arundale* 1971). Again it was held that the payment was compensation, this time for leaving private practice.

These judgments contrast with other and not wholly dissimilar cases where payments were held to be emoluments. In *Riley* v. *Cogan* (1968) a payment to a player to move to a new club, and which was paid on the understanding that he would serve for twelve years or repay a proportion of the fee, was held to be taxable. It was a payment which clearly arose out of services to be performed at the club and this was emphasized by the clause requiring repayment if the contract was terminated early. From the above cases, it should be clear that there will often be plenty of scope for argument about the nature of a lump-sum payment. In deciding whether it is taxable as an emolument, much will turn on the facts in each case. Why was the payment made? What is its true nature?

Other one-off payments

Sometimes lump-sum payments are made which do not arise out of the employment contract. In *Hochstrasser* v. *Mayes* (1960) an employer compensated an employee for a loss he made when he sold his house on transfer to another part of the country. The loss was held to arise from his capacity as a house owner not as an employee. In effect, the agreement was outside the scope of the employment. Similarly, a school teacher's travel allowance paid to cover the expenses of attending parent evenings were deemed not to be emoluments (*Donnelly* v. *Williamson* 1982). The fact that attendance involved voluntary activities which were not part of the duties of the employment appears to have been crucial here.

However, in a more recent case involving civil servants at the GCHQ in Cheltenham who gave up their right to union membership, a compensation payment of £1,000 per person was held to be taxable. The court ruled that the payment was not for forfeiting individual rights but rights which applied to all employees and to which as employees they had become entitled (*Hamblett* v. *Godfrey* 1986).

Ex gratia awards in recognition of long service may be exempt from tax provided they are reasonable. The Inland Revenue has a view as to what is reasonable and its advice should be sought if in doubt. Tips and gratuities normally arise out of the employment and are taxable as part of the earnings from the employment (presumably the waiter would not have been tipped if he had not provided the appropriate service).

Compensation payments

From the above cases it appears that lump-sum payments, which are not a requirement under the contract of employment or paid in return for past or future services, are likely to escape tax under the normal Schedule E charging rules.

However, this is not the end of the story, for specific legislation (s.148 Income and Corporation Taxes Act 1988) exists to bring certain payments which fall outside the normal charging rules into tax. Specifically covered are payments relating to the following:

- Compensation for the termination of the employment contract.
- Breaching or changing the nature of the employment contract.

The legislation applies to cash settlements and the market value of any assets transferred. All but the first £30,000 of a payment falling within the above categories is chargeable to tax (however, the full amount must be included in gross pay for national insurance purposes). This applies provided there is no right to the compensation under the terms of the contract. Where such a right exists the payment derives from the employment contract and hence it is taxable under the normal Schedule E rules. In other words, if the employment contract stipulates compensation if the contract is terminated, breached or changed, the sum is taxable in full.

Completely exempt from tax are payments on termination of employment following death or injury or disability. Statutory redundancy payments and lump-sum payments from an approved pension scheme also escape tax. Non-statutory, but contractual redundancy payments fall under the normal charging rules but, by concession, the Inland Revenue treats them in the same way as statutory redundancy payments, provided they are reasonable in relation to length of service and are not merely made to selected employees.

Restrictive covenants

Legislation exists to prevent restrictive covenants being used to create tax-free terminal payments. Where an individual receives a payment in return for giving an undertaking, for example not to work in the same field of employment in the future, in the hands of the recipient the payment is deemed to have suffered basic rate of tax (though no actual tax is deducted by the payer). The sum is therefore only subject to Income Tax at the higher rate. As the basic rate deduction is purely notional, non-taxpayers cannot reclaim the tax.

The PAYE system

Although people often say they are taxed 'PAYE', this is not strictly correct. Emoluments of employments and offices are taxed under Schedule E of Income Tax; the PAYE procedure is merely a system for *collecting* the tax. Paying the correct amount of tax over to the Inland Revenue without the Revenue needing to issue formal tax assessments is the principle behind the system (ss.203–7 Income and Corporation Taxes Act 1988, also Statutory Instrument no. 334 1973). In so far as the need for tax assessments is drastically reduced, this lowers the cost of administration for government. The cynic might say that it transfers much of the cost to employers!

Basic principles

Under PAYE the tax year is divided into twelve months, each ending on the 5th day of the month. Every time an employer makes a payment of wage to an employee which exceeds the PAYE threshold (in 1991/2 £63.45 a week or £275 per month), he or she is required to deduct tax. The tax is then paid over to the Collector of Taxes within fourteen days of the end of the appropriate tax month, i.e. by the 19th of the following month (because the Income Tax year runs to 5 April, each tax month ends on the 5th). Employees' and employers' national insurance contributions are also collected through the PAYE procedure and paid over to the accounts office. From 6 April 1991, where an employer's average monthly payments of PAYE and NIC are less than £400, payments to the Collector may be made quarterly rather than monthly. This concession should reduce administrative costs for very small businesses and improve cash flow.

By law the employer must operate the PAYE system for all employees including part-time and casual staff and workers supplied by agencies (with certain exceptions). All the necessary forms and instructions will be sent by the tax office. It should be noted that the tax office handling the PAYE scheme may not be the same as that which deals with the company's or business's tax.

The cumulative PAYE system should deduct the correct amount of tax for the year and therefore most employees will never receive a formal Schedule E assessment. Nor will they regularly receive a tax return to complete, though this does not remove the obligation on individuals to notify the Revenue where tax is due. Only where there are emoluments which have escaped the PAYE system (for example, new benefits in kind which have not been reflected in an individual's coding) or a taxpayer realizes that further reliefs are due, should there be any need for the Inland Revenue to issue formal Schedule E assessments after the year end. Another circumstance where the need for a formal assessment may arise is where there are a number of sources of income and higher rate tax has not been fully levied.

Emoluments included

The earnings on which PAYE must be operated are as follows:

- Wages and salaries.
- Bonuses.
- Overtime payments.
- Commissions.
- Round-sum expenses.
- Payments from profit-sharing schemes.
- Holiday and sick pay.
- Certain lump-sum payments, e.g. on termination of employment.
- Drawings on account of future remuneration.
- Vouchers exchangeable for cash.

Wages of sole proprietors and partners are not within PAYE. They are taxed on their profits, not their drawings, under Cases I and II of Schedule D (see Chapter 2).

Operating PAYE

The UK operates a cumulative system so that the amount of tax deducted each month should ensure that there is no remaining tax to pay at the end of the year. To enable the employer to deduct the correct amount of tax, the Inland Revenue issues tax tables to employers and provides a code number for each employee which reflects their entitlement to personal allowances against tax. The code number is derived by adding to the individual's personal allowance entitlement any allowable expenses and other reliefs and by deducting amounts to reflect certain benefits in kind or underpayments of tax in earlier years. The last digit of the total is then disregarded. For example, if someone was entitled only to personal allowances of £3,295, their code number would be 329. Each code number also contains a letter suffix, which denotes a person's tax status as follows:

- **H:** married man (or single person entitled to additional personal allowance).

- **L:** single person (including married women).

- **V:** married man entitled to additional allowances because of old age (age allowance).

- **P:** single person entitled to age allowance.

- **BR:** no personal allowances to be given, all income to suffer tax at the basic rate (this tends to apply in the main where people have two or more sources of income and personal allowances are already fully relieved against the other income).

- **D:** higher rate tax applies (the prefix D is followed by the appropriate higher rate).

- **NT:** no tax is to be deducted.

- **F:** indicates that tax from a pension is to be deducted from current earnings.

- **OT:** no allowances, tax is to be deducted at the appropriate marginal rates.

In addition, the suffix T may be used, which requires an employer to consult his or her tax office before making changes to an employee's coding.

The use of these codes simplifies the alteration of tax allowances following a Budget change. For example, the instruction can go out, raise all code numbers with suffix H by 40 (representing £400 additional personal allowance). Once the employer receives this instruction, the employees' allowances are raised and the PAYE system begins to collect the correct amount of tax given the new allowances.

Three main sets of tax tables are issued to employers, Tables A, B and C. Table A comes in two forms – one for weekly paid employees and one for monthly paid workers. Both forms provide the same information. They show the cumulative total allowances to date for each code number (i.e. the amount of allowances to date in the tax year to which the employee is entitled). These allowances, called 'free pay', are then deducted from the total amount of pay to date to give the taxable pay that week or month. The employer, on consulting Table B, will then discover the total tax due for that employee to date. By deducting the amount of tax paid so far, the amount of tax to be deducted on this occasion is then revealed. Where a taxpayer is liable to higher rate tax, this is also collected by deduction from salary using Table C. An example of how the tax tables work is given in Figure 4.1.

To assist the administration of this system the Revenue issues a working sheet (P11) which guides an employer through the various stages. It also provides space to calculate the amount of employer's and employee's national insurance due. In practice, major employers tend to use their own computerized records which contain the same information and which the Revenue normally accepts.

Changing jobs

Whenever an employee leaves a job, the employer is required to furnish the employee with a form P45 on or shortly after leaving. This gives details of the employee's name, national insurance and PAYE code number and total pay and tax deducted to date. The form is in three parts. The old employer sends Part 1 to his tax office, and the employee passes Parts 2 and 3 to the new employer, who in turn retains Part 2 and sends Part 3 to his tax office. The new employer immediately has sufficient information to begin operating the PAYE system when the first wage is paid and the new and old tax offices communicate to transfer the appropriate records.

Where an employee does not have a P45 for the current year from a previous employer or unemployment benefit office, the employer sends a form P46 to his tax office and issues the employee with a coding claim form to complete (a P15). Where the form provides insufficient details to track down the necessary tax records, the tax office in turn sends a Tax Return to the employee to ascertain entitlement to reliefs and allowances. In the meantime, the employer will normally be required to operate the PAYE system on a 'week 1/month 1' basis (popularly known as 'emergency code'). That is to say, a monthly paid

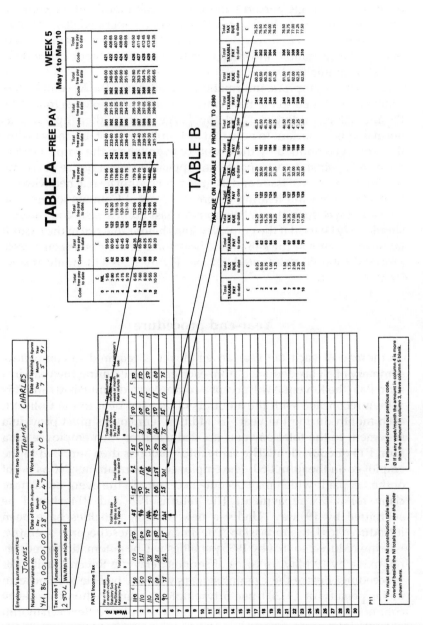

Figure 4.1 How the tax tables work: an example

employee would be given personal allowances equivalent to one-twelfth of the single person's allowance each month and the cumulative procedure for deducting tax would not be operated. This applies unless the employee can certify on the form P46 that he was previously in full-time education, in which case the emergency code is operated but on a cumulative basis.

Once the appropriate information is available to the Revenue, a tax code will be issued to the new employer and the employee (on forms P6 and P2 respectively), and the PAYE system then operates as normal. It is important to note that an employer must use the code for the employee notified by the tax office even where the employee has appealed against it. A taxpayer can appeal against a notice of coding within thirty days of issue and if agreement cannot be reached with the Inspector, request a hearing before the Appeal Commissioners. If a new employee furnishes a P45 from the last tax year, the code shown should only be used if the employee joins before 26 April in the current tax year. Otherwise the P45 should be ignored and the emergency code procedure should be adopted instead. Figure 4.2 is a facsimile of form P45.

Year-end procedure

At the end of each tax year an employer is required to complete a summary of all tax deducted from each employee during the year on a form P35 (the Revenue will accept a computerized equivalent) and this is then reconciled with the amounts of tax paid over to the Collector each month during the year. In addition, employers must provide a statement of the total pay and tax deducted for each employee on a form P14 or equivalent. The same information is then supplied to the employee on the form P60. The employee must retain his P60 as proof of the tax paid; which may become necessary in the event of a future claim for a tax repayment. The returns P35 and P14 should be submitted by 19 May. Under a new system, penalties have been introduced for late submission. The time when these become operative is being reduced so that by 1995 penalties will be automatic for returns not made by 19 May. In cases of serious delay the Revenue will take proceedings before the Commissioners who will be able to impose an initial penalty of £1,200 per fifty employees and, where the delay continues, a further penalty of £100 per fifty employees for each month of further delay.

P45 Details of employee leaving   **Part 1**

		District number	Reference number
1.	PAYE reference		

2. National Insurance number

3. Surname
   Use CAPITALS   Mr. Mrs. Miss. Ms.

   First two
   forenames
   Use CAPITALS

		Day	Month	Year
4.	Date of leaving *in figures*			19

			Code	Week 1 or Month 1
5.	Code at date of leaving			

If Week 1 or Month 1 basis applies, please also write 'X' in the box marked 'Week 1 or Month 1'

			Week	Month
6.	Last entries on Deductions Working Sheet *If Week 1 or Month 1 basis applies, complete item 7 instead*	Week or month number		
		Total pay to date	£	p.
		Total tax to date	£	p

7.	Week 1 or Month 1 basis applies	Total pay in this employment	£	p.
		Total tax in this employment	£	p

8.	Works Number		9. Branch, Contract Department, etc.	

10. Employee's private address _____

_____

_____ Postcode _____

11. I certify that the details entered at items 1 to 9 above are correct.

Employer

Address

Date   Postcode

Instructions to employer
                                                   For Tax Office use

● Complete this form following the 'Employee leaving' instructions on the form P8. Make sure the details are clear on all three parts.

● Detach Part 1 and send it to your Tax Office **IMMEDIATELY**.

● Hand Parts 2 and 3 (unseparated) to your employee **WHEN HE LEAVES.**

● IF THE EMPLOYEE HAS DIED, please write 'D' in this box and send ALL THREE PARTS of this form (unseparated) to your Tax Office **IMMEDIATELY.**

P45   © Crown Copyright 1990

Figure 4.2 Facsimile form P45

PAYE audit

It is a legal requirement that employers operate the PAYE system correctly and this includes keeping all the necessary records and making the necessary returns. If insufficient Income Tax or national insurance contributions are deducted, the Revenue has powers to obtain the amounts unpaid from the employer. In other words, if someone is paid gross who says they will 'sort out their own tax' or says they are 'self-employed' when *in fact* they are not, the legal liability to pay over the missing tax and NIC may fall on the employer. The Inspector can raise an assessment to recover the tax lost (called a Regulation 29 assessment) and can go back six years. He will also now charge interest on unpaid tax which runs from whichever is the later: the fourteenth day after the end of the tax year to which the tax relates or 19 April 1988 (when the interest charge was introduced).

A specialist section of the Revenue, called 'PAYE Audit', is primarily responsible for calling on employers to check whether the PAYE system is being operated correctly. They look particularly for evidence of casual staff and round-sum expenses paid gross, and payments to directors without proper deduction of tax and NIC. Where PAYE Audit finds errors, this will be notified to the local tax office and this may in turn lead to a full investigation of the company or business accounts.

Benefits in kind

In the post-war period, high rates of tax in the UK led to the development of non-cash payments to employees, which escaped tax on their full value. In response, governments introduced legislation to increase the tax on benefits in kind. This legislation also covers the reimbursement of certain employee's expenses by employers. Consequently, some benefits are taxable on all employees, some on only 'higher paid' employees and directors, and others are still not taxable.

Benefits taxable on all employees

Benefits provided by an employer to an employee and which can be converted into *cash* or *money's worth* are taxable on all employees (unless specifically exempted) under the normal Schedule E charging rules. The principle was succinctly stated by Lord Macnaghten in one of the earliest court cases on fringe benefits (*Tennant* v. *Smith* 1892): 'a person is chargeable for Income Tax under . . . Schedule E, not on what saves his pocket, but on what goes into his pocket.' Thus in the case of *Wilkins* v. *Rogerson* (1961) an employee who received clothing costing the employer £14.75 was assessed only on its second-hand value, £5.

However, specific legislation (ss.141–6 Income and Corporation Taxes Act 1988) overrules the normal Schedule E charging rules for the following benefits which are taxable on all employees:

- *Credit cards, credit tokens and vouchers*. Where credit cards, tokens or vouchers exchangeable for goods and services are provided by an employer, the employee is taxed on the cost to the employer of providing the voucher (included are travel season tickets). This means that if there were now a case similar to that of *Wilkins* v. *Rogerson*, where the employee was given a voucher costing £14.75 to spend on clothes, the full £14.75 would be assessable and not the 'money's worth'.

- *Beneficial living accommodation*. Unless the accommodation is *job-related*, the provision of living accommodation by an employer is assessed as a benefit. The benefit is valued at the greater of either the annual value of the property or, where relevant, the rent paid by the employer. The annual value is the gross rateable value for property in the UK, and for a property overseas the rent that could have been obtained. Although the community charge replaced domestic rates in Scotland from April 1989 and from April 1990 in England and Wales, the former rateable value is still used. For new properties a substitute value in line with the old domestic rateable value applies. Where the employee makes a contribution towards the employer's cost of provision, this is deducted from the taxable benefit. Similarly, where a building is partly used for business purposes, normally only the proportion used for domestic purposes is taxed as a benefit. Accommodation available to the employee for only part of the year is assessed on an appropriate proportion of the annual charge. The employee pays the full amount, however, if the property is *available* for the full year but he or she chooses only to use it from time to time.

  As rateable values do not necessarily reflect the true value of properties, a further charge arises if the cost of the property (including the cost of any improvements) exceeds £75,000. The value of the additional benefit is calculated by applying an 'official' rate of interest to the excess of the cost over £75,000 (the 'official' rate varies reflecting national interest rate movements). This value is then taxed as an additional benefit. Where an employer provides as a benefit a property which he has owned for six years or more, the open market value at the time it is *first provided* is substituted for the cost.

'Job-related accommodation' escapes tax but it is narrowly defined to include only accommodation in the following categories:

(a) necessary for the performance of the duties (e.g. lighthouse keeper, publican, security guard); or

(b) provided for the better performance of the duties and where it is customary for accommodation to be provided (e.g. hospital and hotel staff, police housing); or

(c) provided for security purposes (for persons at special risk, e.g. cabinet ministers).

Directors cannot claim exemption under the first two categories unless they are full-time working directors or directors of not-for-profit activities, and they own (directly or through associates) not more than 5% of the company.

EXAMPLE

Widgets Ltd provides its managing director, Paul Widget, with a flat in Kensington which it purchased ten years ago for £90,000. The current market value of the flat is £350,000. The rateable value of the property is £1,200 and the official interest rate is currently 10%. Paul pays rent to the company of £500 a month.

Paul will be assessed on this benefit as follows:

	£
Rateable value of the property	1,200
Plus (£350,000 − 75,000) × 10%	27,500
	28,700
Less rent paid	6,000
Assessable benefit	22,700

If an employer provides services relating to the property, for example a gardener, the cost is charged as a benefit only on higher-paid employees and directors.

- *Benefits in lieu of salary and meeting an employee's expenses.* Where an employee negotiates to forgo salary in return for a fringe benefit, the normal second-hand value rule does not apply. The assessment is on the full value of the salary forgone. For instance, in the case of *Cordy* v. *Gordon* (1925) a husband and wife were employed by an asylum on terms that the employer provided them with board, lodging, laundry and a uniform and in return a sum was deducted from their gross pay. The gross salaries were held to be assessable. This principle was later extended in the case of *Heaton* v. *Bell* (1970) to an employee who accepted a reduction of £2 per week in wages in return for the loan of a car. It was held that he was taxable on the gross wage including the £2. It is important, therefore, in drawing up employment contracts not to state or imply either that the fringe benefit offered is in return for a given salary reduction, or that there is a higher salary alternative in lieu of the benefit.

Where an employer pays debts of the employee, for example a home telephone bill, the employee is taxable on the cost to the company and not on money's worth. Hence in the *Wilkins* v. *Rogerson* case referred to earlier, the full £14.75 would have been taxable if the employee had paid for the clothing and the employer had reimbursed him. This principle was established in the case of *Nicoll* v. *Austin* (1935), which concerned a company paying a director's rates, lighting, heating, telephone and gardening bills. Since the 1930s, special legislation has been passed extending the basis for assessing benefits provided to directors and 'higher paid' employees. The *Nicoll* v. *Austin* judgment remains relevant, however, for other (i.e. lower-paid) employees.

Benefits taxable on higher-paid employees and directors

Today, because of inflation the term 'higher paid' is completely misleading. It applies to anyone earning £8,500 or more *including the value of the benefits in kind* and before deducting allowable expenses – around two-thirds national average earnings! The legislation (ss.154–6 Income and Corporation Taxes Act 1988) also extends the charge to directors no matter their level of pay and to the families or households of higher-paid employees and directors. Moreover, the legislation extends the meaning of the term 'director' to include any person who acts as a director or any person in accordance with whose instructions the directors are accustomed to act (excluding professional advisers). The only exceptions, as in the case of living accommodation discussed above, are full-time working directors and directors of 'not for profit' organizations, and only then provided they do not own more than 5% of the company (and these directors are still caught if they are classed as 'higher paid', i.e. they earn £8,500 or more a year). It is also important to note that benefits do not need to be provided directly by the employer to be assessed. They must merely arise 'by reason of the employment'.

The following are the main benefits chargeable:

* *Cars.* The charge is based on a 'scale charge' which is updated each year and values the benefit according to the age and value of the car, its cubic capacity and in some cases its original cost. The cost for this purpose is not necessarily the price paid by the employer, but the price at which it might have been expected to sell if sold singly in a retail sale (in other words, fleet discounts are ignored). The scale charge for 1991/2 is shown in Table 4.1.

    In recent years, the Chancellor has raised the scale charge ahead of the inflation rate to increase the tax on company cars.

    The charge is reduced on a pound-for-pound basis where the employee is *required* to contribute towards the cost of private use,

Table 4.1 The car scale charge

Original market value	Age of car at the end of the year	
	Under 4 years old 1991/2 £	4 years old or more 1991/2 £
Not exceeding £19,250		
1400cc or less	2,050	1,400
1401cc–2000cc	2,650	1,800
2001cc or more	4,250	2,850
Cars having an original market value exceeding £19,250		
£19,251–£29,000	5,500	3,700
£29,001 or more	8,900	5,900

but not where the employee makes a voluntary contribution. It is also reduced on a pro rata basis when either the vehicle is made available to the employee for only part of a tax year, or where the vehicle is incapable of being used for at least thirty consecutive days.

In order to tax most heavily 'perk' cars, where a car is used for 2,500 miles or less per year on business the scale charge is increased by 50%. Similarly, where two or more cars are provided to the employee, including his family, there is a 50% loading on the scale charge for other than the first car. On the other hand, where a car is used for 18,000 miles or more per year on business, the scale charge is *halved*.

Exempted as benefits in kind and hence the scale charge are cars with no private use and 'pool cars'. To be classified as a pool car, the vehicle must meet all of the following criteria:

(a) it must be available for use by, and actually used by, more than one employee;

(b) it must not normally be garaged at or near an employee's home;

(c) any private use must be only incidental to the business use.

The car scale charge covers the provision of the vehicle, a car phone, the road fund licence and costs relating to maintenance, repair and insurance, but it does not cover the provision of petrol for private motoring, for which there is a separate scale charge, or the costs of a chauffeur or expenses such as parking fees, fines and tolls. The cost of these borne by the employer is assessed in full on the employee, though the employee can make an offsetting expenses claim where appropriate. However, employees are not taxed on the cost of car parking paid by the employer at or near their place of work. In the 1991 Budget the Chancellor proposed to tax for the first time mobile telephones provided by employers, based on a new scale charge of £200 per telephone.

- *Fuel for private motoring.* There is a further scale charge based on the vehicle's cubic capacity where an employer provides fuel for private motoring. This charge is not raised where a vehicle is used for 2,500 miles or less on business, but it is reduced by 50% for business mileages of 18,000 miles or more in the year (it is difficult to identify the logic here). If an employee reimburses *all* the cost of private fuel no scale charge is levied. However, there is no reduction for partial reimbursement.

The fuel scale charge in 1991/2 is shown in Table 4.2.

Table 4.2 The fuel scale charge

	£
1,400cc or less	480
1,401cc–2,000cc	600
2001cc or more	900

- *Expenses connected with living accommodation.* As noted above, the provision of living accommodation is a chargeable benefit on all employees unless it is job-related. Higher-paid employees and directors are also charged where the employer pays the costs of the following:

  (a) decoration and repairs and maintenance;

  (b) heating, lighting and cleaning;

  (c) furnishings.

  The benefit is measured as the cost to the employer less any amounts reimbursed by the employee, or, in the case of furnishings which continue to be owned by the employer, 20% per annum of their market value when first provided. Where the accommodation is job-related (as defined earlier), although the provision of the accommodation escapes assessment, these additional expenses are charged as a benefit. The charge, however, is limited to 10% of the employee's net emoluments (salary plus other benefits in kind less allowable expenses), *excluding* the benefit from the accommodation-related expenses. The cost of providing other benefits related to living accommodation, for example a private telephone line, is taxed in full.

- *Medical expenses.* The payment of medical care and medical insurance is a taxable benefit on directors and the higher paid based on the cost to the employer. Medical costs and insurance necessitated by working abroad on business are excluded.

- *Scholarships for employees' children.* Where a scholarship to a higher paid employee's or director's child is provided directly or indirectly by the employer, its value is taxed as a benefit. The charge can be avoided if it is shown that the scholarship is not a consequence of the parent's employment and that not more than 25% of the scholarship payments made by the employer in the particular year were made by reason of the employment. This takes out of charge a scholarship won by an employee's child in open competition with children in general.

- *Beneficial loans.* Loans made by an employer to a director or higher paid employee or a relative at no interest or low interest rates, are assessed on the cash equivalent of the benefit. The cash equivalent is calculated by applying the 'official interest rate' to the amount of the loan outstanding during the year (pro rata for parts of years). From this any interest actually paid by the employee is deducted. If the resulting amount exceeds a *de minimis* limit of £300 it is charged as a benefit on the full amount (not the balance over £300). Prior to 6 April 1991 the *de minimis* limit was £200. Where interest on the loan would have qualified for tax relief (e.g. loans for the purchase of the employee's home up to £30,000) no assessable benefit arises.

  The charge is extended to loans arranged, guaranteed or in any way facilitated by the employer. Where an employer releases or writes off all or part of a loan, the amount released or written off is assessed as a benefit.

EXAMPLE

Tom Peters, a higher-paid employee of JR plc, on 6 April 1992 received an interest-free company loan of £20,000 to help finance a costly divorce settlement. Assume the official interest rate was 10% until 6 October 1992 and 12% thereafter. Tom was unable to repay the loan and on 6 April 1993 it was written off.

In the year 1992/3 Tom will be assessed on a benefit valued at £2,200:

	£
(£20,000 × 10%) × 6 months/12 months	1,000
Plus (£20,000 × 12%) × 6 months/12 months	1,200
	2,200

In the year 1993/4 he will be assessed on the loan written off: £20,000.

- *The provision of other assets and benefits.* Where a director or higher paid employee or his family or household has the use of assets by reason of his or her employment, for example paintings, a company yacht, or holiday accommodation, the value of these benefits is taxable on the greater of the following:

(a) cost to the employer of hiring or leasing the asset;

(b) or 20% of its market value when first made available to the employee or director.

Where the employee or director contributes to the cost, this is deducted from the benefit charge.

In the case of assets where the ownership is transferred to the employee or director, the benefit is the greater of the following:

(a) market value at the time of acquisition, less the price if any paid by the employee;

(b) or the original market value when the asset was first made available to the employee, reduced by the value of benefits already charged on him or her and any price paid by him or her.

EXAMPLE

Tom King is a director of Kingwing Ltd, who have made available to him the use of a boat owned by the company and moored in the Solent. Its market value when first made available was £15,000, although it cost the company only £12,000.

The taxable benefit on Tom will be £3,000 per annum (20% of £15,000) – the lower cost to the company is ignored. If the boat was then sold to Tom for £1,000 in three years' time when its market value was £8,000, the benefit would be measured as:

	£
Market value when first made available	15,000
Benefit charge for 3 years	9,000
	6,000
Price paid by Tom	1,000
	5,000
Market value at time of sale	8,000
Price paid by Tom	1,000
	7,000

Therefore the chargeable benefit would be £7,000.

Tax-free benefits in kind

Some benefits in kind escape tax altogether. The main ones are as follows:

- Items provided for the employee at his place of work which are used solely for work purposes, for example desk, telephone, etc.
- Meals provided in the employer's canteen or restaurant provided they are available to all staff.
- Luncheon vouchers with a value of up to 15p per day(!).
- The reimbursement of reasonable costs associated with staff relocation, including the costs of temporary accommodation and contributions towards higher housing costs.
- The employer's contributions to pension and superannuation schemes approved by the superannuation funds office and geared to the benefits provided under the scheme.
- Benefits associated with qualifying profit-related pay schemes, profit-sharing schemes, and share option and save-as-you-earn share option schemes (but benefits from share options, etc., outside such approved schemes are taxed) – for further details see below.
- Entertainment including entertainment tickets and vouchers received by employees from third parties, for instance seats at sporting and cultural events, as long as it is not in return for specific services provided or to be provided.
- Car parking spaces at or near the place of employment.
- Travel home when an employee is occasionally required to work late.
- Removal costs reimbursed including reasonable excess housing costs.
- Annual Christmas parties and similar social functions provided to staff generally (the Revenue currently accepts a cost of up to £50 per head; where this is exceeded then the whole cost is assessable).
- Sports facilities provided by the employer and available to staff in general.
- Training courses and educational courses for staff aged under 21, including associated subsistence and travel, and certain scholarships to employees.
- Certain payments under staff suggestion schemes.

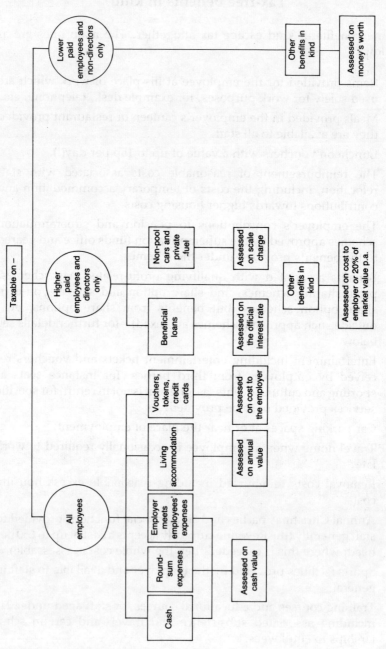

Figure 4.3 Taxable emoluments: a summary

- Modest gifts by an employer for personal reasons unconnected with services in the employment, for example long-service rewards, wedding gifts, etc.
- Since 6 April 1990, nursery provision where the employer provides and manages the facilities and these are not in domestic premises.

Profit-sharing and employee share schemes

Where shares are transferred to employees, under the normal charging rules of Schedule E Income Tax is due on the difference between the market value of the shares at the time of transfer and the price paid by the employee. The exercise of a share option can also trigger a tax charge on the difference between the option price and the market value of the shares at the time of the exercise.

However, in an effort to increase worker involvement in the success of their companies, government has introduced a number of tax privileges for approved schemes which increase employee share ownership. More recently, this has extended to profit-related pay. To avoid abuse, the rules under each scheme are quite complex and the following account is only a broad overview. The rules are subject to change.

Profit-related pay

Employees can receive part of their remuneration tax free under Revenue-approved profit-related pay schemes. The scheme must apply to at least 80% of the workforce (with an option to omit part-timers and new recruits for up to three years). Directors with a controlling interest in the company must be excluded.

The profit-related pay must be calculated at least once a year and all of the payment is tax free up to the level where the profit-related pay is the lower of the following:

- 20% of the employee's total remuneration for the year (benefits in kind and pension contributions excluded), or
- £4,000.

Prior to 1 April 1991, only one-half of the payment was tax free.

Profit-sharing schemes

No charge to Income Tax arises when an option is granted or exercised, or where shares are given or acquired at a preferential price, provided that this occurs under an approved share scheme. Capital Gains Tax will still apply, however, when the employee disposes of the shares.

Under an approved scheme an employer allocates a proportion of the profit to trustees who in turn purchase shares in the company or its holding company on behalf of the employees. In order to qualify the following must apply:

- The relevant shares must be unrestricted and non-redeemable ordinary shares.
- All UK directors and employees with five or more years' service must be eligible to participate.
- The value of shares allocated to each employee annually must not exceed £3,000 (£2,000 prior to 6 April 1991) or 10% of salary if greater, subject to a ceiling of £8,000 (before 6 April 1991 £6,000).

The shares must be held by the trustees for two years and by the employee for a further three years if full exemption is to be obtained. A charge to Income Tax will arise if the shares are sold within this period. Sale within four years leads to Income Tax on either the market value on acquisition by the trustees or the sale price if lower. Sale in the fifth year triggers a charge on 75% of the lower of these two values.

Save-as-you-earn (SAYE) share option schemes

Where employees have deducted from their pay by their employer sums which are paid into a national savings or building society SAYE scheme, they may be granted share options without the usual tax consequence. All employees and directors who work for the company for at least twenty-five hours a week qualify, provided that where the company is a close company (as defined below, p. 213), they do not own, with associates, more than 25% of the company or its holding company. The contributions must continue for at least five years, at which time they will attract a bonus of twelve months' contributions (or after seven years, twenty-four months' contributions). The savings are then used to purchase shares under the option.

The employee's savings under the scheme must be between £10 and £150 per month (from late 1991, £250). When the option is granted, the time at which it shall be exercised must be stipulated and it must be either five or seven years later. The share price under the option must not be less than 80% of the market price at the time the option is granted.

Employee share ownership plans (ESOPs)

Payments by a company to an employee share ownership trust, set up to acquire and distribute shares to its employees, are now deductible in computing the company's taxable profits. There are conditions relating to the nature of the trustees, the distribution of shares and the use of funds. Beneficiaries under the scheme must include all employees employed by the company for five years or more and who have worked for at least twenty hours a week (certain others may also be included). Anyone owning more than 5% of the share capital within the last twelve months cannot be a beneficiary when shares are distributed.

The executive share option scheme

This scheme may be restricted to key employees such as senior executives. Not surprisingly, therefore, it has proved to be the most popular of the share schemes and over 4,700 have been approved, but fewer than 2,000 have been extended to all employees.

Those eligible under the scheme include directors in the UK who work at least twenty-five hours per week and UK employees who work at least twenty hours per week. Excluded, however, are persons who own or have options to acquire more than 10% of the ordinary shares of their company (or its holding company), and their company is a 'close company' at any time in the year preceding either the grant or the exercise of the option.

Shares which receive favourable tax treatment are those which are acquired after three years but within ten years of the option being granted (but not within three years of exercising another option under an approved scheme). The price of the shares must be fixed at the time the option is granted and at a level not manifestly different to their market value at that time.

An employee may not hold unexercised options exceeding the greater of the following:

- £100,000.

- Four times the employee's remuneration of the current or previous year (benefits in kind and pension contributions excluded).

From 1 January 1992, provided a company has an all-employee share scheme, it will be able to grant options under an approved discretionary share option scheme at a discount of up to 15% of market value at the date the option was granted.

Reimbursement of expenses

Round-sum expenses which include an element of 'profit' and all expense payments to directors and higher-paid employees are taxable (s.153 Income and Corporation Taxes Act 1988). However, the employee may deduct expenses actually incurred provided they are allowable under the normal rules relating to Schedule E expenses (see below).

On application, the Revenue may grant a dispensation which allows the employer to pay the expenses without deducting tax at source. This will apply where the allowance would be covered fully by an expenses claim. To economize on administration, the Revenue actively encourages employers to seek dispensations and has produced a leaflet (IR69) which explains the procedure.

Where an employee receives a mileage allowance, this is an emolument of the employment against which technically running costs can be deducted but any excess payment is taxable (*Perrons* v. *Spackman* 1981). So that taxpayers do not have to keep detailed records of mileages and costs, the Revenue has laid down tax-free mileage rates which may be used (see Table 4.3). The basis for calculating the rates changed in 1991.

An employee can, however, claim actual costs rather than the rates shown in Table 4.3 if he keeps all the necessary records and satisfies the Inspector. An employee who 'necessarily' incurs the costs of providing a vehicle for use wholly in the performance of his employment duties

Table 4.3 1991 tax-free rates per mile

	Up to 1,000cc	1,001– 1,500cc	1,501– 2,000cc	over 2,000cc
Up to 4,000 miles p.a.	24.5p	30p	34p	43p
Over 4,000 miles p.a.	9.5p	11.5p	13.5p	16.5p

can claim running costs and capital allowances on the cost of the vehicle (less an adjustment for private usage).

Assessing benefits in kind and expenses

The value of benefits, for example the car scale charge, will commonly be deducted from personal allowances so that the correct amount of tax on the benefits is collected through the PAYE procedure. Where this does not occur, for example a one-off benefit which could not be reflected in the coding issued at the start of the year, or where a larger car scale charge becomes appropriate, tax on the benefits will be collected through a Schedule E tax assessment, which will be issued after the year end, or by adjustment to the following year's code.

At the end of each tax year, an employer is required to make a return to the Inland Revenue of all benefits in kind and expenses provided to higher-paid employees and directors (unless there is a dispensation). The return is made using the form P11D (see Figure 4.4). A form P9D is used to record benefits and expenses of more than £25 given to lower-paid employees and not included in taxable pay. There are penalties for failure to make a return or for incorrect returns.

Expenses

For expenses to be deductible they must have been incurred 'wholly, exclusively and necessarily in the performance of [the] . . . duties' of the office or employment (s.198 Income and Corporation Taxes Act 1988). This is a much tighter rule than the rule for trading expenses under Schedule D where the expenses have to be 'wholly and exclusively', but not 'necessarily' incurred, and where they have to be incurred 'for the purposes of the trade', not in the 'performance' of the trade. The consequence of this much tighter ruling is to exclude expenses in employment which would be allowed if occurred when trading.

The 'wholly, exclusively and necessarily in the performance of the duties' rule has been interpreted in a series of legal cases over many years. The courts have determined that the costs of travelling to and from work are not deductible. In the seminal case of *Ricketts* v. *Colquhoun* (1925) a London barrister who also acted as a recorder at Portsmouth claimed the costs of travelling between London and

**Inland Revenue
Income Tax**

Employer's name _____ PAYE reference _____

Employee's/director's
name _____ NI number

**Return of expenses payments and benefits etc - directors, and employees earning at a rate of £8500 a year or more.
Year ended 5 April 1991**

Please read form P11D (Guide) before completing this form.

You are required to make a return by 6 June 1991 of all expenses payments and benefits relating to -
- directors - *for certain exceptions see form P11D (Guide)*
- employees who are paid at a rate of £8,500 or more including expenses and benefits.

You should not show expenses covered by a dispensation *see form P11D (Guide).*
You are also asked to give details of certain remuneration in Part A below.

A Remuneration

1 Please give details of remuneration paid in the year to 5 April 1991 but earned in another year.

Description and period _____ Amount £ _____

B Cars and car fuel

2 **Cars made available for private use**
If more than one car made available during the year, give details of each car at (a) and (b)

Make and model   (a) _____ cc   (b) _____ cc

	" ✓ "		" ✓ "
Value when new £19,250 or less	☐		☐
£19,251 - £29,000	☐		☐
more than £29,000	☐		☐
First registered on or after 6.4.87	☐		☐
before 6.4.87	☐		☐

Made available to director/employee   from _____ to _____   from _____ to _____

The amount of any wages paid to a driver provided for the director/employee   £ _____
in respect of private journeys

Payment received from the director/employee for the private use of the car   £ _____

	Yes	" ✓ " No	Don't know
Was the car, to your own knowledge, used for business travel - for 2,500 miles pa or less?	☐	☐	☐
- for 18,000 miles pa or more?	☐	☐	☐

3 **Car fuel "scale charges" - cars available for private use**

	Yes	No
Was fuel for the car(s) provided other than for business travel?	☐	☐
If "yes" was the director/employee required to make good the cost of all fuel used for private motoring including travel between home and normal place of work?	☐	☐
If the director/employee was required to make good the cost did he actually do so?	☐	☐

4 **Car owned or hired by director/employee**

Allowances paid to the director/employee in respect of the use of the car and/or running and
overhead expenses   £ _____

Sum contributed by you towards the purchase price, depreciation or hire of a car   £ _____

For official use

P11D (1990)   Printed in the UK for HMSO 12/90 Dd. 0100196 C50,000 (11037)

Figure 4.4   Employer's return for directors and higher-paid employees

Portsmouth and hotel expenses. The claim was dismissed on two grounds: first, that the expenses were not 'necessarily incurred', as the recorder could have lived in Portsmouth, and secondly, they were not 'incurred in the performance of the duties of the employment', which

118

C Beneficial loans

5 Enter details of loans made to, or arranged for, a director/employee (or any of his relatives) on which no interest was paid or on which the amount of interest paid was less than interest at the official rate.

		"√" Yes	No	Don't know
(a)	Were there any loans the interest on which was (or would have been if interest had been payable) not wholly eligible for relief?	☐	☐	☐
(b)	If the answer to (a) is "yes" did the benefit of the loans exceed £200?	☐	☐	☐

(c) *Unless you have answered "No" to (b)* -

* add all the loans together and state the total amounts outstanding at 5.4.90 _____ at 5.4.91 _____

* If the loan was made on or after 6 April 1990 state the amount and the date it was paid. £ _____ Date _____

* If the loan was discharged on or before 5 April 1991 on what date was it discharged? Date _____

* What was the amount of interest paid by the borrower in the year to 5 April 1991 £ _____
  Enter "NIL" if none was paid.

(d) If any loans made by you were waived or written off in the year to 5 April 1991 what was the amount waived etc? £ _____

D Other expenses payments and benefits etc

	£
6 Private medical dental etc attention and treatment or insurance against the cost of such treatment	
7 General expenses allowance	
8 Travelling and subsistence	
9 Entertainment	
10 Home telephone expenses paid or reimbursed { Rental	
{ Calls	
11 Subscriptions	
12 Goods or services supplied free or below market value	
13 Vouchers and credit cards	
14 Cars, property, furniture and other assets given or transferred to the director/employee	
15 Nursery places provided for children of the director/employee	
16 Educational assistance provided for the director/employee or members of his family	
17 House, flat or other living accommodation provided for the director/employee	
Please show address _____ Cost £ _____	
18 Income tax paid to the Collector in the year to 5 April 1991 which a company failed to deduct from a director's remuneration	
19 Other expenses and benefits not shown above eg National Insurance contributions, holidays, private legal, accountancy etc expenses, contributions towards house purchase and other household expenses such as wages and keep of personal or domestic staff and gardening expenses.	
Please give details _____	

Total _____

Less (i) So much of the items entered above as have been made good by the director/employee

(ii) Amounts included above from which tax has been deducted under PAYE

+ _____ =

Net total _____

Declaration

I declare that all particulars required are fully and truly stated according to the best of my knowledge and belief.

Signature _____ Date _____

Capacity in which signed _____

Figure 4.4 – *contd.*

did not begin until he entered court at Portsmouth. Either of these grounds is fatal to a Schedule E expenses claim.

However, in another case (*Pook* v. *Owen* 1969) a doctor who carried on a practice at home but who also was employed at a local hospital was successful in claiming a car mileage allowance from home to the hospital. In this case it was held that the doctor's hospital duties began once he was telephoned at home. Before leaving for the hospital, he gave instructions to the hospital staff so that they were fully prepared on his arrival.

Despite this result, most home-to-work travel costs will not qualify for deduction. Where an airline pilot was on stand-by, but did not start work until he got to the airport, this was distinguished from the case of *Pook* v. *Owen* and travelling expenses were disallowed (*Nolder* v. *Walters* 1930). The same principle applies to other expenses, such as the costs of lodgings and meals and refreshments during the working day, which are the 'necessities of a human being' (Rowlatt, J. in *Nolder* v. *Walters*). Even where an employee has to buy a meal when working compulsory overtime, the cost is normally not deductible (*Durbridge* v. *Sanderson* 1955). In practice, the Revenue usually allows reasonable subsistence and travel costs associated with working away from the normal place of employment.

Expenses specifically disallowed

The following examples of other expenses which have been disallowed give a further taste of how strictly the Schedule E expenses rule is interpreted.

Payment of club subscriptions by a bank manager
Although the manager argued that membership of the club was good for business, the expense was judged not to have been necessarily incurred. It is not necessary for bank managers in general to belong to a club (*Brown* v. *Bullock* 1961). The term 'necessarily' is interpreted as meaning necessary to that *class* of employment not to that particular person's employment. The facts in *Brown* v. *Bullock* were carefully distinguished from the facts in the case of *Elwood* v. *Utitz* (1965), where subscriptions to two London residential clubs were allowed. In this case it was necessary for the employee, who was employed outside London, occasionally to obtain accommodation there. The club subscriptions enabled him to obtain preferential rates.

Fees and expenses associated with educational and training courses borne by the employee
In the past, employees have had great difficulty in claiming successfully that the costs of education and training should be tax

deductible. In the case of *Humbles* v. *Brooks* (1962) expenses incurred by a history teacher in attending a weekend course to improve his knowledge were not allowed. Similarly disallowed were the costs incurred by an articled clerk in sitting the Law Society's examinations (*Lupton* v. *Potts* 1969). In both cases the decision went against the taxpayer because the courts concluded that it was not necessary for the employee to incur the costs and the costs were not incurred in the performance of the duties of their current employment. Even where it was a condition of the employment that the employee should study for certain qualifications, this did not make the expenses deductible. For example, where a lab assistant was required by his contract of employment to attend evening classes to study for a relevant degree, the court ruled that when listening to lectures he was not in the performance of his duties (*Blackwell* v. *Mills* 1945).

The principle that an employee cannot deduct the costs he incurs in obtaining education or training is of long standing. However, the 1991 Finance Act introduced an important change by allowing tax relief for individuals who pay for their own *vocational training*. Basic rate relief is given by deduction at source from qualifying fees. This concession does not at present extend beyond vocational training to more general education, though the course need not be related to an individual's work.

Where the employer directly meets or reimburses *bona fide* education and training costs, these are not normally assessed on the employee.

The costs of clothing

A computer engineer's claim to deduct the cost of a suit failed even though he argued he would never choose to wear the clothing at any other time. It was held that clothing was worn for warmth and decency and therefore was not 'exclusively' incurred in the performance of the duties (*Hillyer* v. *Leeke* 1976).

Expenses specifically allowed

Specific legislation exists allowing certain expenses which might not be deductible under the normal Schedule E expenses rule. The main types are as follows:

- Contributions to qualifying pension and superannuation schemes (an employee can make contributions of up to 15% of earnings and obtain tax relief).

- Certain and limited donations to charities through an approved deduction scheme operated by the employer (in 1991/2 payments of up to £240 per annum).

- Certain subscriptions to professional bodies and learned societies which are relevant to the employment, for example an accountant's professional subscription.

It should also be noted that by concession, the Inland Revenue will for certain occupations agree annual flat rate deductions to cover the costs of protective clothing, books (for lecturers) and similar expenses. These deductions are usually negotiated with the appropriate trade union or professional body.

Entertainment expenses

The position regarding entertainment expenses sometimes causes confusion. The broad principles are as follows. If an employee treats someone to a meal out of his own salary, the cost is not allowable unless it meets the requirements of the 'wholly, exclusively and necessarily' rule. Where the employer funds or refunds the employee's entertainment expenses, he cannot deduct the cost when computing his profits because entertainment costs are specifically disallowed (see Chapter 2). At the same time, if the employee is to avoid being assessed on the payment, he still has to satisfy the requirement that the expense was incurred wholly, exclusively and necessarily in the performance of the duties (although a person has to eat for nourishment, the Revenue has agreed that this does not in itself prevent claiming the costs of subsistence).

Capital allowances

Capital allowances may be claimed against expenditure on plant and machinery (including the cost of a car) *necessarily* provided by the employee for use in the performance of his duties. Normally, however, where plant and machinery is necessary to perform the duties either it will be provided by the employer or an expense allowance will be given to cover the cost. The Revenue takes some convincing that the expenditure is necessary in other cases.

National insurance contributions (NIC)

Class I NIC is payable on the earnings of all employees over 16 years of age. The precise rate of NIC depends upon whether the employee is 'contracted in' or 'contracted out' of the 'state earnings-related pension scheme' (SERPS). There is a lower rate for those who have their own occupational pension scheme or a personal pension plan and hence are contracted out. NIC rates are set each year and the relevant scales are sent to employers along with the annual PAYE documentation.

Once an employee's earnings equal, or exceed, the current lower earnings limit (in 1991/2 £52 per week or £225.99 per month) NIC is due on all of the earnings and not just the amount above the lower earnings limit. This creates an incentive to employ part-time low-paid workers rather than their full-time equivalents. Employees pay what is called the *primary contribution* and employers the *secondary contribution*.

Employees pay the primary contribution only up to a higher earnings limit (which in 1991/2 was £390 per week or £1,690 per month). The Department of Social Security (DSS) issues NIC exemption certificates (an RD950) where no primary contribution need be deducted by the employer. This will apply to employees who pay NIC up to the ceiling in another employment. There is no upper earnings limit, however, for secondary contributions, so these must be made even where a certificate of exemption exists.

Both primary and secondary contributions are collected alongside Income Tax through the PAYE system and should be paid to the Collector of Taxes within fourteen days of the end of each tax month (as mentioned earlier, quarterly accounting for PAYE and NIC may be adopted where total payments average less than £400 per month). The Revenue collects NIC on behalf of the DSS. At the end of each tax year, the total NIC deducted for employees is returned by the employer on the PAYE form, P35. Once again, it is the employer's responsibility to ensure that the correct amount of NIC is paid by employees. The DSS can recover unpaid NIC going back up to six years.

The earnings liable to NIC are the gross earnings before deduction of superannuation contributions or charitable gifts under an approved payroll scheme, although *bona fide* expenses do not need to be included in pay for NIC purposes. Included are amounts credited to directors' accounts and 'golden handshakes' and 'golden hellos'. Benefits in kind, however, which cannot be turned into cash, even though subject to Income Tax, with two important exceptions are not subject to NIC. This further increases the attractiveness of paying employees in the form of fringe benefits rather than cash. The two major exceptions are cars and private fuel. From 6 April 1991 employers' NIC is levied on the appropriate tax scale charges at the end of the tax year.

Where men aged over 65 and women aged over 60 are employed they can obtain a NIC exemption certificate (a CF384) to confirm that no primary contribution need be deducted from their pay. However, the secondary contribution must still be paid. Similarly, some married women and widows are exempt from primary contributions because they so elected before 6 April 1977. No such election now exists and where an employee claims to be exempt they should be asked to produce the appropriate certificate (a CF383). Where the employee is exempt, the secondary contribution is still due. There are special rules relating to employees entering and leaving the UK.

Employers are required by law to pay statutory sick pay (SSP) and statutory maternity pay (SMP) to qualifying employees. In both cases, Income Tax and NIC must be deducted from the payments. The employer may then in turn deduct from the amount paid over to the Collector of Taxes a sum to cover most of the SSP and SMP paid out that month, plus an extra sum to compensate for the employer's NIC contribution on the SSP and SMP. Details of the employer's statutory obligations under the SSP and SMP schemes are outside the scope of this book but can be obtained from the DSS.

Concluding comment

The law places a heavy burden on the employer with respect to the correct taxation of employees' earnings and this has been the primary theme of this chapter. The next chapter reviews how income from business property is taxed.

5

Taxing income from business property

This chapter considers the tax treatment of income arising from property located within the UK. The taxation of foreign earnings is covered in Chapter 7. The main types of income involved are interest on loans and savings, dividends from UK companies and rents from property. Each of these incomes is considered in turn, and in each case how the taxable amount is computed and the basis of assessment receive special attention.

In the case of individuals and partnerships the income is subject to Income Tax, while in the case of companies the income is added to the business profits on which Corporation Tax is levied.

Basic principles

We saw in Chapter 2 that an individual's business profits are taxed on the individual. A similar principle applies regarding the taxation of income from property. Irrespective of whether or not the interest and dividends are from savings built up within the business or the rents are from land and buildings which are perceived to be part of the business assets, so far as the tax system is concerned the resulting income belongs to the proprietor, not the business. The consequent tax assessments are therefore made on the individual.

The same applies to partnerships. Property income is divided between the partners according to their partnership agreement and

125

taxed on each individually. This applies even if the income remains in a partnership bank account or other account. It should be noted that only *income* from property is subject to Income Tax. Capital gains (that is profits from the purchase and disposal of property) are normally taxed under the rules of Capital Gains Tax (see Chapter 6).

One important exception, however, is the profits earned from buying and holding to maturity certain types of securities sold at a discount – for instance Treasury Bills. The difference between the purchase price and maturity value represents the interest on the securities and it is taxed as such.

Since companies are distinct legal entities, interest and rents earned by companies are taxed in the company name. The procedure, which is discussed in detail in Chapter 8, involves adding such income (after any legitimate expenses) to the company's total profit.

Broadly, the two approaches to taxing income from property are as follows:

- The payer of the income deducts tax at source and pays it over to the Inland Revenue.
- The recipient of the income pays the tax.

Where the recipient is a higher-rate taxpayer both procedures may apply with tax at the basic rate being deducted at source and tax at the higher rate being collected by assessment.

Irrespective of whether the income is received gross or net it must be noted on the annual Income Tax Return. Where no Return is received, an individual is still under a legal obligation to notify the Inland Revenue of the income within one year of the end of the tax year in which it arose. Companies must include the income in their taxable profits. Where the rent is paid directly to a person whose usual place of abode is outside the UK, the payer or agent must deduct tax on payment.

Taxing interest

Interest taxed at source

Certain interest on UK government stocks (or 'gilt edged' securities) is taxed at source. That is to say, tax equivalent to the basic rate of Income

Tax on the interest is deducted by the payer, under the rules of Schedule C of Income Tax. This principle also extends to interest on certain foreign public authority bonds, where the interest is paid through a UK paying agent (s.17 Income and Corporation Taxes Act 1988). All other interest arising is taxed under the rules of Case III of Schedule D which are set out below.

Where the interest is paid net of the basic rate tax, the recipient will need to receive a tax assessment only if he is liable to pay tax at the higher rate. It is important to realize that when the Inland Revenue calculates total income it 'grosses up' income on which tax is deducted at source. This can be important for someone close to paying tax at more than the basic rate.

For example, with the basic rate of Income Tax at 25% and a single higher rate of 40%, gross interest on government stock of £1,000 would suffer £250 tax at source. The holder of the stock would receive the net amount of £750 and the tax, £250, would be paid over to the government by the paying agent. The full £1,000, however, is treated as part of the individual's 'gross statutory income' for tax purposes and if the recipient is liable to tax at 40% on this income, then what is called a 'taxed income' assessment will be issued by the Inland Revenue to recover the further £150 (£1,000 × 15%).

The tax on a taxed income assessment is normally due and payable on 1 December in the tax year following the one in which the interest arose. For example, if the income in our example arose some time between 6 April 1990 and 5 April 1991, the additional tax would be payable on 1 December 1991. The only exception applies to an assessment issued late, i.e. within thirty days of 1 December or after that date. In this case – which would occur if for some reason the Inland Revenue were late in learning of the existence of the income – the tax is due and payable within thirty days of the date of issue of the assessment. It is also worth noting that if the holder of the stock is not liable to tax (most usually this will occur where the individual has unused personal allowances to set against the income) a claim can be made to the Inland Revenue for repayment of the tax deducted at source.

A small number of UK government securities pay interest gross, i.e. without deduction of tax at source. The main types are 3½% War Loan and National Savings Bank interest. This arrangement is especially useful for those who are not liable to tax since no claim for a repayment of tax will need to be made. For those who do pay tax, the interest is taxed in the normal way as described below under the heading 'interest paid gross'.

Bank and building society interest

Since 1984/5 interest on bank deposits in the UK has been paid net of tax and the scheme was later extended to building societies. The following discussion is confined to bank interest, but the same principles apply to interest paid by building societies.

Although bank interest is received net of tax, again further tax is due if the recipient pays tax at the higher rate and this is raised through a taxed income assessment. But unlike the tax deducted at source on government securities and on company dividends (see below), it *cannot* be reclaimed where the recipient is not liable to tax. Until April 1991 this worked to the disadvantage of non-taxpayers. From the start of the 1991/2 tax year, however, non-taxpayers have been able to elect to receive their bank interest without tax deducted by completing a simple form.

One further product of the revision of the rules on taxing bank interest has been the abolition of what was known as the 'composite rate'. Previously, tax deducted on payment of bank interest was not calculated at the normal basic rate of Income Tax, but at a notional rate which represented the average rate of tax borne by depositors. From 6 April 1991 bank (and building society) interest is paid under deduction of tax at the normal basic rate. This means that tax-paying savers have suffered a slight *increase* in taxation (the composite rate in its last year of operation, 1990/1, was 22% compared with a base rate for Income Tax of 25%).

It is worth pointing out that bank interest has *always* been paid gross to companies (who include it in their profits which are subjected to Corporation Tax) and the same applies to interest received by bodies normally exempted from tax, notably registered charities and pension funds.

Interest paid gross

If the interest is not paid under deduction of tax, an Income Tax Case III assessment will be issued by the Inland Revenue and the tax will normally be due and payable on 1 January in the tax year (or again within thirty days where the assessment is issued late). For example, tax will normally be payable on a 1991/2 Case III assessment on 1 January 1992. An exception exists for employees paying tax under the PAYE system (pp. 96–101), who often have the tax on their interest collected via an adjustment to their employment tax codes (i.e. their personal allowances are reduced to bring more employment income into tax to recover unpaid tax on the interest).

The main types of interest that an individual in the UK will receive gross are as follows:

- National Savings Bank ordinary and investment accounts (though the first £70 of *ordinary* account interest is exempt from tax).
- Very large bank deposits (currently exceeding £50,000) and on which twenty-eight days' notice of withdrawal has to be given.
- Some UK government securities, notably 3½% War Loan.

Over the years, various methods have evolved to extract interest without paying tax and the Inland Revenue has reacted by passing anti-avoidance legislation. Briefly, where stocks are issued at 'deep discount', the discount is now treated as interest. Similarly, where investors buy stock 'ex-interest' and sell 'cum-interest' – an operation called 'bond washing' – the uplift in value is taxed. A stock is sold ex-interest where the seller is entitled to the imminent interest payment. The purchaser has the right to the next interest payment when stock is sold cum-interest. The bond price, of course, reflects the interest entitlement.

The normal basis of assessment

As in the case of the tax treatment of trading profits (Chapter 2), interest is assessed to tax in such a way that an accurate assessment can be raised some time during the tax year. Since the assessments are normally issued by the Inland Revenue at least thirty days before 1 January, it would often be difficult to assess the correct interest arising through to the following 5 April. In addition, the taxpayer might be asked to pay tax on interest they have yet to receive! Therefore, the normal basis of assessment is on the interest arising in the *preceding* tax year – a PY basis. An important fact to remember is that it is the interest received, including interest credited to accounts which is relevant, not that accrued. For instance, interest may be credited to an account once a year, say 1 December. The interest accruing after 1 December to the following 5 April (the end of the tax year) will not be subject to tax in that year but only in the following year when it is credited to the account.

EXAMPLE

Paula Scott runs an employment advisory service. On 1 June and 1 December 1991 she received interest totalling £3,660 from a National Savings investment account opened four years ago using surplus cash from her business. How will this interest be taxed?

Paula is not trading through a company therefore the interest is deemed to be hers for tax purposes. Interest from National Savings investment accounts is paid gross and it will be taxed under the rules of Case III Schedule D. Since the account has been open for a number of years the interest will be taxed on the PY basis: i.e. interest received in the tax year 1991/2 will be taxed in 1992/3.

Commencements and cessations

The PY basis is advantageous administratively but difficulties arise in the year the interest first arises and when an account is closed. In the first year there is no previous year's interest to tax; while interest received in the final year could not be taxed until the year after the source of the interest (for example, a National Savings Investment account) was closed. This would mean assessing income from a source of income that no longer existed.

To circumvent these problems the following rules (ss.66–7 Income and Corporation Taxes Act 1988) exist:

- In the first year interest arises it is taxed in that year. This is not necessarily the year the investment is acquired. For example, interest first arising on 1 December 1991 on an account opened or security purchased before 6 April 1991, would be assessed to tax in 1991/2. This is known as the 'actual interest' basis.

- Interest arising in the second year is also taxed on an actual basis. This means that, continuing the example, interest arising on 1 December 1992 would be treated as taxable income of the 1992/3 tax year.

- Interest arising in the third and subsequent years is normally taxed on the PY basis. Consequently, one year's interest is taxed twice – in our example, interest arising on 1 December 1992 is taxed as income in 1992/3 (actual basis) and again in 1993/4 (PY basis).

- Interest received in the year an account is closed or investment sold is taxed on an actual basis. Suppose that the account in our example is closed on 31 December 1995. The interest arising on 1 December 1995, plus one month's additional interest credited on closure of the account, will be taxed as income in 1995/6. Also note that the interest arising on 1 December 1994, which on the PY basis would have been taxed in 1995/6 if the account had stayed open, now escapes tax (this is rough justice – it compensates for the fact that interest in the second year after the account was opened was taxed twice!).

It may seem that this system of assessment has an obvious loophole. If the interest on 1 December 1994 had been very high, to avoid tax it would have paid to close the account in the following year. However, like most tax loopholes, it has been closed by the Revenue, which has powers to revise the penultimate year's tax assessment onto an actual basis too. This means that interest in the pre-penultimate year falls out of tax. The Revenue will exercise this right whenever it leads to more interest being charged to tax.

A similar right exists for the taxpayer to *elect* within six years of the end of the tax year concerned, to have the *third year* of assessment after interest first arises revised to an actual basis. If this election is made, the third year's interest and not the second year's, will be taxed twice – in the third year on an actual basis and in the fourth year on the PY basis.

There are certain further complications relating to new deposits, joint accounts, interest received on 6 April and where interest is not paid on an account for a number of years as follows:

- A fresh deposit into an account is technically a new source and therefore should be treated separately in so far as the commencement and cessation provisions are concerned. In practice, however, the Inland Revenue does not normally apply this procedure unless the sum is large. A man who held an account for some years but paid in an extra £2 million expecting the interest on this sum not to be taxed to the following year, found that the courts supported the Revenue's contention that the actual basis applied to the new deposit (*Hart* v. *Sangster* 1957).

- In the case of accounts held jointly, the Revenue treats the interest as shared equally unless the holders declare otherwise.

- In rare cases interest may be paid on 6 April. Where this applies, the first year's interest is assessed as already described (i.e. on an actual basis), but the *second* year's assessment is put onto a PY basis with the taxpayer's right of election for an actual basis applying to that year, not the third year.

131

- If no income arises from a source for six consecutive years the taxpayer may elect to treat the source as having ceased when the income last arose (the cessation provisions will then apply to that year and, at the Inland Revenue's discretion, the previous year). Should income then arise in the future, it is treated as derived from a new source.

In the case of companies, interest is assessed as part of the company's total taxable profits in the accounting period in which it arises. There is no preceding year basis.

Interest which escapes tax

The main forms of interest exempted from tax are as follows:

- Interest on national savings certificates.
- Interest on certain SAYE schemes operated by building societies and national savings.
- Payment on premium bonds.
- The first £70 in interest received each year from National Savings Bank ordinary accounts.
- Interest from 1 January 1991 on long-term savings in tax-exempt special savings accounts (TESSAs) of banks and building societies.
- Interest on children's bonus bonds under national savings.

Taxing dividends

Dividends from UK companies are subject to Income Tax under Schedule F of the Income Tax Code (s.20 Income and Corporation Taxes Act 1988). Whenever a UK company pays a dividend to its shareholders (and certain other types of 'qualifying distributions', see pp. 206–7 for details), the dividend is paid along with an appropriate 'tax credit' (see Figure 5.1). Since the dividend is paid out of profits on which Corporation Tax is levied, the individual's basic rate Income Tax liability is treated as covered by the company's payment of its Corporation Tax. In other words, part of the Corporation Tax payment

PETROLEUM COMPANY p.l.c.

Ordinary Shares of 25p each

Payment No.

Quarterly Dividend
payable 7th February, 1994

	Holding as at 30.11.1990	Non-elected Shares	Elected Shares	Rate (p)	Tax Credit	Amount Payable
ORD. SHARES	105	105		3.950000	1.38	4.15
			0	See Accounting Statement	0.00	0.00
				Totals	1.38	4.15

JOHN SMITH
1 FORTUNE CRESCENT
HARROGATE

Warrant No.

Account Code

I certify that Advance Corporation Tax of an amount equal to that shown as tax credit will be accounted for to the Collector of Taxes.

This voucher should be retained and will be accepted by the Inland Revenue as evidence of tax credit in respect of which you may be entitled to claim payment of relief.

Elected Shares are those shares on which you have elected to participate in the Share Dividend Plan. Non-elected Shares qualify for the full cash payment.

Figure 5.1 Example of a dividend voucher showing the tax credit

is *imputed* to the dividend as a tax credit (a method known as the 'imputation system').

The tax credit effectively covers the recipient's basic rate tax liability leaving, where appropriate, only the higher-rate tax to be raised through a 'taxed income' assessment. As in the case of interest received, the tax charged in the taxed income assessment is normally due and payable on 1 December in the year following the year in which the dividend arose. In calculating an individual's liability to tax at the higher rate, the *gross* amount of the dividend (dividend plus tax credit) must be added to other incomes of the year.

Where a UK company receives dividends from another company the procedure is different. This is discussed in Chapter 8.

Rental income

Provided that the business is not *trading* in property, then income derived from land and other property situated within the UK is subject to Income Tax under Schedule A. The possible exception is income from furnished lettings which is normally taxed under Case VI of Schedule D. This distinction is important, as we shall see, especially in terms of the treatment of any losses from lettings.

The principles of Schedule A

Income taxed under Schedule A includes the following:

- Rents from land, including ground rents (in Scotland, feu duties and ground annuals).
- Rents from unfurnished and sometimes furnished buildings.
- Rents from other property.
- Premiums relating to leases.
- Other miscellaneous receipts, for instance parking fees, fees for displaying advertising, payments for granting a right of way or other right over property (known as *wayleaves*) and sporting rights on land.

Where part of the business premises are let, the resulting income will normally fall within Schedule A. Correctly, the income should *not* be included as part of the trading income of the business but should be separated out. This is necessary not least because the rules on expenses relating to Schedule A income are different to those for trading profits taxed under Case I Schedule D. This is a good example of the importance of the Income Tax Schedules in the administration of the UK tax system. Also, a correct separation of the profits from trading is necessary in other contexts, notably the treatment of losses and in the determination of the amount of profit against which a proprietor can make pension contributions. However, the Revenue will usually raise no objections to adding the income to trading profits where the rental income is derived from part of the business premises and there are no material tax implications.

The tax treatment of companies involved in letting property as a business is covered in the discussion of 'investment companies' (p. 201 below).

The charge to tax

The charge to tax under Schedule A is based on the *entitlement* to rent, i.e. the amount of income *due* in the tax year which need not be the same as the amount received. Where annual rental accounts are drawn up the Inland Revenue may be willing to treat the income and expenditure in these accounts as the income and expenditure of the tax year in which the account year ends. However, where a tenant has absconded and the landlord has taken all reasonable steps to trace and recover the lost rental but failed, or where the landlord waives the right to rent to avoid hardship to the tenant, the Inland Revenue will normally omit the lost rent when calculating the tax payable. But in other cases the *full rent due* is taxed, even where the tenant pays the rent late. If rent lost is subsequently recovered, an adjustment is made to the assessment for the year when the rent should have been paid. There is a requirement to inform the Inland Revenue within six months of the recovery (s.41 Income and Corporation Taxes Act 1988).

Treatment of premiums

Some leases involve the payment of a premium when the lease is granted. One example of a premium is so-called 'key money' (a cash sum which was originally to obtain the key to property rented!). The incidence of premium payments varies geographically within the UK reflecting local custom and practice, but it is especially likely to be found in connection with commercial leases.

If premiums were able to escape Income Tax then there would be an incentive for landlords to demand large premiums in return for correspondingly lower rentals. To close this obvious tax loophole, premiums are subject to tax under Schedule A. The amount of the premium is taxed in full in the year it is received subject to a deduction of 2% for each complete year of the lease after the first year. Therefore, where a lease is for more than fifty years, any premium paid escapes Income Tax. For example, the amount taxable of a premium of £10,000 on a twenty-year lease appears below. A lease is normally regarded as being for the period for which it was granted except where there are grounds for believing that it will be terminated before this date.

	£
Premium	10,000
	3,800
less 2% × (20 years − 1 year) treated as rental income in the year received	
	6,200

Note that the £3,800 will be treated as sale proceeds for disposal of an interest in land and will be subject to Capital Gains Tax (see p. 175 above). Also, where the payer of the premium is trading or lets the property, part of the premium can be deducted as an annual expense against the resulting income. The amount deductible is the amount of the premium subject to tax divided by the length of the lease. In the example £6,200/20 = £310 can be deducted each year during the life of the lease from trading income or rentals.

If the tenant pays a sum to alter the terms of the lease or the terms of the lease require the tenant to carry out certain repair or improvement work, the landlord is treated as having received a premium equivalent to the cost. There are also provisions for taxing payments made on the granting of a sublease out of a head lease and, in certain circumstances, the assigning of a lease.

Schedule A expenses

In calculating the amount charged to tax, certain expenses incurred by the landlord may be deducted from the income. The expenses which can be deducted are essentially those relating directly to (a) the property; and (b) the period in which the property is let or available for letting (s.25 Income and Corporation Taxes Act 1988).

Allowable expenses
The following expenses can normally be deducted from income when calculating Schedule A profits:

- Repairs and maintenance on the property (but not improvements) incurred by the landlord and related to the period in which the property is let, available for letting or being prepared for letting (see 'Period of ownership' below).
- Rent payable (say to a superior landlord).
- Local authority rates and water rates of the tenant where the landlord has agreed to make the payment.
- The cost of services provided to the tenant by the landlord, for instance security services.
- Accountancy and legal costs relating to the preparation of accounts, maintaining records and the pursuit of defaulters (but not charges arising out of the acquisition or disposal of the property – except by concession the acquisition of a lease of twenty-one years or less – these are taken into account in calculating the Capital Gains Tax liability when the property is sold).
- Wages of maintenance and other staff.
- Costs relating to the finding of tenants and the collection of rents.
- Insurance premiums relating to the property (but not against loss of rents).

Interest payments
Interest paid on loans used to purchase or improve the property for letting is *not* deductible as an expense when calculating the Schedule A profit. However, subject to certain conditions it is allowed as a deduction from the taxpayer's total income when calculating the actual tax liability. This means that the tax assessment will show the interest deduction separately. The effect on the tax liability will often be the

same as allowing the interest as a deduction. An exception occurs where the interest paid exceeds the rental income. This is discussed in further detail under the heading 'Schedule A losses' below.

The relevant conditions (s.355 Income and Corporation Taxes Act 1988) to obtain relief for interest payments relate to the use of the property. To be eligible for relief, the interest paid must relate to property let at a commercial rent for more than twenty-six weeks in any fifty-two-week period, or be available for letting in this period, or the property must be in the course of being prepared, for instance repaired, ready for future letting.

It should be noted that there is no ceiling on the size of the loan limiting interest relief, as exists for interest on mortgages secured on an individual's domestic residence.

Period of ownership

To be deductible the expenditure must relate to the period of letting or a period in which the property is available for letting.

A particularly tricky area concerns what are called 'void periods'. A void period is one in which the property is not being let. This could occur because there is a gap between the time at which the property was acquired and it was first let. Expenditure during this period is allowable provided that it relates to repairs necessitated because of events which occurred *after* the property was acquired. For example, the property might have suffered flood or gale damage. However, if it amounts to being repairs or improvement of a property bought in a dilapidated state, then this will be treated as capital expenditure and will not be allowed against rents. Furthermore, the void period must be one in which the property was empty. If the property was bought, used as a domestic residence and then let, repairs relating to the period in which the property was a domestic residence, may not be deducted.

In addition to a void period following the acquisition and first letting of the property, there could be a void period between tenancies. This may occur, for example, when the property is available for letting or is being repaired ready for reletting. Expenditure in this period will normally be allowed against the future rental income.

In both cases, however, there is an overriding proviso. The lettings must be at a 'full rent'. That is to say, the rental charge must be on a commercial basis so that, taking one year with another, it is at least sufficient to cover outgoings on the property. For example, if the tenant of a property was charged an artificially low rental, as might occur if it was let to an associated business, a relation or a friend, expenditure on repairs following the letting will not be allowed against rent from subsequent leases. Expenditure relating to a tenancy not at a 'full rent' can only be set off against income from *that tenancy*.

EXAMPLE

Walter Griffin purchased an office building. Before the building could be used he spent £20,000 on urgent repairs to the roof. The offices were then let on 1 June 1991 on a 15-year lease to an advertising firm at a rent of £12,000 per annum payable in advance. The lessee also paid key money of £5,000. In the first six months further repair work costing £1,800 was undertaken following a violent storm two weeks before the letting; £1,500 was covered by insurance. The insurance premium is £1,600 per annum. Walter estimates the management charges at £300.

The Schedule A assessment for 1991/2 will be on:

		£
Rents		12,000
Plus premium	5,000	
Less (15 − 1 year × 2%) × 5,000	1,400	
Assessed as rental	——	3,600
		15,600
Less:		
Management charge	300	
Insurance premium	1,600	
Repairs (net of insurance recovery)	300	2,200
Taxable Schedule A		13,400

Expenditure on improving a property, as opposed to repairing and maintaining it, is considered to be *capital* expenditure and cannot be deducted in calculating the Schedule A profit. It can, however, be added to the cost of the property and taken into account when calculating a future liability under Capital Gains Tax provided the improvement is reflected in the property at the time of disposal (Capital Gains Tax on property is discussed in Chapter 6).

It is also worth noting that capital allowances may be available on certain types of capital expenditure: for example, expenditure on industrial buildings and on lifts and swimming-pools and certain other amenities in buildings. In addition, plant and machinery used in maintaining the property or administering and managing the leases may qualify. The general rules relating to capital allowances were discussed in Chapter 3.

139

The tax assessment

As with assessments on interest, the tax on Schedule A income becomes due for payment on 1 January in the year of assessment (once again unless the assessment is issued late, in which case it is thirty days after the assessment is issued). For example, a timely assessment to tax on rental income in the year to 5 April 1992 would normally become due for payment on 1 January 1992. This means that the assessment is issued three months before the end of the year when the true Schedule A liability can be determined. Therefore, the Inland Revenue issues an initial assessment which is adjusted if necessary after 5 April. The initial assessment will automatically be adjusted once the Revenue is notified of the actual profits (there is no need to appeal against the initial assessment). Depending upon whether the final profit figure is less or greater than the provisional profit figure on which tax has already been paid, an appropriate refund or further assessment on the balance of tax due will be made. It is important to note that income under Schedule A is always taxed on an actual basis; the preceding year basis never applies.

In determining the Schedule A profits to be included in the initial assessment, the Revenue takes the previous year's agreed profits (i.e. the final profit figure agreed after the year end). However, this may either overstate or understate the true profits, where property has recently been sold or new property has been rented out. In this case, the Inspector should be informed before 1 January so that the initial assessment reflects the change.

Leaving aside companies receiving income from property which is trading income, the rules relating to income from property are essentially the same for companies paying Corporation Tax as for sole proprietor and partnership businesses subject to Income Tax; that is to say, companies calculate their profits from rental income during an accounting period in exactly the same way, adopting the rules of Schedule A of Income Tax. But once the profit is derived, it is added to the trading profits and any bank interest and other taxable incomes, and this global sum becomes the total profit on which the Corporation Tax is due.

Schedule A losses

It is quite conceivable that once allowable expenses have been deducted from income a loss arises. This is most likely to occur where the landlord is responsible for some or all of the repairs to the property (*a landlord's repairing lease*) rather than where the tenant is responsible for all or most repairs (*a tenant's repairing lease*). The treatment of Schedule A losses is made more difficult by the different types of leases. The rules are as follows:

- The first rule is that Schedule A losses can *never* be set against other taxable income (for example, trading profits or employment income) in order to reduce the tax due on these incomes. This is so even though 'trading losses' *can* be set off against Schedule A profits (for details see pp. 56–9 for Income Tax and pp. 203–5 for Corporation Tax).

- Profits and losses incurred on properties let at a 'full rent' and under landlord's repairing leases are *pooled*. This means that a loss on one property is offset against profits from other properties provided they are also let on landlord's repairing leases. Any remaining loss is then carried forward against pooled profits in future years.

- Losses from properties let under tenant's repairing leases can be carried forward against profits earned from *that particular property* in future years. Alternatively, they can be offset against any current or future year profits in the pool just referred to (though profits and losses of tenant's repairing lease properties are never themselves pooled). Any remaining balance of the loss is then carried forward against the same property's profits. The loss on one tenant's repairing lease cannot be set off in the current year or future year against profits from other properties let on a tenant's repairing lease.

- Properties let at less than a 'full rent' are likely to incur losses. However, since the property is not being let commercially, it would be unreasonable to expect losses incurred to be allowable against profits earned from other properties. For properties let at less than 'full rent', the loss can only be carried forward against profits derived from the *same property* and while under the *same tenancy*.

EXAMPLE

Simon Howard owns four properties which he leases as follows:

- A property at 10 High Street used as a shop and let at a rent of £10,000 per annum; Simon is responsible for repairs.
- A property at 18 Northern Way used as an office and let at £12,000 per annum; again Simon is responsible for repairs.
- A property used as a shop at 15 High Street and let at a rent of £8,000 per annum; the tenant is responsible for repairs.
- A house at 16 Cedar Grove which is let to Simon's aged parents at a peppercorn rent of £100 per annum; Simon meets all repair bills.

The income from the properties would be assessed to Schedule A as follows in any year:

	10 High Street £	15 High Street £	18 Northern Way £	16 Cedar Grove £
Rents	10,000	8,000	12,000	100
Expenses (say)	1,500	2,000	14,000	450
Profit/(loss)	8,500	6,000	(2,000)	(350)

Schedule A assessment:

	£
Pooled income	14,500
Less loss	2,000
Taxable Schedule A	12,500

The loss on the tenant's repairing lease property can be set against the income from the two landlord's repairing lease properties which are pooled. The loss on 16 Cedar Grove cannot be set off against rents from other properties because it is not let at a 'full rent'. The loss can only be carried forward and relieved against rents on 16 Cedar Grove in future years and while it is still let to Simon's parents.

We discussed earlier that, subject to certain conditions, interest on loans incurred to acquire or improve a property were not deductible when calculating profits from a rental but could be allowed against an individual's total income when it came to computing the tax due.

Hence, interest can never create a Schedule A loss. The interest can be set off against profits in the same year from *all* of the taxpayer's commercially let property (not just the profits of the property to which the loan relates). Any surplus interest can then be carried forward and set off against profits from letting property in future years. Similarly, capital allowances are deducted separately in the tax assessment after the Schedule A profit or loss is derived. Where capital allowances exceed the Schedule A profits, any balance can be carried forward and set against taxable profits in future years. For companies, the interest actually paid in the year is relieved as a charge (see p. 202).

Table 5.1 contains a summary of the tax rules regarding income from land and buildings.

Furnished lettings

Furnished lettings are treated differently to other let property and are usually assessed to Income Tax under Case VI of Schedule D rather than Schedule A. However, the method of calculating the amount taxable is broadly the same. In particular, the due date for payment of the tax remains 1 January in the year of assessment and the same types of expenses can be deducted from income. Furnished lettings, however, include furnishings which suffer wear and tear. To allow for this, the taxpayer can either claim the cost of *renewing* furnishings (known as the 'renewals basis' – note that in this case the cost of the *original* furnishings cannot be claimed), or he can make a deduction of 10% of the rent receivable (after any portion relating to the tenant's rates). The latter method is by far the most common in practice –

Table 5.1 Taxing income from land and buildings: a summary

Property let under: Landlord's repairing lease	Tenant's repairing lease	Lease at a nominal rent
Pool profits and losses on properties; carry forward any losses against future profits in the pool	Treat each property separately; carry forward any losses against future income from the *same* property or set against profits from (pooled) landlord's repairing leases	Treat each property and each tenancy separately; carry forward any losses against future income from the same property and the same tenancy

143

though the Inland Revenue will usually accept either of the above methods provided it is followed consistently.

Losses incurred can be set against any Case VI incomes of the year or future years but not incomes assessed under other Cases of Schedule D or the other Income Tax Schedules, including Schedule A. Provision exists, however, to elect, within two years of the end of the tax year concerned, to have the rent divided between that part which relates to the property and that which relates to the furnishings (a fair division will have to be agreed with the Inland Revenue). The furnishings proportion of the income is then assessed under Case VI of Schedule D and the property part under Schedule A.

This will be advantageous where a taxpayer has Schedule A profits from properties under landlord's repairing leases but has incurred a loss on the property portion of the furnished lettings income. This loss can then be set against the Schedule A profits. It is also worth considering where there are losses on other properties and a profit on the property portion of the furnished lettings income. In this case, all or part of the latter profit may be covered by the Schedule A losses.

Furnished holiday lettings

While furnished lettings are taxed under Case VI of Schedule D, the profits of hotels, boarding-houses, etc., are taxed as the profits of a trade under the rules of Case I Schedule D (see Chapter 2). There are, however, borderline cases, for example holiday lets of flats and houses. In the early 1980s the courts decided that the profits from such lets arose from the ownership of property and did not amount to trading (*Gittos* v. *Barclay* 1982 and *Griffiths* v. *Jackson* 1982).

This meant that the resulting profit did not benefit from the more generous rules on expenses, capital allowances, loss relief and payment of tax (two instalments rather than one) under Case I; that the income was not 'relevant earnings' for pension purposes; and that the reliefs under Capital Gains Tax for business assets were not available (as detailed in pp. 168–73).

In response to pressure from the tourist industry, in 1984 legislation was passed which, while leaving the income within Case VI, extended to holiday lettings the above benefits of Case I treatment. To obtain these tax benefits, however, the property must be as follows:

- Available for letting for 140 days in a twelve-month period.

- Be commercially let for 70 days.
- Not be let to any one person for more than 31 days during seven months of that period.

There is a method for averaging the letting periods to meet these requirements where a person lets more than one property as holiday accommodation. Interestingly, in the legislation 'holiday accommodation' is not defined and hence it appears that it does not have to be at a recognized holiday resort.

Concluding comment

The focus of this chapter has been the tax treatment of investment *income*. In the next chapter we consider the allied subject of the taxation of *capital gains*.

6

Taxing capital gains

Capital Gains Tax is the taxation of the increase in the capital value of an asset between the date of acquisition of the asset and the date of its disposal. When the distinction was first drawn between income and capital for the purposes of assessing Income Tax, the result was predictable. People tried to prove that the money they received was in fact capital, and that, therefore, they were not liable to pay tax. The introduction of Capital Gains Tax in 1965 put an end to such arguments when many of the capital receipts which were the subject of discussion became liable to Capital Gains Tax.

The predicament lies now in the decision as to whether the taxation of a receipt under the Income Tax rules would prove to be less favourable than an assessment under the rules of Capital Gains Tax. This was a primary consideration when Capital Gains Tax used to be taxed at a low rate in comparison with the highest rates of Income Tax. However, the Budget of 1988 introduced significant changes to the manner of charging Capital Gains Tax, so that capital gains are now charged at a rate equivalent to the recipient's marginal rate of Income Tax. In 1991/2, therefore, individuals pay Capital Gains Tax at a rate of 25% or 40%. The law on capital gains applies to companies though they pay Corporation Tax on their gains at either 25% or 33% depending on their status as a 'small company' or not (see p. 197).

A further measure was introduced in 1988 which stated that only capital gains which have accrued since 31 March 1982 will be taxable. This change was introduced to overcome the previous difficult problem of computation which arose following the introduction of an allowance for inflation when computing capital gains (*the indexation allowance*).

The capital gain accruing after that date was subject to indexation relief while the rest of it was not.

This chapter will examine the scope of the tax on capital gains which may arise as the result of a disposal of capital assets. We will discuss the topic within the following categories in order to achieve an overall understanding of the principles of capital gains: the distinction between capital and income; the charge to Capital Gains Tax and the significance of resident status; the meaning and scope of disposal of assets; gains and losses; allowable expenditure; reliefs and exemptions; allowable losses; and the computation of Capital Gains Tax.

The distinction between capital and income

The distinction between *capital* and *income* receipts is necessary because it is usually only income receipts which are chargeable to Income Tax, while capital receipts normally attract Capital Gains Tax.

The judges have poetically likened the difference between capital and income to the difference between a tree and its fruit, where the tree is analogous to the capital and the fruit is analogous to the income. In a general sense this is quite useful in gaining an understanding of the concepts. To place it in a business context, if a person receives dividends from his or her shares in a company, his or her dividends will be taxed as income, while the sale of the shares will be liable to Capital Gains Tax. However, the decision as to whether a receipt is to be regarded as income or capital is not always as straightforward as the analogy suggests, as we have already had cause to discuss in Chapter 2 in the review of trading receipts. As Lord Denning has commented:

The question revenue expenditure or capital expenditure is a question which is repeatedly asked by men of business, by accountants and by lawyers. In many cases the answer is easy; but in others it is difficult. The difficulty arises because of the nature of the question. It assumes that all expenditure can be put correctly into one category or the other; but this is clearly not possible. Some cases lie on the border between the two; and this border is not a line clearly marked out; . . . . It is like the border between day and night, or between red and orange. Everyone can tell the difference except in the marginal cases; and then everyone is in doubt . . . .

There are two basic tests to be applied to the receipt in question in

147

order to try to establish its nature. The first test is to assess whether the receipt relates to the *permanent structure* of the business. An example of this might be plant or machinery, so that on its sale it would be treated as a capital receipt. The second test relates to the distinction between *circulating* and *fixed capital*. The characteristic of a fixed capital asset is that it is retained in the business for the purpose of making profit – machinery is such an example. The principal characteristic of circulating capital, on the other hand, is that it is purchased in order to be used or sold – the raw materials of a business being an example.

However, although these tests are useful, they are not definitive and it is necessary to look at precedents to see how a particular type of receipt might be treated.

Payments in lieu of trading receipts

These are generally regarded as revenue receipts. For example in the case of *London & Thames Haven Oil Wharves Ltd* v. *Attwooll* (1966) compensation in respect of loss of profits following damage to a wharf was paid, and was treated by the courts as an income receipt because it was in lieu of profits.

Recurring payments

Again these are more likely to be treated as income receipts unless the payments are obviously of a capital nature. The rule is therefore of greatest significance in borderline cases.

The sale of 'know-how'

This will only be treated as capital receipts if the sale accompanied the sale of all or part of the business and both parties have not elected otherwise.

Payments in compensation for restrictive covenants

These are regarded as capital receipts. The payment of £15,000 to Sir Laurence Olivier in the case of *Higgs* v. *Olivier* (1952), in return for him agreeing not to work for another film company, was held to be a capital receipt because it was an agreement not to exercise his profession (certain payments in connection with restrictive covenants are now subject to higher-rate Income Tax, see p. 94).

Receipts from the sale of business assets

Again these are treated as capital receipts. However, if the seller continues to profit from the asset after its sale, by virtue of a subsidiary agreement, the profit will be charged as income.

Receipts for the destruction or sale of profit-making apparatus

This is regarded as capital and taxed accordingly. The case of *Barr, Crombie & Co. Ltd* v. *CIR* (1945) concerned a fifteen-year contract between shipping managers and a client which was terminated after only eight years, compensation being paid for the remaining years which the contract had to run. The compensation was treated as a capital receipt since the loss of the contract prejudiced almost all of the company's business.

It should be noted that where a business trades in assets, for example an investment company, the liability to tax will arise under Schedule D Case I.

The charge to Capital Gains Tax

As was indicated in the introduction to this chapter, in broad terms capital gains liability may exist whenever a capital profit arises, whether it concerns either a trading or a non-trading situation. However, since the tax was not introduced until April 1965, there can *never* be a charge on gains accruing before that date. This is very much a general indication of the position, and it is necessary to look at the wording of the statute (s.1 Capital Gains Act 1979) to establish the true scope of the tax: 'Tax shall be charged in respect of capital gains, that is to say chargeable gains computed in accordance with this Act and accruing to a person on the disposal of assets.'

Immediately, it can be seen that the Act distinguishes between a capital gain and a chargeable gain. This is a significant point to note because although all chargeable gains will arise from capital gains, not all capital gains will give rise to a chargeable gain. Before a chargeable gain can arise three elements must be established as follows:

- There is a chargeable person.
- There is a chargeable disposal.
- There is a chargeable asset.

These three factors are the foundation stones of the charge and will be discussed in some detail within this chapter.

Residence

An individual is liable to pay Capital Gains Tax for any part of a year of assessment in which he or she is either *resident* or *ordinarily resident* in the UK (see Chapter 7 for details of residence and ordinary residence).

The factor of ordinary residence was included as an alternative condition of charging to discourage taxpayers who have been resident and ordinarily resident in the UK from going abroad for an entire year of assessment and thus becoming non-resident and being able to dispose of their capital assets abroad, free of tax (*Reed* v. *Clark* 1985). Therefore, where a person is resident, or ordinarily resident, a liability to Capital Gains Tax will arise on any chargeable gain realized by him or her in 'any part of the world' unless he or she can establish that he or she was not domiciled here. If the person is not domiciled in the UK, he or she will still be liable to pay tax on the chargeable gains which arise within the UK, but where gains are realized in respect of the disposal of assets outside the UK, they will not be chargeable unless the gains are 'paid, used or enjoyed in or in any manner or form transmitted or brought into the UK'.

Where the person is not resident or ordinarily resident in the UK but carries on a trade, profession or vocation here through a branch or agency, the liability to Capital Gains Tax is on the gains which arise from the disposal of assets situated in the UK and which have been used for the purpose of the trade prior to the capital gain arising.

For people who have been carrying on a trade, profession or vocation in the UK through a branch or agency and who then discontinue the venture in the UK, with the result that the assets are no longer subject to Capital Gains Tax, the Revenue will still impose a capital gains charge which will be calculated as if the person had disposed of the asset just before ceasing trading and then bought the asset for market value on the same day. Where there is a genuine transfer of a branch or agency there is a possibility of avoiding the charge.

There are four categories which are exempt from Capital Gains Tax. They are: registered charities, approved pension schemes, local authorities and friendly societies.

Assessment

Capital Gains Tax for individuals is payable on 1 December following the tax year in which the gain is made. For example, a chargeable gain arising on 1 July 1991 will be assessed to tax for the year 1991/2, and the tax will be payable on 1 December 1992. The Capital Gains Tax year is the same as the Income Tax year, 6 April to 5 April. The only exception is where the assessment is issued late, i.e. after 1 November, in which case the tax is due thirty days after the date of the assessment. For companies the chargeable gain is added to the company's profits and charged to Corporation Tax in the usual way (see Chapter 8).

Individuals must declare all gains to the Revenue even where a tax return is not received, unless they do not give rise to a Capital Gains Tax liability. Penalties and interest can be levied by the Revenue for failure to declare a chargeable gain or for a late return of the gain.

The disposal of assets

In this section the meaning of both *assets* and *disposals* will be discussed. We will then move on to examine a number of special situations which are regarded as a disposal of assets even though, on the face of it, they do not appear to fall within the general definition. These include the following:

- Capital sums which derive from assets.
- Compensation and insurance.
- Hire-purchase agreements.
- The shift in value of a controlling shareholding.
- Debts.
- Options.

The opposite situation will then be considered; that is, events which on the face of it look as though they should give rise to a charge because they appear to fall within the definition of a disposal of assets, but which are in fact deemed not to be chargeable disposals. These are the following:

- Death.
- Foreclosure of mortgages.

Finally, the timing of the disposal will be examined.

Assets

It will be remembered that Capital Gains Tax is levied on the gain accruing on the disposal of assets. Assets are defined by the legislation (s.19 Capital Gains Act 1979) to include all types of capital asset, both tangible and non-tangible. So buildings, options, debts and even currency other than sterling will all fall under the title of 'assets'.

The case law on the area indicates that the term 'assets' includes any right that could be turned to account (*Zim Properties Ltd* v. *Proctor* 1985). For example, if a company is paid £50,000 by one of its employees who wants to be released from his obligations under a contract in order to take up a higher-level job, this could be regarded as an asset even though the rights of an employer under a service contract could not be transferred or assigned. It would be sufficient to show that the employer could turn his or her rights to account.

The law makes provision for the exemption of certain assets from Capital Gains Tax. Among those exemptions are the following items:

1. Principal private residence (though when part of the residence is used exclusively for business purposes, the gain attributable to that part may be taxable). There is an exemption up to a maximum of £40,000 for homes let wholly or partly by owner occupiers.
2. Private motor cars.
3. Chattels sold for less than £6,000.
4. Wasting chattels.
5. UK Government and company loan stocks.
6. Surplus on life assurance policies.

Disposals

Disposals are not specifically defined by the law, but they should be accorded the everyday meaning of the word, which includes any method by which the owner divests himself of the ownership of the asset. It is not necessary that the owner disposes of his entire interest in the asset, it is sufficient to show that he has disposed of part of it (for example, a factory owner selling off part of his land), or that he has placed his assets within a settlement (see pp. 262–5) and declares himself to be the trustee of the settlement in which the asset is held for the benefit of others.

Deemed disposal of assets

The following situations may be deemed to be a disposal of assets where a charge to Capital Gains Tax will arise despite the fact that an asset has not actually been acquired by any person.

Capital sums derived from assets

Consider the following example: Fred sells some shares and in return gets an immediate payment plus the right to receive some more money in the event of the shares being floated and then being sold at a greater price than he was paid for the shares. A flotation of the shares does take place and as a result Fred receives a payment. Here, the payment would be regarded as a capital sum derived from an asset and thus would be taxable. Fred's right to the payment is an asset and the sum of money which he received was derived from that asset even though the person paying the sum did not receive an asset in return (*Marren* v. *Ingles* 1980). This example demonstrates the principle that where a capital sum is derived from an asset, notwithstanding that no asset is acquired by the person paying the capital sum, a liability may arise.

Compensation and insurance

If an asset is damaged and the owner receives some money in compensation, or insurance money, and he fails to repair the asset, the money received will be deemed to be a part disposal. If, however, he uses the payment to restore the asset to its former glory, he will not be regarded as making a disposal.

Where an asset is lost altogether, and the owner receives compensation or an insurance payment, the following three choices are available:

1. He can use the money to replace the asset, in which case he can make a claim to postpone paying the tax on his gain by 'rolling it over' until he finally disposes of the asset.

2. He may choose to keep the money and not replace the asset, in which case he will be taxed on any gain from the disposal.

3. Finally, he may be able to replace the asset at a lower price than the money received in compensation. He is then only liable for the part of the gain which he did not use in replacing the asset.

Hire-purchase

In the event of a hire-purchase agreement being entered into where the ownership of the asset will pass to another person after the expiry of a period of time, the asset will be treated as having been disposed of at the beginning of the hire-purchase agreement. If the hirer fails to pay on the agreement, so that the asset reverts to the original owner, the tax will be adjusted accordingly. It should be noted that the profits from a hire-purchase business are subject to Income Tax under Case I Schedule D rather than Capital Gains Tax.

Options

The general rule is that the grant of an option is regarded by the Revenue as the disposal of an asset. For purposes of Capital Gains Tax, it is necessary to distinguish between a traded and a non-traded option. A traded option will be regarded as a taxable disposal, whereas a non-traded option will not be regarded as a Capital Gains Tax disposal and therefore no allowable loss will arise.

Debts

A debt is an asset for the purposes of Capital Gains Tax. Therefore, if the debt is satisfied wholly or in part, this may be treated as a disposal of assets. This only applies where the person holding the debt is not the original creditor.

A shift in value of controlling shares

Where a person who has a controlling interest in a company acts in a way which reduces the value of his controlling shares or interest and passes that value into other shares or interests in the company, he or she will be deemed to have made a disposal of assets. These provisions also cover value shifting which may take place within a group of companies.

The timing of a disposal

In the majority of cases it is very easy to say when a disposal takes place – parties to the agreement will agree on a price and the asset will be exchanged for the agreed consideration. Sometimes, though, the contract for sale will pre-date the conveyance of the asset, or a contract may be made but the terms are never fulfilled.

In the case of the former situation, the disposal is deemed to take place at the time when the contract was made, rather than at the time the asset was conveyed. If the contract is one under which a condition must be fulfilled before completion can take place, the disposal will be held to have occurred at the time the condition was satisfied. In the latter case, where completion of the contract never actually takes place then no disposal will be deemed to have occurred.

Situations not treated as disposals

This brief section will deal with events which appear to fall within the category of transactions which should fall to be taxed as disposals, but which, nevertheless, the legislation deems to be non-disposals.

Death
When a person dies, the value of his or her assets is usually charged to Inheritance Tax (see Chapter 10). To avoid a double charge, death is not a taxable event for Capital Gains Tax purposes.

Mortgages
If a mortgagee gains possession of an asset because the mortgagor has defaulted on his or her payments, this will not be treated as a disposal of assets.

Other exempted disposals
It should be noted that the following four other cases are deemed not to be disposals for the purposes of Capital Gains Tax:

- Gifts to non-profit-making bodies for the public benefit.
- The sale of works of art to national institutions.
- Gifts to charity.
- Payments to the Inland Revenue in respect of Inheritance Tax.

Computing the gains

The essence of the Capital Gains rules is taxation of the amount by which the value of an asset has increased between the date of its acquisition and the date of its disposal. This section will explore the way in which the gains and losses which affect businesses are calculated. The basic premise behind the numerous rules and regulations is that to find the gain, the original cost of the asset must be subtracted from the amount of consideration which was received when the asset was sold. However true this statement may be, it would be unrealistic to give the impression that the calculation is so simplistic. Often the price which was originally paid for the asset has to be altered, either because statute has intervened (for example, to deem that the cost should only relate back as far as 31 March 1982) or because various items of expenditure have to be added to the original price paid. There are also numerous allowances which are important in arriving at the final taxable figure.

Consideration

The consideration is usually the price which has been paid in return for the asset. However, there are some important exceptions to the norm which are discussed below.

Alternative Income Tax charge

The first of these exceptions relates to sums which count as receipts for the purpose of Income Tax computations. If the sum does fall into this category, it cannot also be consideration under the Capital Gains Tax rules. An example of this is where an individual is given a large gift of money by an employer. This would not attract liability to Capital Gains Tax because it will be charged under Schedule E as a receipt for Income Tax purposes. Equally, if expenditure on an asset is allowable as a deduction for Income Tax purposes, it will not also be allowed for Capital Gains.

The second exception relates to assets which are acquired by a trader otherwise than as trading stock, but then the assets are used as trading stock. This might be the case, for example, if a trader begins a business with stock that was given to him as a gift earlier. The law will treat the proprietor as having sold the assets for market value at the time of transfer to trading stock.

This important exception not only relates to trading stock which has been provided by others. Whenever a trader appropriates assets to his or her trading stock, their market value must be recorded in the accounts. When the trader sells them, he or she will be charged under Schedule D Case I on the increase in their value from the market price attributed to them at the time of the appropriation, to the price gained on sale. The regulations then state that a Capital Gains charge must be paid on any increase in the value of chargeable assets that took place up to the time of their appropriation.

However, the trader is allowed to make an election either to reduce the market value recorded in the accounts for stock by the amount of the capital gain or to increase the recorded market value by the amount of the allowable loss. The election will be made where the amount of Income Tax he or she will have to pay on the resulting extra profits will work out to be less than the amount of Capital Gains Tax that the gain would otherwise attract. This is best explained with an example:

EXAMPLE

Nectarine runs an Art Gallery. In 1988 she buys a Picasso painting for herself and hangs it over her mantelpiece at home. She paid £2,500 for the painting. In 1989 the painting has increased in value to £3,250 when she appropriates it to her trading stock at the gallery. In 1990 she was able to sell the Picasso for £3,750.

In the absence of an election, she will be treated as having acquired the painting for trading stock at a price of £3,250 and then having sold it at £3,750, which leaves her with a trading profit of £500 to account for. She will also be liable to pay Capital Gains Tax on the appreciation in value of the painting on the difference between its original purchase price (£2,500) and its value when appropriated to trading stock (£3,250), i.e. £750.

Nectarine could choose, however, to elect to treat the painting as transferred to her trading stock at its original value of £2,500. This would give her a trading profit of £1,250 and no Capital Gains charge.

Bargains not made at 'arm's length'

Another exception to the price paid automatically being the consideration relates to bargains which are not made at arm's length. In such cases market value is substituted. This aims to dissuade people from charging a very low price for an asset which is worth much more, in order to avoid Capital Gains Tax. The most common example of this is where 'connected persons' – notably family members or partners – pass assets from one to another and there is deliberate lowering of the price of the asset. Figure 6.1 summarizes the definition of 'connected persons' in families. It should also be noted that if a loss is incurred on a disposal to a connected person, the loss may only be offset against chargeable gains arising from further disposals to that person.

For example, if Julie happens to find a Ming vase on a market stall, pays a low price to the unsuspecting stallholder, and then gives the vase to her nephew on the occasion of his twenty-first birthday, she will be treated as if she had sold it for its full market value.

A further exception exists where the form of consideration that is received for the asset is incapable of being valued. So if Bert transfers to Ethel his interest in a time-share apartment in Spain in return for her support in being elected as chairman of the local Green Party, he will be deemed to have received the market price for it.

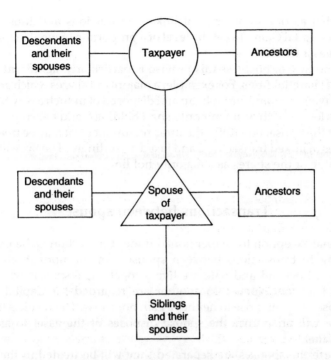

Figure 6.1 'Connected persons'

Linked transactions

The next exception relates to assets which are disposed of by a series of linked transactions. The following three factors must be established in order for this to apply:

1. The transactions must be made by one person.
2. The transactions are made to connected persons (see above).
3. The transactions all occur within six years of each other.

An example of the type of situation envisaged by the legislation might be where a person owns a set of ten valuable coins. Individually the coins may be valued at £300 but as a set they may have a value of £5,000. If the owner were to give the coins individually to connected persons within a six-year period, then the first gift would be treated as if the consideration was £300. However, the next gift would be regarded as one in a series of linked transactions and thus would attract Capital Gains Tax at the level of a proportion of what the set was worth as a whole.

In the case of business this proviso is particularly significant in the case of shareholdings. For example, a majority of shares which are held in a private company are split up and disposed of in such a way that the shares look as if they are minority shareholdings, and hence are worth less. If the transaction fulfils the three requirements it may be treated as a series of linked transactions and taxed accordingly. The tax will be on the value of the shares as a majority holding.

Transactions between spouses

The final exception to be mentioned under this section is the position relating to transactions between spouses. In the normal situation, where a husband and wife are living together, disposals which are made from one spouse to another are regarded for Capital Gains purposes as giving rise to neither a gain nor a loss. The result is that no charge will arise until the spouse disposes of the asset to another individual.

Where the spouses are separated they will be treated in the same way until the end of the tax year in which they separated, but from then until they obtain a divorce they will be regarded as connected persons (*Aspen* v. *Hildesley* 1982).

Allowances

In this part of the chapter we will look at the allowances which are available in respect of deductions from the consideration that was given, or deemed to have been given, for the asset. The allowances will be considered under the following headings:

- The cost of acquiring the asset.
- Incidental costs expended in acquiring the asset.
- Expenditure incurred in enhancing the value of the asset.
- Expenses incurred in defending the title of the asset.
- Costs incidental to the disposal of the asset.

The final part of the section will describe the types of expenditure which are not allowable as a deduction even though they would appear to be covered by the above categories.

The cost of acquiring the asset

The amount of money, or money's worth, which was given 'wholly and exclusively' for the purpose of acquiring the asset is deductible. If the asset has not been acquired in the sense that it was bought as a whole entity, but instead has been put together by the taxpayer, the amount of money it cost to buy the materials to create the asset will be allowable.

Incidental costs expended in acquiring the asset

Costs which are incurred 'wholly and exclusively' when acquiring the asset will be allowable. Examples of the sorts of costs which are envisaged are fees paid to professional advisers, advertising costs, or costs incurred during a conveyance of property.

Expenditure incurred when enhancing the value of the asset

If the taxpayer spends money on the asset in order to increase its value, and at the time when the asset is eventually sold, the value of the asset has been increased due to this expenditure, the amount expended will be allowable. For example, if a person builds an extension onto a property which increases its value, the expenditure incurred will be allowable. If the person had attempted to get planning permission for the extension and had thereby incurred costs, but the application was turned down, this expenditure would not be allowable, because the end result was not an increase in the value of the property.

Expenditure incurred in defending the title of the asset

If costs are incurred 'wholly and exclusively' for the purposes of protecting, or defending the title to the asset, they will be allowable unless they have already been allowed for Income Tax purposes.

Costs incidental to the disposal of the asset

The legislation will allow 'expenses reasonably incurred in ascertaining the market value' of the asset, as well as all the usual costs and fees which were allowed on acquisition of the asset. There are, however, some categories of expenditure which are specifically excluded from the list of allowable expenditure.

Part disposal of assets

Separate provisions are made for *part disposals of assets*. In this event, the cost will be apportioned according to the amount of the asset which is sold and that which still remains in the ownership of the taxpayer. There is an equation which is used to compute this apportionment.

$$\frac{A}{A+B}$$

where A = the amount or value of the consideration for the disposal before deducting the costs of sale, and B = the market value of the part not disposed of.

EXAMPLE

Angus buys a large Victorian house for £120,000 at which time he pays £10,000 in fees to his solicitor. He then converts the house into five separate dwellings which costs him a further £70,000. He then sells one of the flats for a purchase price of £60,000 but he incurs a further expenditure of £4,000 in conveyancing fees. The market value of the remaining dwellings is £240,000.

The apportionment would be worked out in the following way:

	£	£
Proceeds of sale		60,000
Costs of disposal		4,000
		56,000
Allowable expenditure	120,000	
	10,000	
	70,000	
	200,000	

In the equation, $A = 60,000$

$B = 240,000$

$$\frac{A}{A+B} = \frac{60,000}{300,000} = \frac{1}{5}$$

Allowable deduction $= 1/5 \times 200,000$ $= 40,000$

Gain $= 16,000$

(the effect of indexation is not included).

Angus may now carry forward the remaining allowable expenditure (£160,000) which will again be apportioned when he sells the next dwelling.

Where the partial disposal proceeds are 5% or less of the value of the whole at the time of the disposal (or 20% for land and buildings where the proceeds do not exceed £20,000) an election may be made simply to deduct the proceeds from the cost of the asset taken into account in a future disposal. This delays the chargeable gain and overrides the normal part disposal calculation.

Expenditure which is not deductible

Expenditure which is allowed against income

Because of the principle that Income Tax and Capital Gains Tax are mutually exclusive, it follows that any expenditure which is allowable for Income Tax purposes will not be allowed for Capital Gains. It is not always easy to decide whether the expenditure is of a capital nature or an income nature. An example of a capital expenditure would be the cost of making improvements to a factory building, which would be allowable for Capital Gains Tax purposes. The cost of maintaining and repairing the building would be regarded as income and thus not allowable.

Insurance and interest paid on a loan

Where the taxpayer has entered into a loan in order to purchase an asset he or she will not be able to claim the interest on the loan as a capital deduction. A similar principle is applied to payments made on policies which insure the asset. Businesses may, however, be able to deduct such expenses in computing their trading profits for Income Tax or Corporation Tax purposes.

Indexation allowance

Capital Gains Tax was often accused of being a tax on inflation. The rise in the value of an asset between purchase and sale could be largely or wholly the result of inflation. The introduction of the indexation allowance from March 1982, however, has to a large extent overcome this problem. It works in the following way. If Gerald buys an asset for £500 in 1990 when the inflation rate was 10% and then sells the asset in 1991 for £600, he has made a gain of £100 on the deal; but in real terms inflation has eaten away one half of the gain. The indexation allowance thus allows him to take into account the effect of inflation by letting him increase the cost of his acquisition and thus reduce his taxable gain. The use of the indexation allowance can have the effect of turning a gain into a loss for the purposes of Capital Gains Tax if the rate of inflation exceeds the rise in value of the asset (Schedule 19 para 2).

The calculation of indexation allowance is made according to the following formula:

$$\frac{\text{RPI in the month of disposal} - \text{RPI in month of acquisition (if later, 31 March 1982)}}{\text{RPI in month of acquisition (if later, 31 March 1982)}}$$

The figure is always taken to three decimal places as follows:

Taxing capital gains

Calculation of indexation adjustment:

RPI in month of disposal	= 135.4
RPI in month of acquisition	= 110.5
Indexation adjustment	= 135.4 − 110.5

$$= \frac{135.4 - 110.5}{110.5}$$

$$= 0.225\,339$$

$$= 0.225$$

(rounded to 3 decimal places)

The Revenue periodically publishes tables of the indexation allowances. They are regularly reprinted in tax journals and can be found in most public libraries.

EXAMPLE

Alex owns a freehold pet shop which he bought in 1978 for £8,000. Suppose that he sells the premises in March 1991 for £80,000. The market value of the pet shop in March 1982 was agreed at £26,000.

The market value at March 1982 is used (see 'Rebasing' below) and the indexation adjustment is 0.654 between March 1982 and March 1991.

	£
Sale proceeds	80,000
Less market value March 1982	26,000
	54,000
Less indexation allowance (£26,000 × 0.654)	17,004
Capital gain	36,996

Where there is a part disposal, the usual rules of apportionment will apply and the indexation allowance will only relate to the apportioned expenditure which is allowable on the part disposal.

The purchase of shares is a particular problem in this respect, due to the fact that they are habitually bought at different prices and at different times. To get over this problem all the shares that were bought after 5 April 1982 are regarded as part of the same 'pool' and are known as the 'new holding'. The expenditure of the new holding is primarily an addition of two elements: first, the acquisition cost of all the shares in the holding; second, the indexation allowance (with shares acquired before April 1985 'indexed up' to that date). After this stage, the indexation allowance will be applied on each occasion when a transaction in the shares takes place.

Rebasing

The Budget of 1988 introduced a further measure to mitigate the effects of inflation. Basically the legislation allows a taxpayer to rebase any assets held on 31 March 1982 and which are disposed of on or after 6 April 1988. He will then be deemed to have disposed of the asset on 31 March 1982 and then immediately to have reacquired it at its market value on that date with no charge to Capital Gains accruing. However, unless an election is made for this new rule to apply to all of the taxpayer's disposals, it is necessary to compare the gain calculated under the new and old rules. The lower gain is then chargeable. Where losses result under both rules, the lower loss is taken. If the two calculations produce a gain on the one hand and a loss on the other, the transaction is treated as a no gain/no loss.

EXAMPLE

Freda bought 1,000 shares in Tinkle Ltd, a private company, in 1975 for £15,000 which she sold in March 1991 for £50,000. The market value at 31 March 1982 has been assessed at £10,000. The indexation figure is again 0.654. No election has been made.

	Rebasing 31/3/82			Pre-Finance Act 1988 rules
	£	£	£	£
Proceeds of sale		50,000		50,000
Less cost of acquisition			15,000	
Market value at 31 March 1982	10,000			
Indexation allowance (0.654)	6,540	16,540	9,810	24,810
Capital Gain		33,460		25,190

NB: The gain of £25,190 achieved under the pre-1988 rules will be taken as the chargeable gain since it represents the smaller figure.

The election to calculate gains and losses on *all* assets using the value at 31 March 1982 must be made within two years of the end of the year of assessment for individuals, or accounting period for companies, in which the first disposal following the introduction of the new rule is made.

Reliefs and exemptions

As is undoubtedly becoming obvious to the reader by this stage, Capital Gains Tax has as many exceptions to the rules as it has rules. This section focuses on yet more reliefs and exemptions which are applied to the disposal of capital assets. Some of these are extremely important for the manager who either wishes to delay or mitigate the tax.

Annual exemption

The legislation (s.5 Capital Gains Tax Act 1979) allows the first part of a person's annual gain to be exempt. The allowance is announced each year and in 1991/2 stood at £5,500 (except for trusts, where the sum is £2,750). Therefore, if a person has total chargeable gains in 1991/2 of £12,000, £6,500 of these gains will actually suffer tax.

Losses

The basic principle with regard to losses is that they should be computed in the same way as gains. A Capital Gains loss can be defined as the excess of allowable expenditure over the consideration received. Losses in a year are first set off against gains in that year, and the net amount is chargeable. Where the losses in any one year exceed the gains made in that same year, the amount of 'surplus loss' may be carried forward and used to set off against gains which arise in subsequent years. Losses in a year which are set against the gains of that year cannot be restricted so as to leave an amount chargeable which is then covered by the annual exemption. This would leave more losses to carry forward. When utilizing losses brought forward from earlier years, they can be so restricted.

Capital Gains losses may not be transferred among a group of companies. This means that it is essential that group transactions in chargeable assets are funnelled through one company in the group.

From 1991/2, trading losses of sole traders and partnerships can be set off against capital gains made in the same or the following tax year. The relief is given after losses on capital disposals in the year but before capital losses brought forward from earlier years.

Relief for losses incurred on business loans

If a loss occurs on a loan which was made for business purposes to someone who is resident in the UK, the loss may be allowable for the purposes of Capital Gains Tax.

Charities

When an asset is given or sold at undervalue to a charity, the disposer will not be subject to the usual rule that the asset must be treated as having been transferred for market value. It will be deemed to incur neither a gain nor a loss.

Roll-over relief

The usual rule is that when a business asset is sold, it may give rise to a charge. However, the existence of 'roll-over relief' enables this charge to be deferred if the business asset is replaced by another business asset. The charge will then be deferred until such time as the replacement asset is sold. This sequence of events can continue for long periods of time, indeed until such time as the business itself is sold. At this stage it may then be possible for an individual to claim 'retirement relief' (see pp. 171–2). If the roll-over relief is being claimed by a company, because the company has a perpetual existence, the relief may be available indefinitely. The relief is computed by deducting the gain from the cost of the replacement asset, so that the gain is increased when it is eventually disposed of.

There are three basic conditions to be met before the relief can be allowed as follows:

1. The replacement of the asset must occur within a period beginning one year before the disposal and ending three years after the disposal.

2. The asset disposed of and the replacement must both belong to

one of the following group of assets (though not necessarily the same group):

(a) fixed plant and machinery (i.e. not moveable machinery, e.g. earthmoving equipment);

(b) land and buildings;

(c) goodwill;

(d) ships or aircraft;

(e) satellites, space stations and spacecraft;

(f) milk and potato quotas.

Also, by concession, sale proceeds can be used to carry out improvements to existing assets and to acquire a further interest in an existing business asset – for example, the freehold reversion where a person already holds the leasehold interest.

3. Where only part of the proceeds of the disposal are used for replacement, there will be an immediate charge to Capital Gains Tax on that part not rolled over. Full relief will arise where all the proceeds of the disposal are reinvested.

EXAMPLE 1

In March 1991 Daniel sold his ironmonger's shop (the building) for £240,000. He had bought it for £80,000 in June 1979. Its market value at 31 March 1982 was £120,000. In February 1992 he bought a building which he used as a fish-and-chip shop for £200,000 – that is, £40,000 less than the proceeds of the sale of the ironmonger's.

Sale in May 1988:

	£
Proceeds	240,000
Market value 31 March 1982	120,000
	120,000
Indexation allowance (0.654 × £120,000)	78,480
Gain	41,520
Non-reinvested proceeds (£240,000 − £200,000) chargeable to Capital Gains Tax 1988/9	40,000
Gain 'rolled over'	1,520

Deemed acquisition cost of the fish-and-chip shop in a future Capital Gains computation:

	£
Cost	200,000
Less 'rolled over' from previous shop	1,520
	198,480

EXAMPLE 2

Gareth sold his toyshop building in July 1990 for £60,000, producing a gain of £40,000, and immediately reinvested the proceeds in a new freehold for a sweetshop. If we assume that the sweetshop cost the following three amounts (1) £12,000, (2) £37,000 and (3) £70,000, and ignore the effect of indexation, the effect of roll-over relief on each of these transactions would be as follows:

	(1) £	(2) £	(3) £
Non-reinvested proceeds	48,000	23,000	NIL
Capital gain chargeable 1990/1	40,000	23,000	NIL
Base cost of new shop	12,000	37,000	70,000
Less gain rolled over	NIL	17,000	40,000
Deemed cost of new shop for Capital Gains Tax	12,000	20,000	30,000

In relation to an individual who is carrying on a number of different businesses, the relief on a transaction from one business can be rolled over against the acquisition of an asset in another business. Similarly, for companies which form part of a 75% group, gains in one member of the group can be rolled over against acquisitions in another.

Hold-over relief

If the asset which has replaced the original asset is a 'depreciating asset', it is not possible to apply for roll-over relief. Instead, another form of relief is utilized which again allows for the deferment of Capital

Gains Tax. A depreciating asset is defined as a 'wasting asset' or one which will become a wasting asset within ten years – i.e. an asset with a life of less than sixty years. Wasting assets are discussed in more detail below.

Provided that the same three basic conditions which had to be fulfilled to obtain roll-over relief apply, the tax on gains on depreciating assets can be deferred to the earliest of the following three dates:

1. The date on which the replacement asset is disposed of.

2. The date on which the replacement asset ceases to be used for the purpose of the business.

3. The ten-year anniversary date of the acquisition of the replacement asset.

A form of hold-over relief also used to apply to most assets gifted between individuals. One of its main purposes was to provide tax relief on gifts which may have been liable to both Inheritance Tax and Capital Gains Tax. However, the legislation with regard to the hold-over relief underwent significant changes in 1989, so that the relief is now restricted mainly to disposals of certain business assets and for certain disposals relating to trusts (see pp. 179–80).

Retirement relief

At the end of an individual's working life in business, an important relief is available to mitigate the liability which arises to Capital Gains Tax on the sale of that business. It works in such a way that the first £150,000 of the gain is exempt from Capital Gains Tax, while half the gain between £150,000 and £600,000 is also exempted. These limits may be subject to change, and the current figures should be confirmed with the Tax Inspector. To qualify for this relief the following three conditions must be met:

1. The retirement age is 55 or above, or the person is retiring before 55 due to ill-health.

2. The retiring person has owned the business for ten years. If he or she has not done so, there is a sliding scale of relief available at 10% of the full relief for each year of ownership (pro rata for parts of a year, but with no relief if the business has been owned for less than a year). A further provision exists to cover the situation where a

person has acquired the business from his or her spouse, in which case the period of the person's ownership will be deemed to include the spouse's previous period of ownership.

3. The assets which are to be the subject of the relief must be 'chargeable business assets'. The most important examples of chargeable business assets are land and buildings, plant and machinery (excluding private cars) and goodwill. Investments in stocks and shares, etc., and current assets such as debts, cash and stock are excluded categories.

The relief is computed in the following way: first, the gains on the disposal of the assets are calculated in the usual manner; secondly, the retirement relief is applied to reduce the total of the gain.

EXAMPLE

Freda is 69 years old and sells her knitting business in 1992 for £160,000 (all are chargeable business assets). She has owned the business for a period of nine years which means that she may claim a 90% relief. The purchase price of the business including indexation is taken to be £15,000. Freda is therefore entitled to the following relief:

90% × £150,000 = £135,000

Calculation of the chargeable gain:

	£
Proceeds of sale	160,000
Less purchase price (including indexation adjustment)	15,000
Gain	145,000
Less retirement relief (£135,000 + [½ × £10,000])	140,000
Chargeable gain	5,000

This form of relief is also relevant where there is a sale of shares by the directors of 'family' companies. There are stringent rules which prevent people who are only investors in the company from gaining relief. It must be established that the person who makes the disposal is a full-time working director of the company. This person must also be shown to hold either at least 25% of the voting rights in the trading company, or to hold at least 5% of the voting rights with members of his family holding more than 50%.

The computation here is slightly more tricky. The gain on the shares disposed of is calculated by bringing the value of the assets of the company at the time of sale into account and allowing relief only on the proportion of the gain in the value of the shares relating to the chargeable business assets.

Transferring a business to a limited company

It is worth noting that where individuals or a partnership make the decision to transfer their business into a limited company as a going concern, where the consideration received is in the form of shares or loan stock the payment of Capital Gains Tax can be deferred until their disposal.

Relief for shares in unquoted companies

A person who subscribes for shares in an unquoted company and who then makes a loss when they are disposed of, will have an allowable Capital Gains loss. The choice is available, however, for this loss to be claimed against income as if it were a trading loss. The relief may be claimed in respect of the year in which the loss occurred, or if any balance of loss remains, for the following year. The following four criteria must be established in order to make use of this provision:

1. The shares must have been issued from the company as opposed to being bought from another shareholder.
2. The company must be UK-registered and have operated as a trading company for six years, or for a shorter period, provided it has not been an investment company.
3. The disposal must have been at 'arm's length', or regarded as a deemed disposal because the shares have become of negligible value, or a distribution on the winding up of the company.
4. A claim must be made within two years of the relevant tax year in which the loss was sustained.

Wasting assets

We have already mentioned the term 'wasting assets'. We will examine here the significance of the term and the exemption which applies in relation to 'tangible moveable property' which is a wasting asset. A summary is provided in Figure 6.2.

Chattels

There are two concepts which need to be defined, the first being 'tangible moveable property': essentially this refers to chattels, although it also extends to cover such items as insurance policies. The other concept is a 'wasting asset', which is an asset having a predictable life not exceeding fifty years (s. 37 Capital Gains Tax Act 1979). Assets which are tangible moveable property and wasting assets are fully exempt from Capital Gains Tax, unless they are business assets on which capital allowances are available. Where the asset has been in use partly as a business asset and partly for private use, the gain will only attract partial exemption.

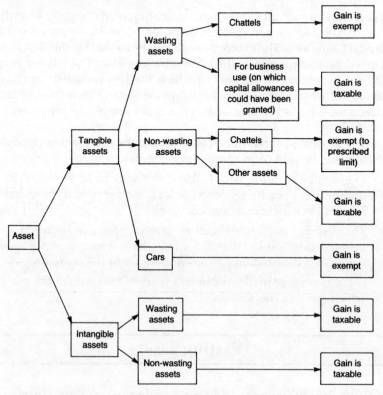

Figure 6.2 Summary of the taxation of wasting and non-wasting assets

174

Chattels which are not wasting assets – i.e. they have a predictable life of over fifty years (examples might include antiques, paintings and jewellery) – are exempt from Capital Gains Tax where the consideration for the disposal does not exceed £6,000. Where the consideration exceeds £6,000, the chargeable gain is limited to five-thirds of the excess of the disposal value over £6,000.

Leases

When a short lease is assigned, this requires a special calculation to be made on the disposal. The law deems a short lease not to waste away at the same velocity each year, but instead regards it as wasting slowly in the first years and accelerating as the period of the lease continues. A short lease is one of less than fifty years. Long leases are not wasting assets and are taxed in the normal manner.

Capital Gains Tax on the disposal of leases and Schedule A tax on premiums

Where a sublease is granted out of a lease this will have implications for both Income Tax and Capital Gains Tax. The relationship is dependent on whether the disposal is made out of a short lease or a long lease. If it is made out of a short lease the assessment to Income Tax under Schedule A in respect of the premium is calculated in the usual way (see pp. 135–6 above). The amount not subject to Income Tax is then charged to Capital Gains Tax. However, premiums in respect of the grant of leases of more than fifty years' duration are charged only to Capital Gains Tax.

Shares and securities

Earlier in the chapter we have looked briefly at the treatment of shares under Capital Gains Tax. As this is one of the more important areas where Capital Gains Tax impinges on business, this section will explore the regulations in greater detail. Many of the rules apply to both quoted and unquoted shares and securities, but occasionally the law makes a distinction between the two.

Some securities are entirely exempt from Capital Gains Tax. These fall into the following categories:

- Corporate bonds issued after 13 March 1984 by a quoted company.
- National savings certificates, premium bonds and some other non-marketable savings.
- Gilt-edged stocks.

Pooling

The system of 'pooling' was created to deal with the problems which arise when a holding of shares of the same class in the same company was acquired by several separate purchases. Two difficulties are evident here: the precise identification of which shares are being sold, and the resultant problem of differing indexation allowances. To circumvent these issues, identification rules exist; wherever a sale takes place it is essential to have an acquisition date and this will be determined by the following rules:

- Acquisitions and disposals which take place on the same day are matched and are not pooled.
- Acquisitions which are made within nine days of the disposal are matched on a 'first in first out' basis and no indexation is allowed, neither do the shares enter the pool.
- Shares acquired after 31 March 1985 are pooled.
- Shares acquired between 31 March 1982 and 31 March 1985 are separately indexed within the pool.

When shares are purchased in several transactions after 31 March 1985, and each time shares enter or leave the pool, the whole pool will be indexed from the last date of indexation except if the first two above rules apply. Where shares were purchased during the period from April 1965 (when Capital Gains Tax was introduced) and 31 March 1982, a separate calculation will be required.

Valuation of shares

It is obvious that a value must be placed on the shares before computation can take place. In respect of unquoted shares a professional valuation must be sought and then negotiated with the Revenue. For quoted shares, the price quoted on the Stock Exchange on the date of acquisition is the starting-point. There is then a choice of the following methods of assessing the value:

- '¼ up' from the lower of the buying and selling prices on that day, or
- The middle point of the highest and lowest recorded prices at which bargains were made on that day.

The same method of valuation applies when the quoted shares are sold. The value of the shares will be taken to be the lower of the two figures. The term 'quoted' shares excludes shares traded in the unlisted securities market.

Reorganizations

There are a number of ways in which a company reorganizes or affects its share capital. The main methods are as follows:

- Bonus issues.
- Rights issues.
- Take-overs and mergers.
- Capital distributions.

Bonus issues
A bonus issue is an allocation of extra shares to existing shareholders. Because the shares are acquired at no cost, no indexation is required and the shares are simply added to the appropriate share pool.

Rights issues
Additional shares are sold to existing shareholders at a privileged price. Indexation is applied to the amount paid, and the appropriate share pool is indexed up in the ordinary way.

Take-overs and mergers
Shares which are acquired because of a take-over or merger by way of a share-for-share exchange are regarded as having been bought at the cost of the original shares. Therefore, no gain or loss is deemed to have arisen at the time of the take-over except if the parties have received

cash. A chargeable gain will arise on that part of the consideration received as cash.

Capital distributions

A capital distribution for the purpose of Capital Gains Tax is a repayment of share capital. It will be dealt with in different ways, depending on the size of the distribution. However, the general rule is that the distribution will be regarded as a part disposal of an asset and treated in the normal way. If the disposal is less than 5% of the value of the shares, the Revenue has the discretion to allow any gain to be rolled over by treating the distribution as a deduction from the cost of the shares for the purposes of calculating any gains or losses on future disposals.

The link between Inheritance Tax and Capital Gains Tax

Although the general principle in relation to the Income Tax Schedules is that they should not overlap, the same is not entirely true of the two capital taxes – Inheritance Tax and Capital Gains Tax. Table 6.1 summarizes the relationship between the two. Generally, credit is given where payment is made under one of these taxes and a liability arises under the other.

Partnerships and Capital Gains Tax

For the purposes of Capital Gains Tax, all partnership assets, including the goodwill of the business, are treated as though each of the partners owns a fractional share of each asset. The partnership deed should, therefore, reflect the interest of the partners in each asset if this is different from the ratio in which they divide the profits from trading. When the ratio in relation to profit-sharing alters, there is deemed to be an acquisition of a new interest in the assets by the partners whose profit share is enhanced, and a disposal of an interest by those partners whose share of the profits is diminished. However (provided no payment is made), no gain or loss occurs on such disposals because the

Table 6.1 The relationship between Inheritance Tax and Capital Gains Tax

	Cash gift	Property gift	Sale at market value	Sale at undervalue	Death
Inheritance Tax	Not taxable (provided donor survives 7 years)	Not taxable (provided donor survives 7 years)	Not taxable	Taxable (unless donor survives 7 years)	Taxable
Capital Gains Tax	Not taxable	Taxable	Taxable	Taxable	Not taxable

consideration for the transaction is held to be equal to the current balance sheet values of the assets.

Capital Gains Tax and trusts and settlements

For the purposes of Capital Gains Tax any property which is held in trust (with three exceptions) is regarded as 'settled property' (s.46 Capital Gains Act 1979). The three exceptions are as follows:

1. Bare trusts – that is where the property is held for a beneficiary who is absolutely entitled against the trustee.
2. Property held for two or more persons who are jointly entitled to the property.
3. Property held for any person who would be entitled to the property but for being an infant or under some disability.

Apart from these three examples, all other trusts are relevant for Capital Gains purposes. When a settlement is created, this is treated as a chargeable disposal of assets by the person setting up the trust – the 'settlor'. If the settlor is living when he or she creates the trust, he or she can utilize the normal Capital Gains Tax exemptions with the result that if he or she settles exempt or non-chargeable assets (e.g. money or principal residence) he or she will not be liable to Capital Gains Tax. There is also provision to roll-over gains and treat them as reducing the trustee's acquisition cost when property is transferred into a discretionary trust, or business assets are involved.

179

A charge to Capital Gains Tax will arise at the time when property in the trust ceases to be trust property. When a sale of assets is made by the trustees of the settlement, they will be liable to Capital Gains Tax. They are allowed only half of the individual's annual exemption (in 1991/2, £2,750). However, where a beneficiary under a trust transfers his interest to someone else, this will not usually be a chargeable disposal for Capital Gains Tax. Also, when a beneficiary becomes absolutely entitled to assets of a discretionary trust, the trustees and the beneficiary may jointly elect for the tax liability to be deferred. The beneficiary's deemed cost for a future gains calculation is then reduced by the gain rolled over. In the case of interest in possession trusts, gains on business assets may be similarly deferred.

A tenant for life is a person who has an interest in the trust property which persists during his or her lifetime. When a tenant for life dies and the property is thus disposed of, the legislation provides that the death will give rise to neither a chargeable gain nor an allowable loss. The result of this is that the value of the assets at the time of the tenant for life's death becomes the new 'base value' for the trustees.

At the time of writing, a consultative document has been issued by the Revenue which considers several possible Income Tax and Capital Gains Tax changes for UK trusts. The key principle is that property held in trust should in general be taxed neither more lightly nor more heavily than property held by individuals. Changes are also proposed to the taxation of settlors where they, their spouses, or children can benefit from the trust.

Complex anti-avoidance legislation exists to minimize the opportunity to reduce the tax burden by the transfer of assets to overseas trusts or through the migration of UK trusts. The above comments are only a brief introduction to the taxation of trusts; it is a difficult area where expert advice should be sought.

Concluding comment

Our discussion of taxation so far has been primarily concerned with income and capital gains arising within the UK. The next chapter deals with the complex issue of the tax treatment of foreign income and gains.

7

Taxing foreign earnings

So far we have been primarily concerned with the taxation of income and gains arising within the UK. We now turn to the tax treatment of foreign earnings. In this chapter we review the rules on residence and domicile introduced in Chapter 1; consider the tax treatment of income and gains from overseas for both individuals and companies; and conclude by looking at the general rules on double taxation relief.

The vast majority of UK taxpayers are resident and domiciled in the UK. Therefore, they are subject to UK tax on their *world-wide* income and gains. In other words, the fact that certain profits or gains arose outside the UK is immaterial. It is important to recognize, however, that those who are not UK resident and domiciled do not necessarily escape UK tax.

In respect of individuals, income arising on foreign securities or possessions is subject to Income Tax under Cases IV and V of Schedule D, while capital gains arising outside the UK will, in most cases, be subject to UK Capital Gains Tax in the normal way. Turning to companies, UK companies are liable to UK Corporation Tax on their foreign as well as their domestic earnings, and companies not UK resident are taxed on profits derived from operations in the UK through a branch or agency.

Foreign incomes and gains taxed in the UK may also be taxed in the country of origin. Similarly, a foreign company trading in the UK may find income and gains taxed here and in its country of residence. To relieve the burden of double taxation, agreements have been negotiated with most countries. In addition, it is important to recognize the current movement within the European Community towards fiscal harmony. In the 1990s this will increasingly affect the administration of taxation in Europe. Already there has been some, if limited, progress towards harmonizing VAT, and in the future other taxes may be brought more into line. This should simplify the taxation in one European country of earnings arising in another.

The rules on residence and domicile

Individuals

Chapter 1 introduced the fact that a taxpayer's residence, ordinary residence and domicile status are important in determining the manner in which income and gains are taxed in the UK. This applies both to income and gains arising within the UK and income and gains arising overseas.

Residence
It has been established that an individual is deemed to be resident in the UK in any given tax year if he or she was or did any of the following:

- Ordinarily resident in the UK throughout but temporarily abroad.
- Present in the UK for 183 days or longer, excluding the dates of arrival and departure (the 'six-month rule').
- Made 'frequent and substantial' visits to the UK, which is usually interpreted to mean visits averaging ninety days or more each year for four or more consecutive years.
- Had accommodation available for his or her own use in the UK and made one or more visits to the UK in that tax year (this rule does not apply, however, to someone who retains a home in the UK while working full-time abroad).

Also, it has been decided that UK residence extends to a boat in UK territorial waters and oil rigs in certain parts of the UK continental shelf.

Quite obviously, therefore, it is not easy to spend much time in the UK and remain non-resident. There is also nothing in principle to stop an individual being resident (or ordinarily resident) in more than one country in any tax year, though double taxation rules may clarify in which country they are to be treated as resident for tax purposes.

Ordinary residence

The term ordinary residence suggests a greater degree of permanence than the term resident. It has been defined as 'a man's abode in a particular place or country which he has adopted voluntarily and for settled purposes as part of the regular order of his life for the time being, whether of short or long duration' (*R.* v. *Barnet London Borough Council, ex p. Shah* 1983). In other words, it is associated with the place where a person normally resides. Therefore, if a person is resident in the UK, he or she will also be deemed to be ordinarily resident if the residence is 'habitual'. An individual entering the UK with the intention of staying here permanently is treated as ordinarily resident from the day of arrival.

In strict terms a person is resident and/or ordinarily resident for the whole of a tax year or not at all. If, therefore, a person normally resident in the UK went abroad on 1 June 1991, he would still be technically resident and ordinarily resident for the whole of the tax year 1991/2. This would mean that his overseas earnings after 1 June 1991 to at least the end of the tax year would be taxed in the UK. By concession, however, the tax year will normally be divided so that, in our example, UK tax would only apply up to 1 June 1991. This arrangement applies provided the person has left the UK for *permanent* residence overseas or is going abroad to *take up employment*. Similarly, someone arriving from abroad with a view to *permanent* residence in the UK usually will be deemed resident and ordinarily resident only from the date of arrival. People coming to the UK with the intention of staying for at least four years will normally be judged to be ordinarily resident from the date they arrive.

To take advantage of this concession, when leaving the UK the tax authorities will require evidence that the individual is intending to reside abroad with some permanence, for example the sale of the family home or the purchase of a home overseas. Where such evidence is not forthcoming, the Inland Revenue may postpone a decision for three years and then make any necessary and retrospective adjustments. There is a right of appeal against a Revenue ruling on residency status to the Special Commissioners and thence to the courts. The appeal must normally be made in writing to the Tax Inspector within three months of the ruling.

There are also special rules relating to those who work abroad full-time under a contract of employment. In these circumstances, an individual will be deemed not resident and not ordinarily resident in the UK for the whole period of the employment, and hence the overseas earnings will be exempt from UK tax, provided all of the following conditions are satisfied:

- The duties of the employment are performed wholly overseas, or where duties are performed in the UK, they are *incidental* to the duties abroad.
- The absence from the UK includes a complete tax year (6 April to 5 April).
- Visits to the UK do not either average three months or more each tax year or equal six months or more in any one tax year.

Overseas earnings may well, however, suffer tax in the country where the employment takes place.

Quite clearly the rules on residence status are such that taxpayers going overseas must be careful about retaining accommodation in the UK for their own use, the number of subsequent visits they make to the UK, the length of their stay, and the timing of their exit from the UK.

Domicile

Whereas a person can be simultaneously resident in more than one country, at any given time he can only be domiciled in one. The law on domicile in England and Wales states that persons are domiciled where they have their permanent home, i.e. the place they intend to return to when away from it. Most people acquire their domicile at birth – known as the 'domicile of origin' – which is normally the domicile of the father or, in cases of illegitimacy, the mother. It is not necessarily the country in which the person is born. A person over the age of 16 can, however, acquire a different domicile during life – known as the 'domicile of choice'. This requires the person to sever totally their ties with the country of their domicile of origin and to have the firm intention of permanent settlement in their new domicile. It is important to realize that living in a country for a long time may not in itself be sufficient to alter a person's domicile status. Indeed, it is difficult to cast aside an existing domicile.

Companies

The issue of domicile is rarely relevant to companies. However, a company is considered to be domiciled where it is incorporated and this domicile can be changed only in very exceptional circumstances.

Taxing foreign earnings

The definition of company residence until recently derived from the leading case of *De Beer Consolidated Mines Ltd* v. *Howe* (1906), in which the House of Lords established that the residence of a company depended not on where it was registered, but where it really kept house and did its 'real business'. Its 'real business' was carried on where the *central management and control* actually took place. Therefore, this was a question of fact which required scrutiny of the course of business and trading. If a company's 'central management and control' was exercised from the UK, it was held to have UK residence even if board meetings were held abroad and its shareholders were resident overseas.

The location of the central management and control remained the main test for the determination of company residence until the Finance Act 1988 which issued the first statutory definition. Since 15 March 1988, a company newly incorporated in the UK is automatically regarded as resident in the UK, notwithstanding that its central management and control are exercised abroad. There is an intention to extend this rule to all companies after 15 March 1993. If, however, a company is incorporated abroad, its UK residence will still depend on the management and control test. The new definition means that it is no longer possible for a company incorporated in the UK to cease to be resident here, but it is possible for a 'non-UK' company to cease to be resident in the UK by moving its central management and control outside the country.

A UK resident company is liable to UK Corporation Tax on its world-wide profits including the profits from branches and agencies overseas, but not the profits of foreign subsidiary companies unless they are paid over to the UK company. By contrast, a company not resident in the UK is liable to Corporation Tax only on profits derived from a branch or agency operating in the UK. Simply trading *with* the UK is not in itself sufficient to establish the existence of a branch or agency. There must be actual trading operations taking place *within* the UK (*Firestone Tyre and Rubber Co. Ltd* v. *Lewellin* 1957).

Where a UK company has an overseas subsidiary and it is managed and controlled abroad then its profits may escape UK tax. The UK holding company would be charged only on payments received from the subsidiary: that is to say, interest on loans (under Case IV) and dividends (under Case V of Schedule D).

At the same time, however, losses incurred by an overseas branch or agency are automatically included in computing a UK company's Corporation Tax profits, but losses stemming from a subsidiary cannot be deducted ('group relief' for losses extends only to UK resident companies, as explained in below, pp. 210–11). For this reason, if intending to trade in a country with tax rates lower than the UK's, it appears advisable to start out trading through a branch, so that initial losses are deducted from domestic profits, and transfer the trade to an overseas subsidiary once profits begin. Before embarking on such a course, however, it is essential to seek detailed legal advice.

Anti-avoidance legislation relating to *dual residence, transfer pricing* and *controlled foreign companies* exists to avoid tax being lost where companies operate outside the UK.

Companies which have dual residence

In some cases a company may have dual residence. This is possible when a company has been incorporated in the UK but trades in a country which uses management and control as its primary test of residence. In order to prevent a substantial loss of revenue from these dual-residence companies, new rules have been introduced which restrict reliefs, notably for losses and capital allowances (s.404 Income and Corporation Taxes Act 1988).

If the situation arises that a company is liable to be charged in both the UK and the foreign jurisdiction on the *same* profits, it may be possible for the company to avail itself of double taxation relief (see pp. 191–3).

Transfer pricing

Purchases and sales between a UK company and an overseas subsidiary, or companies within a multinational grouping, could take place in such a way that profits are diverted into low-tax havens. For example, the UK company might sell its products to an overseas subsidiary at a no-profit price. In these circumstances, the Inland Revenue has the right to substitute an 'arm's length' (i.e. commercial) price in calculating the taxable profit of the UK company. The Revenue also has powers to obtain details necessary to their enquiry into the relevant transactions.

Controlled foreign companies

Where a company is resident outside the UK in a country with a substantially lower rate of profit tax but is controlled by persons resident in the UK, the Inland Revenue can apportion its profits between the members and so bring profit into charge to UK Income or Corporation Tax. The original intention behind this measure was to prevent the accumulation of income where tax rates are lower than in the UK. The legislation has succeeded in reducing the attractiveness of setting up subsidiaries in tax havens.

There are also restrictions relating to foreign subsidiaries of UK companies issuing shares or debentures, the transfer of such shares and debentures, and the transfer of a trade to a non-resident company.

The importance of residence and domicile status

A person's residence and domicile status have an important bearing on the taxation of income and gains. In particular, someone resident in the UK is liable to UK Income Tax on income wherever that arises, whereas someone not UK resident is only taxed in this country on income arising here. The following are further important factors:

- In the main, only people resident in the UK benefit from the personal allowances available to set against income liable to UK tax. The primary exception relates to British subjects resident abroad who may claim a proportion of the relief.

- Bank and building society interest and interest on certain government securities may be paid gross to those not ordinarily resident in the UK.

Another distinction relates to the taxation of foreign income. Those not domiciled within the UK and British subjects who are resident but not ordinarily resident in the UK are generally taxed only on foreign earnings *remitted* (paid or transmitted) to the UK. The rules, however, are more complicated for employment income.

Employment income

The three Cases of Schedule E were outlined in Chapter 4 and these Cases determine how employment income is to be assessed. The broad rules are as follows:

- An individual resident and ordinarily resident in the UK is taxed under Case I Schedule E on their income wherever it arises, even if it is not remitted to the UK. Where, however, a person is employed abroad for a continuous period of 365 days or more but remains resident in the UK, he or she benefits from a deduction of 100%, i.e. the overseas emoluments escape UK Income Tax. 'Continuous period' is defined as one which excludes a time when the taxpayer is in the UK for more than 62 consecutive days (excluding the day of departure but including the day of arrival) and periods in the UK which together exceed in total one-sixth of the period of the tour to date (periods abroad plus periods in the UK).

- An individual resident but not ordinarily resident in the UK is subject to Income Tax on his or her employment income arising within the UK under Case II of Schedule E and on foreign earnings, in so far as they are remitted to the UK, under Case III of that Schedule.

- An individual not resident in the UK is subject to UK Income Tax under Case II Schedule E but only on his or her employment income arising within the UK.

- Where a person is employed abroad and becomes not resident and not ordinarily resident in the UK for the period of the contract, the resulting income escapes UK tax.

There are special provisions relating to expenses *incurred by the employer* in providing board and lodging for an employee while abroad, and for the cost of providing or reimbursing travelling expenses associated with working abroad. Similar concessions exist for non-UK domiciled people employed by foreign employers in the UK. Although such expenses are normally liable to tax as income of the employment (see p. 106), these provisions remove a charge to Income Tax on the costs borne by the employer. The costs of two return journeys for a spouse and child each year to visit an employee working abroad for at least sixty days are also exempted from tax. It should be appreciated that these concessions apply only where *the cost is met by the employer*. If the employee meets the costs directly, he cannot claim them as expenses for Schedule E purposes (this may not seem equitable but it is the law).

Profits from trading overseas

Sole traders and partnerships resident in the UK but exporting overseas or undertaking all or part of the trade overseas are taxed on the full profits resulting under the normal Case I Schedule D rules (as detailed in Chapter 2). In other words, the fact that the trade is carried on wholly or partly abroad has no tax consequence.

Where partnerships are concerned, a UK resident partner is assessed on his or her share of the profits under Case I Schedule D where the control of the business lies in the UK, but under Case V Schedule D where the control lies abroad. It is important to realize that what is decisive here is where the *control* of the business lies, not where the actual trading occurs. Because the basis of assessment differs between Cases I and V of Schedule D, the Case under which the profits are taxed can have important tax consequences. In particular non-UK-domiciled people and UK-domiciled people not ordinarily resident in the UK are taxed under Case V only on income *remitted* to the UK. By contrast, a Case I assessment is on the profits of the trade *wherever they arise* and irrespective of the amount paid into the UK.

It is no easy thing, however, to convince the Revenue that a business is controlled overseas. In all cases it will be a question of fact; legal documentation will be supportive only. For example, even where a trade was carried on wholly in Canada by a person resident in the UK, and he took no part in its management, it was held by the House of Lords that the profits were taxable under Schedule D Case I. In this case, the fact that the taxpayer could at any time take control of the business was decisive (*Ogilvie* v. *Kitton* 1908).

Losses on trades carried on abroad are computed, and can be relieved, essentially in the same way as losses of a UK trade – as detailed in pp. 56–62 above. The main distinction relates to setting the losses against other income to obtain a tax repayment. Losses on trades carried on abroad can only be set off against profits from other overseas trades, foreign emoluments under Schedule E (foreign wages and salaries, etc.) and pensions from overseas.

Income from securities and possessions outside the UK

Income from *securities* of overseas governments and interest on foreign mortgage loans and on loan or debenture stock issued by foreign companies are technically taxed in the UK under Case IV of Schedule D. By contrast, dividends and rentals from overseas, along with foreign pensions and profits from a business carried on and controlled wholly outside the UK, are treated as income from *possessions* outside the UK and are taxed under Schedule D Case V. The main exception is where the income (for example, a dividend) is paid through a UK paying agent who deducts basic rate tax at source. In this case the income is assessed under Schedule C.

The rules (s.65 Income and Corporation Taxes Act 1988) for assessing income under Cases IV and V of Schedule D are identical and therefore there is no need to be too concerned about the distinction between the terms securities and possessions, though the former implies some underlying guarantee. For persons resident in the UK (excluding companies), income under both cases is normally assessed on the *preceding year* basis, but with the *actual* income of the year assessed in the opening two years and the closing year (the basis of assessment is the same as for interest taxed under Case III Schedule D, as detailed in pp. 129–35).

For example, foreign dividends arising in the year to 5 April 1991 will be taxed in the UK as income of the tax year 1991/2, unless dividends on the shares first arose, or the shares were sold in that year, in which case the dividends would be treated as income of 1990/1. Notice that the opening year is the year in which the first dividends were paid. This is not necessarily the year in which the shares were acquired, whereas the closing year is the year the shares were sold. There is provision under Cases IV and V to treat a source as having ceased when no income has arisen from it over the last six years. The last year the income arose is taken to be the year of cessation. Should income arise from the source in the future, at the time this occurs it is treated as a new source. It is also worth noting that foreign annuities and foreign pensions are taxed at only 90% of the amount arising.

Turning to people who are resident but not domiciled in the UK, or a person who is a British subject and resident but not ordinarily resident in the UK, the charge is only on the income remitted to the UK. In other words, someone resident in the UK who is not UK-domiciled, or not ordinarily resident, and who receives £10,000 in foreign rentals, but remits to the UK only £3,000, will be taxed in the UK only on the £3,000. Not surprisingly, to prevent abuse the term 'remit' has been defined widely to include any commercially recognized form of remittance.

Case V losses from trading can be fully relieved against either future profits from the same trade or other overseas earned income. Losses from letting foreign property can be set off against future income from the same property. In computing profits or losses on these sources, the expenses deductible are similar to those for Case I (UK trading profits) and Schedule A (UK rents). There can be no losses from income on securities under Case IV.

Income within Cases IV and V received by a UK company is assessed to Corporation Tax in the accounting period in which it arises (see Chapter 8).

Capital gains

Where an individual is domiciled and resident or ordinarily resident in the UK, Capital Gains Tax is charged on gains from the disposal of assets no matter where they are situated. Similarly, a UK resident company is liable to Corporation Tax on world-wide gains from the disposal of its assets. If an individual is not domiciled in the UK but is UK resident or ordinarily resident, he or she is liable to pay Capital Gains Tax on disposals of assets located within the UK, and on gains arising from foreign assets but only in so far as they are remitted to the UK. Someone outside the UK residency rules is chargeable to Capital Gains Tax only if trading through a UK branch or agency. Liability arises on disposal of the assets of that branch or agency (Capital Gains Tax Act 1979).

Double Taxation Relief (DTR)

Foreign income and gains of UK residents are liable to UK tax but are also likely to be taxed in the country in which the income and gains arise. Similarly, in many cases non-residents of the UK pay UK tax on income and gains arising within the country, while also paying tax on the same income and gains in the country in which they are resident. In other words, income and gains may be taxed twice.

This could lead to an alarming tax burden. To avoid this result, international double taxation agreements exist (under s.788 Income and Corporation Taxes Act 1988). Typically an agreement between the UK and another country will embrace the following:

- A definition of residence to avoid 'dual residence'.
- A decision on where income and gains should be taxed.
- The manner in which credit should be given in the country where the individual is resident for any tax paid in the country where the incomes or gains arise.
- Special provisions for taxing persons such as students, teachers and visiting diplomats.
- The levying in the country of source of preferential rates of tax for certain types of income.

Under double taxation agreements between the UK and another country, normally certain types of income are taxed in only one of the countries. It is important, therefore, to consult the appropriate agreement for detailed guidance. But where under the agreement an income remains taxable in both countries, or where no double taxation agreement exists, DTR is typically given by means of a deduction of foreign tax suffered from the UK tax liability (known as *unilateral relief*).

Withholding tax

In many countries, when interest, dividends and other incomes are paid to foreigners, tax is deducted at source. This is commonly referred to as 'withholding tax'. But the income will most likely also suffer tax in the country in which the recipient is resident. To give DTR, in the UK the basic procedure involves the Inland Revenue giving credit for the tax already paid against the person's UK tax liability on the income. This credit cannot, however, exceed the UK tax liability on the income. Consequently, the taxpayer bears the higher of the UK tax or the foreign tax.

Underlying tax

Where a UK company has 10% or more of the voting control in an overseas company, a credit may also be obtained for what is termed the 'underlying tax'. The purpose of this relief is to reflect the fact that companies abroad often pay dividends out of taxed profits.

An example should clarify the operation of the DTR provisions as they relate to relief in the UK for both withholding tax and underlying tax.

EXAMPLE

A company resident in the UK owns 30% of a Ruritanian company. This company made a gross profit of £100,000 on which it paid Ruritanian tax at 20%. The company made a dividend payment of £25,000, deducting Ruritanian withholding tax of 15%.
The UK company receives:

		£
Gross dividend	25,000 × 30%	7,500
Less withholding tax	7,500 × 15%	1,125
		6,375

Taxing foreign earnings

The UK tax position is:

	£
Gross dividend received	7,500
Grossing up for underlying tax 7,500 × 100/80	9,375
Therefore, the withholding tax is £1,125 and the underlying tax is £1,875 (total £3,000)	

The UK tax assessment (Case V) on this income will be:

	£
9,375 × 33%*	3,093.75
DTR	3,000.00
Net UK tax payable	93.75

*Note: Assuming a Corporation Tax rate of 33%

DTR claims must be made within six years of the end of the relevant year of assessment for Income Tax and the accounting period for Corporation Tax. With regard to Corporation Tax, DTR is given before the ACT set-off (see pp. 207–8 below).

A summary of how the different incomes and gains of UK-domiciled and UK-resident individuals are taxed is contained in Table 7.1.

Table 7.1 The taxation of income and gains: a summary

Source	Assessed under	Normal basis of assessment*
Income from foreign securities	Case IV Schedule D	Preceding year's profits
Income from foreign possessions	Case V Schedule D	Preceding year's profits
Profits from trading overseas but where the trade is deemed to be controlled from the UK	Case I Schedule D	Preceding year's profits
Profits from trades controlled outside the UK	Case V Schedule D	Preceding year's profits
Emoluments from employments outside the UK	Schedule E	Actual emoluments of the year
Gains on disposals of assets world-wide	Capital Gains Tax	Gains in the year

*Note: Except for companies, where it is the income arising in the accounting period.

8

Taxing companies

In earlier chapters of the book, both Income Tax and Capital Gains Tax have been discussed. It should be remembered that neither of these taxes directly applies to companies. Companies pay tax on both their income and their capital profits by way of Corporation Tax.

Under the British Law a company is a distinct legal person, but it is also an artificial person, who can in reality only operate through its directors or shareholders. Because of this strange concept of legal personality the basis of the taxation of companies is to 'strip aside the corporate mask' and look at the reality of the situation. The result is that the legislature has to use two systems of taxation: the *profits* of the company are taxed by one method, and the *distribution* of profits to shareholders by another.

This chapter will discuss both of these systems of payment starting with the taxation of the profits of a company which give rise to a liability to Corporation Tax, moving on to how the distribution of the profits is taxed by the use of advance corporation tax and tax credits. The new method of 'pay and file' will be examined, as will the significance of where a company resides for the purposes of taxation.

Liability to Corporation Tax

In order to understand when a company will be liable to pay Corporation Tax, it is first necessary to define, as far as is possible, who, or what, is a company. Under the legislation for the purposes of

Corporation Tax a company is regarded as 'any body corporate or unincorporated association' but does not include a partnership, a local authority or a local authority association (s.832 Income and Corporation Taxes Act 1988). In the case of *Conservative and Unionist Central Office* v. *Burrell* (1982), the Court of Appeal considered the meaning of the term 'unincorporated association'. Lawton, L. J. defined it in the following words:

> two or more persons bound together for one or more common purposes, not being business purposes, by mutual undertakings, each having mutual duties and obligations in an organization which had rules which identify in whom control of it and its funds rested, and on what terms, and which could be joined or left at will.

It can be seen from the complexity of this definition that there may often be some dispute as to who falls to be taxed to Corporation Tax. It has been held for example that the Rotary Club is an unincorporated association and therefore has a potential liability, but clubs which are formed on a yearly basis in order to save for Christmas or annual holidays are treated as having no liability.

The charge to Corporation Tax

Corporation Tax is imposed on the 'profits' of the company. This includes both the income and capital gains of the organization. No liability arises to Income Tax on the income, equally no liability to Capital Gains Tax arises on the chargeable gains. The determination of what is treated as income of the company is, however, based on the principles of Income Tax assessment. The income which falls to be taxed is aggregated with the chargeable capital gains in order to assess the total profits.

The period of assessment

The period of assessment for Corporation Tax is by reference to a 'financial year' (FY). In comparison with the variety of systems available under the Income Tax regulations, the method of assessment is relatively straightforward. The FY runs from 1 April to 31 March and each FY is labelled according to the year in which it began. So, for example, the financial year 1991 runs from 1 April 1991 to 31 March 1992.

Although Corporation Tax is charged according to financial years, the basis of assessment is the 'accounting period' (AP) of the company. This period is usually determined by the company's accounting date (the date to which it prepares its accounts) but it must not exceed twelve months in length.

Where accounts for more than twelve months are prepared, they form two or more APs. For example, accounts of eighteen months form one AP of twelve months and a further AP of six months. It is very possible that the FY and the AP will not coincide and in such cases the profits of the relevant period are apportioned according to the length of the AP which falls into the respective financial years. Each proportion of the profit is then taxed at the level of Corporation Tax which was imposed in the particular FY.

EXAMPLE

Superritch Ltd makes up its accounts to 30 September each year. In the period of account ending in September 1991 its trading profits were £6,000,000.

To determine the liability to Corporation Tax, first the accounting profit must be apportioned to each FY. October to March 1991 falls in FY 1990; therefore the profit in this period is taken to be:

$6/12 \times £6,000,000 = £3,000,000$

April to September 1991 falls in FY 1991; therefore the profit in this period is taken to be:

$6/12 \times £6,000,000 = £3,000,000.$

Apportioning the profit in this way will have no consequence if the Corporation Tax rate is the same in both financial years, but it will be significant if the rates vary.

There will, of course, be no need to apportion profits where the period of account is for a twelve-month period ending on the 31 March – in which case the accounting period and the financial year coincide.

The rate of Corporation Tax

The current practice of the government is to set the rate in advance. The rate for FY 1991 is 33%.

Small companies

There is a distinction between the rate of tax levied on 'small companies' and 'large companies'. A small company is defined as one where the profits of its accounting period do not exceed a given limit (hence, the company may not be 'small' in the sense of its business interests at all – ICI could benefit from 'small companies relief' if its profits in one year were sufficiently low). This limit is periodically reviewed. For 'small companies' the rate of corporation tax is mitigated and in FY 1991 stood at 25%.

Where the profits of a company exceed the lower limit, in FY 1991 £250,000, but do not exceed a higher limit, in FY 1991 £1,250,000, there is a system of tapering relief available. This means that the company will be entitled to obtain a marginal relief on the normal rate of Corporation Tax.

It is not possible for a large company to split itself into a number of smaller companies in order to avoid paying the higher rate of Corporation Tax, because the lower and upper limits are divided by the number of associated companies. For example, where there are two associated companies, the lower and upper limits in FY 1991 were £125,000 and £625,000. Similarly the limits are reduced pro rata for APs of less than twelve months to prevent another obvious means of bringing profits below the limits.

Payment of Corporation Tax

'Pay and file'

The Finance Act 1987 introduced a new system of payment of Corporation Tax. These provisions have not yet come into force, but are imminent and were announced in advance so that companies would have time to prepare themselves. The procedure is called 'pay and file' and will standardize the dates for the payment of the tax. Currently, Corporation Tax for a particular accounting period is payable nine months from the end of that period.

There are, however, companies which were established before Corporation Tax was introduced in 1965. Special provisions existed for these companies which used to enable them to delay the payment of tax for anything up to a year. These provisions have now been abolished and the new 'pay and file' regulations will apply to *all* accounting periods, although transitional rules operate to reduce the hardship on those companies which enjoyed the benefit of delaying payment in the past.

When the new system comes fully into operation, Corporation Tax will be paid by a company nine months after the end of its AP, even if its profits have not been finally assessed. The payment will be made on the basis of a provisional self-assessment of its taxable profits by the company. In order to encourage the prompt payment of Corporation Tax, interest will begin to accrue from the date the payment was due. If it later transpires that tax has been overpaid, the company will be entitled to apply, in writing, for the excess to be repaid. The amount of overpaid tax plus the interest will then be returned to the company. Where the taxable profits are underestimated, interest will accrue on the amount of the underpayment of tax.

In order to speed up the process of final assessment of tax, the legislation has been amended so that accounts must be received *not later* than one year after the end of the accounting period to which they relate. Penalties will be levied for the late submission of accounts, including the imposition of a fine of up to £1,000 or, if the accounts are over eighteen months late, a percentage of the tax due may be demanded in addition to payment of the Corporation Tax for that period.

When assessing the amount of Corporation Tax to be paid, this will be influenced by three factors: the payment of 'advance corporation tax', the amount of Income Tax deducted at source for payments made to the company and double taxation relief. The significance of the first two factors will be examined later in this chapter. Double taxation relief was discussed earlier, pp. 191–3.

The importance of where a company is resident

The question of whether a company is resident in the UK is a significant one because companies which are regarded as being resident here are liable to pay Corporation Tax on all profits wherever they arise. Until 1988 there was no statutory definition of residence, so that the Inland Revenue had to look to the courts to provide a test for residency. The test they utilized was one of 'management and control'. However, as has been discussed in detail in Chapter 7, the Finance Act 1988 now states, in effect, that any company which has been incorporated in the UK on or after 15 March 1988 is to be treated as resident here, notwithstanding that its management and control are exercised abroad.

If, however, a company is incorporated abroad, its UK residence will still depend on the management and control test. The new definition means that it is no longer possible for a company newly incorporated in the UK to cease to be resident here, but it is possible for a 'non-UK' company to cease to be UK resident by moving its central management and control overseas.

Even where a company is deemed to be non-resident it may still be liable to pay Corporation Tax. This occurs where a company not resident in the UK carries on a trade here through a branch or agency. It will then attract Corporation Tax on its 'chargeable profits' arising in the UK.

The computation of profits

When considering the computation of profits, it is important to remember that the profits which are charged under Corporation Tax are made up of two elements, income and chargeable gains.

Income

The position regarding the income of companies is that it will be charged in accordance with the principles of Income Tax. This means that all the same schedules apply, except where any section in the legislation refers specifically to 'individuals'. Therefore, in order to compute the amount of income liable to Corporation Tax, reference must be made to the Income Tax Schedules and the Cases relevant to the source of the company's income (Schedules E and F would not, for example, be relevant, as these only apply to the taxation of 'individuals'). In accordance with these principles, the exemptions which are available under Income Tax may also be utilized by companies unless the section specifies 'individuals' only.

An example in this regard is pre-trading expenditure. A company which incurs expenditure in the three years before it begins to trade, may obtain relief for that expenditure as if it had been incurred on the day the trade's first transaction took place. The expenditure must, of course, be allowable under the 'wholly and exclusively' rule or specific legislation (see Chapter 2 for details). It is applied in a slightly different way than under the rules of Income Tax, in that for the purposes of Income Tax pre-trading expenditure is used as if it were a loss sustained in the year of assessment in which the trading commenced.

Where a company receives income net of Income Tax, for example from a building society source, the gross amount will be included in the company's income, but the amount of tax deducted will be given as a credit against the company's Corporation Tax liability. If it transpires that the company is not liable to pay any, or only a minimal amount of Corporation Tax, it is at liberty to reclaim the excess Income Tax deducted. As will be discussed at a later stage, the receipt of dividends by a company is treated in a quite different way from other income.

If a company pays yearly interest on a bona fide UK bank loan, this may be deducted from its income. However, other interest payments and annuities and annual payments are not so deducted, but instead are regarded as 'charges on income' (the meaning and use of charges on income are discussed later in the chapter).

Chargeable gains

The chargeable gains of a company are computed according to the Capital Gains Tax legislation, except again in so far as the latter relates to 'individuals' only.

There used to be a distinction between the manner in which Corporation Tax was levied on income as opposed to capital gains. These rules applied until 1987 when the regulations were changed and the distinction between the treatment of income and capital was removed. Basically, any capital gains made by a company are taxed along with income, at the rate of Corporation Tax currently in force.

Deductions

Just as individuals are entitled to make deductions to reduce their tax liability, so companies are able to reduce the profits which are chargeable to Corporation Tax. They may make use of the deductions available under the Income Tax and Capital Gains Tax regulations in so far as they relate to Corporation Tax (note that dividends and other appropriations of profits are not deductible). However, there are two categories of deductions which deserve special mention: capital allowances and management expenses.

Capital allowances

Companies are entitled to claim capital allowances in much the same way as individuals (see Chapter 3). However, they are treated as a trading expense rather than as a deduction against the assessment (which is the case for Income Tax). A balancing charge is treated as trading income. The period for which allowances are granted is the AP of the company in question.

There are two major ways by which the capital allowances may be granted. The first is by deducting the allowance from the relevant income for the appropriate accounting period, e.g., trading income, Schedule A income, etc. The second method is used when there is insufficient relevant income received during the particular accounting period. Here the allowance may be carried forward indefinitely and used to the benefit of the company at a later stage. However, where a capital allowance effectively creates a trading loss, then it will be regarded as part of that loss for loss relief purposes (see below, pp. 203–5).

Management expenses

The general rule is that where a company's income arises from trading activities, the expenses of managing the company are allowable under the normal Schedule D Case I rules as detailed in Chapter 2. The situation is different when the income of the company is derived from investments. Where this is the case, the expenses of managing the investments themselves are deductible directly from the investment income, but the expenses of managing the company are not.

The legislation does not permit, however, sums disbursed as expenses of management to be deducted from the overall profits of resident investment companies. In other words, there is a separate category of company 'management expenses'. An 'investment company' is defined as being a company whose business consists wholly or mainly in the making of investments, and one whose principal income emanates from those investments. Examples of the types of companies envisaged by the statute are savings banks and some life insurance companies.

The meaning of 'management expenses' is less easy to define, as there is little help in the statutes. However, cases such as *Hoest Finance Ltd* v. *Gumbrell* (1983) have given the term a fairly wide construction. So expenses such as salaries and wages are included, but expenses which are closely connected with a particular transaction, for example a stockbroker's commission on a sale of investments, will not be covered under this heading (but will be directly deductible from the investment income).

Charges on income

It will be remembered from the discussion of Income Tax that charges on income are annual payments which usually have to be made net of Income Tax, and which are deducted from a person's total income when computing the person's tax liability. A company receives similar treatment when calculating its liability to Corporation Tax. Charges on income cannot be deducted from income in calculating the company's trading profits. They come into play after the total profits have been calculated. Another important feature to stress is that any payment which could be deducted by a company when computing profits must be treated as such, and may not be regarded as a charge on income.

Charges on income include the following:

- Yearly interest, for example loan or debenture interest but excluding interest on UK bank loans and overdrafts.
- Patent royalties.
- Annual payments, for example covenants.
- Interest charged on capital, for example where there is a substantial capital expansion scheme.
- Certain one-off donations to charities.

There are various types of annual payments, however, which may never be regarded as charges on income. The most important examples are the following:

- Interest on overdue tax, and dividends and other distributions made to shareholders by the company.
- Payments not made under a liability for valuable and sufficient consideration.

The latter example was discussed in the case of *Ball* v. *National & Grindlays Bank* (1973). Here, the employees of the company spent most of their working lives abroad. Accordingly, those with children chose to educate them in boarding schools in England. In order to prevent discontent and resignations, the company entered into covenants to pay trustees monthly sums to be applied towards the education of the employees' children. The Court of Appeal held that these payments could not be regarded as charges on income because no valuable consideration had been given in return by the recipients. The acquisition of the undoubted business advantage of having contented employees was not sufficient to fulfil this requirement.

The relief for losses

There are two types of losses sustained by companies for which relief is available: *trading losses* and *non-trading losses*. This section of the chapter will discuss the way in which the legislation allows a company to mitigate its loss by reducing the amount of Corporation Tax paid.

Trading losses

A trading loss is a loss which is derived from a company's trading activities and not from other possible sources of income.

There are three main ways in which a company can gain relief in respect of trading losses. The first method enables a company to carry forward its trading loss and set it off against future profits from the *same trade* – the trade must not change. A claim for this relief must be made within six years of the termination of the accounting period in which the loss was made. The carry-forward provisions are only available where there is no subsequent substantial change in the ownership of the company and its trade. This works against individuals who buy a company merely in order to take advantage of accumulated losses. These provisions will come into play when within three years of each other the change in ownership is accompanied by a major change in business. The meaning of this latter term was explored in the case of *Willis* v. *Peeters Picture Frames* (1983). Here the company had changed the manner in which sales and distribution of the same product were carried out. The Revenue sought to argue that this represented a major change in business. However, the Court of Appeal found that this was not the case and that such changes did not represent a major change in the nature and conduct of the trade.

The second method of relief is the 'sideways' relief which enables a trading loss to be set off against any profits (including chargeable gains) which occur in the same accounting period. In order to avail itself of this relief, the company must make a claim within two years of the termination of the accounting period when the loss occurred.

EXAMPLE

Flexible Ltd incurs a trading loss of £120,000. In the same accounting period it receives interest of £30,000 and rent of £40,000. The trading loss could be relieved against the other income of the same accounting period. The relief would be calculated as follows:

	£
Schedule A income	40,000
Schedule D, Case III income	30,000
Total profits	70,000
Less trading loss	70,000
Profits chargeable to CT	Nil

This would leave a balance of trading loss not so far relieved of £50,000.

It is also possible for a company to gain relief against profits of preceding accounting periods providing that it was engaged in the same trade during that period. Again, the claim must be made within two years of the end of the accounting period in which the loss was sustained. Up until 31 March 1991 the trading loss incurred in a twelve-month AP could be set against profits of the preceding twelve-month AP or of APs totalling twelve months. From 1 April 1991 the relief has been extended so that a trading loss can be carried back for up to three years.

The third relief enables a company which has ceased trading to carry back its terminal losses – that is, loss sustained in the last twelve months of trading – and set it against trading profit made in the preceding three years, setting the loss against profits of later years first. This, fairly obviously, is the last relief available in the life of a company, therefore all other reliefs should be claimed before this one. The limitation period for claiming the relief is six years from the cessation of trading.

204

Non-trading losses

Companies may incur losses other than trading losses. In the case of a transaction carried out within Schedule D Case VI, the only relief available is to set the loss off against profits gained from another Schedule D Case VI transaction either in the same accounting period, or in any subsequent period.

Capital losses can be taken into account only against chargeable gains which occur in the same or a later accounting period. They may not be set off against income profits. The same principle is followed for losses incurred under Schedule A, for example where a company spends more in maintaining a property than it receives in rent. The loss may be set against other Schedule A profits (using the rules detailed on pp. 140–3) or set against future Schedule A profits.

Taxing dividends and distributions

It should be remembered that the rules relating to the computation of company profits do not allow the dividends and distributions of a company to be treated as expenses or charges on income. Therefore, the Revenue has devised a separate system for assessment which involves taxation at source and which is known as the 'imputation system'. The system requires the company, on making a distribution, to make a payment to the Revenue which is equal to the basic rate of Income Tax on the gross amount of the distribution. This payment is known as 'Advance Corporation Tax' (ACT).

The ACT in 1991/2 is equal to 25/75ths of the amount of the distribution. This fraction is subject to change from time to time. The individual who is the recipient of the dividend is then liable to pay Schedule F Income Tax on the grossed-up sum. So, for example, if he were to receive £7,500 he would be liable to Schedule F tax on £10,000. The distribution has a 'tax credit' attached to it which is equal in amount to the ACT, i.e. £2,500 which satisfies his liability, if any, to basic rate Income Tax. Therefore, this is truly a system of taxation at source.

The most important feature of the system is the concept of ACT, which links the taxation of company profits to the taxation of distributions. The ACT provides a credit for the company which can be set against the company's Corporation Tax liability (leaving what is referred to as the 'mainstream' liability). Equally, ACT forms a link between the company and its shareholders because, as already mentioned, it provides a basic rate tax credit for the shareholder – the system is summarized in Figure 8.1.

The next section will examine the process in more detail and focus on the following issues: the definition of a distribution, how a company uses ACT, the meaning of 'franked payments', how companies use their tax credits and the meaning and use of 'franked investment income'.

Distributions

A distribution is very widely defined in the legislation (s.209 Income and Corporation Taxes Act 1988) to include the following:

- Dividends including 'capital dividends'.
- Any other distributions in respect of shares not being a repayment of capital.
- Bonus redeemable shares or debentures.
- Interest on certain securities which have share characteristics or interest above a normal commercial rate.

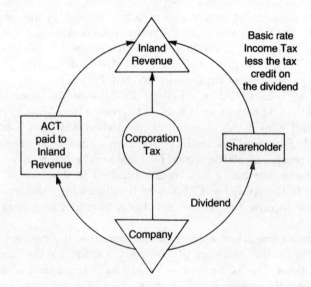

Figure 8.1 The system of tax credits

- Transfers of assets to shareholders at below market value or acceptance of assets from members at above market value.
- Bonus issues followed by a repayment of share in capital.
- A repayment of share capital followed by a bonus issue.
- Premiums paid on redemption of shares or securities.

To be subject to ACT, the payment must not only be capable of being categorized as a distribution, but must further fall within the definition of a 'qualifying distribution'. This essentially is defined to mean any distribution by the company except issues of bonus redeemable shares and bonus debentures. The discussion which follows relates only to 'qualifying distributions'.

Advance Corporation Tax (ACT)

It has been established that when a company makes a qualifying distribution it must, in addition, pay a sum which represents the basic rate of Income Tax in the hands of the shareholder. The sum of a qualifying distribution plus the ACT is called a 'franked payment'. To illustrate this point with an example, if with an ACT rate of 25/75ths a company makes a qualifying distribution worth £7,500, it will make a franked payment of £10,000 (the gross distribution, including a credit for Income Tax paid at a rate of 25%).

In respect of the timing of payment, ACT differs from 'Mainstream Corporation Tax' (MCT) in that instead of being payable nine months after the accounting period, it becomes due within fourteen days of the *end of the return period* in which the distribution was made. Companies normally make quarterly returns to the Revenue on the usual quarter days – 31 March, 30 June, 30 September and 31 December. Where the company's AP ends on a different date, a return is also made on that date. The return, made on a form CT61Z, details all the ACT payments made and dividends received with their tax credits in the quarter. A separate part of the form provides for details of payments the company made under deduction of Income Tax and payments received on which Income Tax was deducted by the payer. Any net amounts of ACT deducted by the company are paid over to the Collector when the form is submitted after crediting for tax credits received. Similarly, net Income Tax deducted is paid over after crediting the Income Tax deducted on payments received.

How companies make use of ACT

As the name implies, Advance Corporation Tax is an advance payment of Corporation Tax! This means that the amount of MCT will thus be reduced when the company makes distributions within the relevant accounting period.

In order to prevent companies making huge distributions which reduce their mainstream liability excessively, a company is only entitled to offset a maximum amount of ACT which is equal to 25% of the aggregate of the company's profits including chargeable gains for the period. Sometimes this will mean that there is a surplus of ACT which cannot be used in a particular period. There are a number of ways in which the excess may be treated: it may be carried forward and used against future MCT liabilities, it may be carried back against earlier Corporation Tax liabilities for a maximum of six years, or it may be surrendered for use by a subsidiary company. By so doing, the company (or its subsidiary) will be able to reduce its MCT liability, or obtain a repayment of some of the MCT already paid.

EXAMPLE

Barmy Ltd makes up its accounts to 31 March each year. For the accounting period to 31 March 1992 it has income of £600,000 and chargeable gains of £100,000. It pays qualifying distributions of £750,000 in the same period. Its liability to Corporation Tax will be calculated as follows:

	£
ACT liability 25/75 × £750,000	250,000
Corporation Tax 33% × £700,000	231,000
The company can only set off ACT of 25% × £700,000	175,000
MCT liability	231,000
Less ACT	175,000
	56,000
This leaves a surplus of ACT	250,000
Less set-off	175,000
	75,000

which can be carried forward, carried back, or surrendered to a subsidiary company.

When companies receive distributions

Companies are not liable to Corporation Tax on the distributions which they receive from other UK resident companies. However, because most of the distributions received will be qualifying distributions, the company which paid the distribution will have already had to pay ACT. The result of this is that the distribution will have an accompanying 'tax credit'. The question then arises as to what is to be done with the tax credit.

Companies which are liable to pay Corporation Tax are entitled to use these distributions to reduce the amount of tax they must pay in respect of their own distributions. The statute deems the company to have received income equal to the distribution plus the tax credit. This is known as 'franked investment income'.

EXAMPLE

Smart Alec Ltd made a qualifying distribution of £75,000. The amount of ACT due would be £25,000 (with the rate of ACT at 25/75ths).

If Loveless Ltd held 10% of the shares in Smart Alec Ltd, Loveless will receive 10% of the distribution, i.e. £7,500.

That sum also has a tax credit of £2,500. Therefore, the franked investment income of Loveless would be £10,000.

Franked investment income may be used by the company to 'frank its own income'. This allows a company which is paying out distributions for which it is liable to pay ACT, and at the same time receiving distributions on which it is entitled to tax credits, to only become liable to pay ACT when the amount of the ACT liability is greater than its entitlement to tax credits. This is, of course, a fair solution, since the Revenue is already in receipts of funds which represent the amount of the tax credit.

As with ACT, the situation may arise where there is a surplus of franked investment income. When this occurs the principal course open to the company is to carry the surplus forward into succeeding accounting periods indefinitely. This means that franked payments can be made without paying over ACT until the surplus is used up. An alternative exists where in the same AP as the surplus franked investment income arises, the company has unrelieved trading losses. The opportunity exists for the company to offset the loss against the franked investment income and obtain an immediate refund of the relevant tax credit.

Groups of companies

Because of the nature of the trading world today, no discussion of company taxation would be complete without an examination of the way in which the Revenue treats groups of companies. Strictly, in law each company within a group retains its own legal personality. As such, the Revenue should treat individually each company within a group. However, the tax legislation has made concessions to economic reality and recognizes associations of companies.

For the purposes of taxation, the legislation defines a subsidiary as a company controlled by another company: for example, a company will be regarded as a 51% subsidiary of another company if not less than 51% of its ordinary share capital is owned directly or indirectly by that other company.

Where a group exists special provisions apply. An example of these special provisions exists where payments of dividends are made by one company in the group to another company within the same group. Here, the payer and the recipient are entitled to elect jointly that the dividend shall be paid without the addition of ACT. This also means that there will be no tax credit attached.

An election may also be made in respect of a charge on income with the result that a payment can be made between group companies without deduction of tax. Normally, remember, such payments have to be made under deduction of Income Tax and the tax paid over to the Revenue using the CT61Z procedure.

Where a group structure consists of a holding company and a number of subsidiaries each being 75% subsidiaries there are further tax advantages open. This comes under the heading of group relief.

Group relief

A subsidiary company within a group, as described above, may surrender any trading losses, excess charges or excess management expenses in the case of investment companies to another company in the same group provided all companies are resident in the UK. The group relief thus allows one group member to claim the losses of another group member in the current AP and set them against its total profits when computing its liability to Corporation Tax (s.403 Income and Corporation Taxes Act 1988).

Although there are undoubted benefits in this respect, strict anti-avoidance legislation operates to ensure that there is no exploitation of group relief. In particular the rules do not permit the temporary formation of groups merely to make use of these tax advantages.

Consortium relief

The group reliefs apply also to a consortium. A consortium for these purposes consists of several UK companies which jointly control at least 75% of the ordinary share capital of another, and further that each member of the consortium holds at least 5%. For example, if Layout Ltd was owned 100% by Marble Ltd, Granite Ltd, Stone Ltd and Ore Ltd but is not classified as being a subsidiary of any of those four companies, any trading loss which is sustained by Layout Ltd could be surrendered to the owning companies, the amount which they receive depending on their individual holdings. Equally, where a loss is incurred, for example by Stone Ltd, this may be surrendered to Layout Ltd. However, the offset will only be allowed against the proportion of Layout's profit which is attributable to Stone Ltd.

Surrendering ACT to subsidiaries

In addition to our earlier discussion of the use of ACT, there is an option available which relates only to groups of companies. This allows a holding company to surrender all or part of its current ACT (relating to its dividends only), to a 51% subsidiary. The relief is not available in reverse (i.e. it does not allow subsidiaries to surrender ACT to holding companies or other subsidiaries in the same group) neither does it apply to a consortium.

The transfer of assets in a group of companies

There is an important and useful rule relating to the transfer of assets from one member of a group to another. It states that when assets are transferred in this way, they are deemed to be transferred at a price which does not give rise to a profit or a loss. In order to qualify, the companies must be linked by a shareholding of at least 75%. Because group loss relief does not apply to capital losses, it is extremely beneficial for companies within a group to be entitled to transfer assets without incurring tax. For example, all the sales of the group may be put through just one of the companies within the group so that the offset of profits and losses may be used to their maximum effect.

Companies which purchase their own shares

Recent legislation permits limited companies to buy their own shares subject to very stringent safeguards. A company is allowed to purchase the shares out of money which is raised by a new issue of shares raised specifically for the purpose, or out of profits which are available to pay dividends. The strict safeguards include the following matters:

- A statutory declaration must be made to the effect that the company is solvent and will remain a going concern for the following year.
- Publication of the purchase in the *London Gazette*.
- A right of dissenting creditors and shareholders to object.
- Provisions which may require past shareholders and directors to contribute to the assets if the company becomes insolvent.

Unlimited companies are allowed to buy their own shares without any restrictions being placed on them.

Generally, the regulations state that any payment made by the company to its shareholders in respect of the purchase of its own shares must be taxed as a distribution, except to the extent that the shareholder receives back the amount he or she subscribed for the shares. However, in certain circumstances it is possible for the shareholder in an unquoted trading company to fall outside this general rule, so that he or she is treated as not having received a dividend on the purchase of the company's own shares. It is required, however, that the shareholder bring the proceeds into his or her Capital Gains Tax assessment. The relief is available when either the purchase of the shares was made wholly or mainly to benefit the trade and not for the purposes of avoiding tax, or that the payments made to the shareholder were applied towards Inheritance Tax liabilities arising on death and for which he or she is liable (this will be relevant mainly in cases of hardship).

The shareholder must also show that he or she is resident and ordinarily resident in the UK and that he or she has owned the shares for at least five years. It must further be established that his or her percentage holding in the company has been reduced by at least 25% and that he or she does not retain a holding in the company exceeding 30%.

It is necessary for the company to obtain clearance from the Revenue before the transaction takes place. Because of the reduction in Income Tax rates and the fact that Capital Gains Tax is now charged at the same rates, there are possibly more tax-efficient ways of realizing the value of a shareholding than by a company purchasing its own shares, and the significance of the relief has therefore been diminished.

Close companies

This section of the chapter relates to the numerous companies which exist in Britain which are run by a small number of individuals, perhaps family members, or friends who have come together to go into business. Often, such companies are set up to make use of the advantage of limited liability, or are used as a haven for an individual to store his or her income in a company, later bringing it out of the company at lower rates of tax than it would otherwise attract. Where a company is under such close control, there is also the possibility of other tax advantages. For example, the individual may choose to store the profits of the company while taking other benefits from the company such as a car, interest-free loans, a company flat, etc.

For many years governments have sought to defeat this form of tax avoidance by means of special legislation relating to 'close companies'. There is a strict definition of what constitutes a close company. It is basically as follows:

- A company which either is under the control of five or fewer participants or which has any number of participators who are directors.

- A company where the five or fewer participators, or the participators who are directors, are entitled on the winding up of the company to the greater part of the assets.

Excluded are companies controlled by non-close companies, and quoted companies where more than 34% of the voting power is beneficially held by members of the public and there has been at least one share dealing in the preceding twelve months (unless 'principal members' of the company hold more than 85% of the voting power: a principal member is one with 5% or more of the company's voting power and being also one of the five largest shareholders).

The government's attitude to close companies has recently changed quite dramatically. The new approach is a result of the realization that the old restraints on close companies were stifling many genuine attempts at business, and penalizing many more people than those who merely wanted to avoid paying tax. Accordingly, the old 'apportionment rules' which allowed the Revenue in some circumstances to treat a close company as having distributed undistributed income, have now been abolished (for accounting periods beginning 31 March 1989).

A close company is still restricted, however, in two ways. First, in relation to benefits enjoyed by participators, and secondly, for loans made to participators. A participator is usually a shareholder in the company, but might also include loan creditors (excluding banks which make loans in the normal course of their business), and any persons who are entitled to secure for themselves the benefit of assets or income of the close company.

Benefits

In relation to benefits enjoyed by participators where the participator in question is not a director or higher-paid employee, the benefit must be treated as a qualifying distribution and taxed accordingly. This means, in effect, that it will not be allowed in computing the close company's adjusted profit for the purposes of Corporation Tax liability. When the participator is also a director or higher-paid employee the benefit will instead be taxed under Schedule E of the Income Tax code (see pp. 102–110).

Loans

With respect to loans to participators, including directors and higher-paid employees who are also participators, if the close company makes a loan, it must pay an amount equal to the current rate of ACT to the

Revenue, which will be returned on repayment of the loan. Loans by companies include overdrawn directors' loan accounts. There are two exceptions to the rigours of this rule: if the loan is made in the normal course of business, or if the loan does not exceed £15,000 and is made to a full-time working director of the company who does not hold more than 5% of the company's ordinary share capital. Note that the tax is equal to the current rate of ACT; it is not, however, ACT and therefore none of the set-off provisions relating to ACT applies. Provision exists for the Revenue to charge interest on tax paid late.

Close investment companies

A 'close investment company' is defined broadly as being a close company as follows:

- It is neither a trading company nor a member of a trading group.
- Nor is its business mainly concerned with investing in landed property for letting to unconnected persons.
- Nor is it a company which mainly invests in other companies which are carrying on these first two activities outlined above.
- Nor is it a managing company which is concerned with the above first two activities.

These companies are now charged to Corporation Tax at the full rate whatever the level of their profits, and they are not able to benefit from the small companies rate or marginal relief. A further restriction is placed on the close investment company in that the right of the members to receive payments for excess tax credits is restricted where the relevant distribution is a payment made by the company on the purchase of its own shares, or the Tax Inspector regards the distribution as unusually large.

Going public

As a complete contrast to the previous section we turn now to look briefly at the implications for companies which decide to 'go public'. The primary advantages of going public lie in a change in status of the company in terms of profile and credit rating. Also, new shares can be issued to the public to increase investment and, finally, existing shareholders may be able to realize some of their investment if they desire it.

On the other hand, the status of public company also involves accountability to the public in the form of published accounts, vulnerability to take-over bids and the possible increase in the market value of shares now that they are marketable will increase the likelihood of shareholders becoming liable to Capital Gains Tax and Inheritance Tax. Where share exchanges and other transactions in securities are involved, clearance should be obtained from the Revenue to ensure that no unforeseen tax liabilities arise. In general, expert tax planning is required before the decision to 'go public' is taken.

Deciding whether to incorporate

There are a number of factors as follows to be considered when a business is deciding whether or not to incorporate:

- *The tax rate on profits.* There is a relatively favourable rate of tax for companies as opposed to individuals, in particular if the company is regarded as a small company.

- *The tax rate on gains.* These attract the same tax rates as income. However, there is a disadvantage in some ways in being a company in this respect. For example, if a company sells a chargeable asset, the company pays Corporation Tax on the gain, and if the proceeds are paid out to shareholders as dividends they are subject to ACT and Income Tax, and if paid out as extra remuneration to directors they are subject to Income Tax and NIC. If not paid out, when the shares are eventually sold the value of the gain will be reflected in the sale price and more Capital Gains Tax will be payable.

- *Date of the payment of tax.* Companies are required to pay ACT fourteen days after the end of the return period in which the dividends are paid, and Corporation Tax nine months after the end of the accounting period. Individual traders usually have significantly more time in which to satisfy their tax liability.

- *The payment of stamp duty*. This used to be a factor, but Stamp Duty is now being abolished on the sale of shares, and is not incurred on most business assets (except land). It accords with the position under a partnership whereby no Stamp Duty is payable on partnership assets.

- *Reliefs*. These are equally available for both companies and unincorporated businesses with regard to retirement or death, but it is undoubtedly easier to transfer a business in the form of shares, so that shareholders in a company may be in a more favourable position to mitigate the potential problem of Inheritance Tax. However, company directors must satisfy more conditions than sole traders and partners to qualify for the relief.

- *Transfer costs*. This is a consideration as it may be costly in terms of tax (see below) and other expenses to change a business into a company, or, more particularly, a company back into a business.

- *Expenses*. The rules on deducting expenses are much more stringent for directors than for the self-employed.

- *Losses*. Business trading losses can be set off against other income of the trader, perhaps leading to a useful tax repayment. This is not possible for company losses.

- *NIC*. A trader pays the lower Class II NIC contributions whereas directors pay Class I contributions. But consequently entitlement to unemployment benefit and the state earnings-related pension is lost.

- *Raising finance*. A company can often raise finance more easily than an unincorporated business because it can offer a floating charge over its assets as security. A company also has the advantage of limited liability should the business fail, whereas sole traders and partners (unless limited partners) are liable for the business debts to the extent of their private assets. This advantage is eroded when banks and landlords require personal guarantees from the company's directors.

- *Accounts*. There are statutory obligations imposed on companies regarding the submission of audited accounts which do not apply to sole traders and partners.

217

- *Drawings*. There is no tax on business drawings. PAYE must be operated on directors' remuneration.

- *Pensions*. There is no limit to total contributions made by a company to a company pension scheme as long as the scheme provides for no more than the maximum approved benefits. Therefore, pension contributions, which are a deductible business expense, can be used to eliminate taxable profits. This can work to the benefit, in particular, of someone setting up in business who has to date no pension scheme. He or she can provide for a more generous pension than could be obtained under a self-employed personal pension (see pp. 271–3), while at the same time reducing his or her company's taxable profits. Moreover, the directors can be trustees of a self-administered pension scheme. Therefore, subject to the constraints on behaviour laid down by trust law, they can loan money to the company and buy and own the company's premises.

Transferring a business to a company

When the business ceases trading the normal Income Tax cessation provisions apply, so it is important to time the switch carefully. Capital assets are treated as transferred at their market value, and a balancing charge may arise under the capital allowances rules. However, where at least 75% of the trade continues to be under common ownership an election can be made to avoid a balancing charge. The assets are transferred at their written down values and the company claims capital allowances in its first accounting period based on those written down values. Also, the trade may be treated as not having ceased which means that the Income Tax cessation provisions are not invoked (see pp. 49–51).

A Capital Gains Tax liability may arise because chargeable assets are deemed to have been disposed of at open market value. Given the rules regarding the interaction of Capital Gains Tax and capital allowances, this provision will tend in the main to catch gains from goodwill and on land and buildings. But as long as the entire business (excluding cash balances) is transferred to the company in exchange for shares in the company, the chargeable gains can be rolled over, thus lowering the base cost of the shares in a subsequent disposal. The CGT is therefore postponed and may be avoided when the shares are sold; for example, if the shareholder can claim 'retirement relief' or disposal occurs at death (not a chargeable event). There is also provision affecting transfers of only some of the business assets to the company. The assets transferred are not treated as a supply for VAT purposes providing they are used in the same kind of business and the company is registered for VAT. Where only part of the business is transferred, that part must be capable of operating separately. The company may take over the existing VAT registration number. Where a VAT charge arises on a transfer, the company will claim the VAT as input tax. It is important to remember that unused trading losses cannot be carried forward to the company. However, subject to certain conditions, they can be set off against any income the transferor obtains from the company by way of dividends, salary, etc.

Reversing a business out of a company

Briefly, this can lead to the following unfortunate tax consequences:

- The company's unused losses are lost because the trade ceases.
- A Capital Gains Tax charge may arise on the value of the company's shares.

There are also legal hoops to jump through and the costs of liquidating the company may be appreciable.

Reconstructions and amalgamations

Reconstruction refers to the splitting of a company into two or more separate concerns. Amalgamation is the reverse process. If either event occurs for bona fide commercial purposes it does not lead to a Capital Gains Tax charge.

Where a company is reconstructed and this involves the transfer of the trade to a new company, trading losses cannot be carried forward unless 75% of the ordinary share capital of both companies belongs to the same shareholders at some time beginning one year before the reconstruction and two years after it.

219

Company take-overs and demergers

The entitlement to carry forward loss relief and surplus ACT is not affected provided within a period of three years there is not a change in ownership of the company (more than 50% of ordinary share capital transferred) and a change in the nature and conduct of the trade. The carry forward of a trading loss and ACT may also be lost if the change in ownership occurs after the company's trade was reduced to a small or negligible level.

Where a company is taken over, the parent company may wish to transfer some of the trade or some assets to itself or another subsidiary. Provided that there is at least 75% common ownership before and after the transfer, the trade is treated as continuing. Also, the transfer will be deemed to have taken place on a no gain/no loss basis for CGT purposes.

Stamp Duty (1991/2 at 1%) applies where assets are purchased using a written contract. Where the consideration for land is less than £30,000 no duty is payable. Shares and debentures issued in exchange for the shares in a victim company are subject to Stamp Duty at the time of writing at 0.5%. However, it is intended to abolish Stamp Duty on stocks and shares in the near future.

Where shareholders of the victim company are offered shares or debentures in the acquiring company in return for their shares, subject to certain conditions, no immediate Capital Gains Tax charge arises. Where there is part payment in cash, this will be chargeable.

Demergers can lead to complex tax problems. However, subject to certain conditions, where a company is split and the shareholders receive shares in another company, this will not be treated as a qualifying distribution.

Concluding comment

This chapter has detailed how the worldwide income and gains of UK companies are taxed. In the next chapter we turn to the taxation of goods and services in the UK and especially the VAT system.

9

Taxing sales

Value Added Tax is charged on the supply of goods or services in the UK, and on the importation of goods into the UK. The distinction between revenue and capital expenditure, which as we have seen in earlier chapters is important in other areas of tax, does not apply to VAT. The system for taxing sales is essentially different from the other main forms of taxation in that it is the only one which is based on the concept of indirect taxation. Its introduction in this country came as a response to the requirements that were imposed upon the UK in anticipation of joining the EC in 1973.

The legal basis for the imposition of VAT is found in the Value Added Tax Act 1983 as amended by subsequent Finance Acts and statutory instruments. It is important to remember that VAT law in the UK is subject to EC law and is, therefore, very much influenced by decisions taken in the European Court as well as the British courts and VAT tribunals. The idea of indirect taxation is well known in the EC. It works in a way that places the ultimate burden of paying the tax on the consumer, while it is the supplier who adds the tax to the goods or services initially and who is then able to reclaim the added tax. It is businesses, therefore, which are the principal administrators of this tax. The standard rate of VAT stood at 15% until 1 April 1991, when it was raised to 17.5%. Goods and services suffer VAT either at the standard rate, or zero rate, or are exempt from VAT.

The VAT system is administered by Customs and Excise officers and it is to them that a registered business must submit their return. This chapter will examine the operation of the VAT system. In particular it will deal with the people who are required to be registered, and how registration works; what is meant by the supply of goods and services and under which headings those goods and services are classified; exemptions and importations; as well as the special treatment of groups of companies, partnerships and agents.

Certain goods and services sold in the UK are also subject to other taxes which we mention briefly here in passing. The main types are Customs and Excise Duties, and duties on gaming and car tax. Beers, cider, wines and spirits, and tobacco are subject to Excise Duty. The rates are complicated and subject to change at each Budget. Duties on alcohol are broadly linked to original gravity or alcohol level; while tobacco duties vary for cigarettes, cigars and other types of tobacco products. Hydrocarbon oils are also subject to duties and these vary according to the type of oil or petrol. The gaming licence duty comprises a small fixed charge on application for a licence and a rate of duty depending on the gross gaming yield. Certain imports into the UK are also subject to Customs Duties in accordance with EC import regulations. Finally, the Car Tax is levied at a rate of 10% on the wholesale value of cars.

Liability to pay VAT

A person is liable to pay VAT when a registered taxpayer fulfils the following criteria:

- He or she makes a supply of goods or services which is taxable – known as a 'taxable supply'.
- The supply is made during the course of business, or in the furtherance of business.
- The supply is made within the UK or in the Isle of Man.

If these conditions are fulfilled, the registered person will charge VAT to his or her customer and this form of VAT is known as 'output tax'. Where the recipient of the taxable supply is also registered for VAT, and the goods or services he or she receives are for the purposes of furtherance of his or her business, the VAT for which he or she is liable is known as 'input tax'. These two concepts are the central feature of the system. Registered traders are permitted to deduct the input tax which they suffer on goods or services supplied to them from the output tax which they charge to their customers. This means that at each step along the road of producing goods or supplying services, the net tax paid is the value added at that particular stage of production.

EXAMPLE

Whizzo Ltd manufacture de luxe washing machines which are subject to the standard rate of VAT. These are sold to Young Ltd, a wholesaler, and they then sell them to Zap Ltd, a retail outlet. Zap Ltd then sells a washing machine to Fred who is the ultimate purchaser. The costs of these transactions are as follows:

Whizzo Ltd sell to Young Ltd for £300 per machine
Young Ltd sell to Zap Ltd for £480 per machine
Zap Ltd sell to Fred for £900

Fred will ultimately pay 17.5% VAT on his purchase of £900, i.e. £157.50. This is collected by Zap Ltd who pay the £157.50 to the Customs and Excise. However, before doing so, Zap Ltd may deduct all the VAT which they have suffered on their purchases. This includes the VAT which has been charged by Young Ltd on the supply of the washing machine (£480 at 17.5% = £84), as well as any incidental VAT costs suffered as a result of the supply (the provision of stationery for example). The end result of the accounting process is that Whizzo Ltd, Young Ltd and Zap Ltd will be able to deduct the VAT paid on their inputs from the VAT collected on their outputs.

The administration of VAT

The collection of VAT is administered by the government department of Customs and Excise and its authority is exercised through a network of local and regional officers, who deal with the registered persons whose businesses operate within their area. It is their responsibility to deal with matters such as registration, tax assessment, bad debt claims and the value of supplies. The record-keeping procedures of taxable persons are monitored by a system of 'control visits', whereby VAT officers visit premises to ensure that accurate records are being kept. If there is a disagreement between the department and the person being taxed it is possible to appeal to a VAT tribunal and from there, on questions of law only, to the High Court.

Various enforcement powers and penalties are available under the legislation to deal with parties who fail to comply with the regulations.

Who is a taxable person?

VAT is only levied on 'taxable persons'. The meaning of this term is clearly defined in the legislation (s.2 Value Added Tax Act 1983) and includes any person who makes or intends to make *taxable supplies*. It is further stipulated that such persons are required to be registered for VAT and indeed must be so registered before being entitled to charge VAT on outputs or reclaim VAT on inputs. A 'taxable person' includes individuals, partnerships, and any company, club, society or trust.

The term 'business' has been given a very wide meaning by the courts. In the case of *Commissioners* v. *Morrison's Academy Boarding House Association* 1978 it was held that the vital element of a business was not the existence of a commercial purpose, or indeed the intention to make profit. It was, instead, to demonstrate a course of activities carried out over an appreciable period with such frequency as to amount to a recognizable and identifiable activity of the potentially taxable person, and also that the activities predominantly concerned the making of taxable supplies to others for consideration. The principal exception to activities which may have a large proportion of these characteristics but are nevertheless deemed not to be a business, occurs where such activities are in essence carried out as a hobby, and the taxable supplies are merely incidental to that recreational activity. Charities also benefit from certain VAT reliefs.

The VAT fraction

With a standard rate of VAT of 17.5%, the amount of VAT payable on gross takings is found by applying the 'VAT fraction', 7/47ths. For example, with gross takings of £9,876.54 the amount of VAT is £1,470.97.

Registration

It is important to remember that it is the 'person', and not the business, who is registered for VAT. This means that all the taxable business enterprises of the individual are covered by his or her registration. Whether a person needs to register depends on the amount of taxable turnover he or she has over a period of one year. The limit is changed annually, reflecting, in broad terms, the effect of inflation, and in 1991/2 applies to sales exceeding £35,000.

In essence, it is obligatory for a person to register when the following applies:

- At the end of any month, the value of his or her taxable supplies in the period of one year ending at that time has exceeded the stated limit, unless the Commissioners are satisfied that for that period of one year beginning at that time, the value of his or her taxable supplies will not exceed the stated limit.

- There are reasonable grounds for believing that in a period of thirty days commencing at any time the value of his or her taxable supplies will exceed the stated limit.

It is thus necessary for the potentially taxable person to make a regular judgement on the amount of his or her taxable supplies. If the taxable turnover exceeds the registration limit, the Customs and Excise must be notified, on Form VAT1, within thirty days after the end of the relevant month or within thirty days after the date on which grounds for registration first existed. There are penalties for failing to register and for late registrations. A trader may apply for cancellation of registration if the turnover for the forthcoming year is unlikely to exceed a given limit, £33,600 in 1991/2.

Voluntary registration

A person is allowed to register for VAT even though his or her turnover does not meet the published limit. The particular advantage of this rule is that unless a person is registered for VAT, he or she will not be allowed to recover the input tax paid to his or her suppliers. Voluntary registration may be a wise choice where the business is primarily concerned with sales to businesses who are registered for VAT. In this situation, the registered businesses will wish to reclaim VAT on their purchases, and this requires registration by the supplier, who in turn will be able to reclaim VAT on his inputs. Voluntary registration is also advantageous to the small business which may wish to engender confidence in its customers by the suggestion that the business's turnover is larger than it is! In order to be accepted, the trader must prove to the Customs and Excise that he or she is carrying on a business and that he or she does make taxable supplies in the course of, or in furtherance of, his or her business.

Groups of companies

If a business is operating within a group of companies, it is possible for the group to elect for a single registration. This has the effect of vesting the VAT concerns in one of the group companies, which is known as the 'representative member'. The benefit of this is that intragroup supplies are not liable to VAT and this reduces the administration costs. However, all the members of the group continue to be jointly and severally liable for tax submitted on the VAT Return of the representative member. The criteria for enabling companies to avail themselves of this facility are laid down by statute. Two or more UK-resident companies are eligible to be treated as a group if either one company controls each of the others, or one 'person' (i.e. company, partnership, or individual) controls all of them.

Divisional registration

Where a company is divided up into a number of self-accounting bodies, the company may apply for divisional registration. The divisions then administer the tax separately, but they do not become separate taxable persons. The prime advantage is that of administrative cost-saving and the company must come within the conditions laid down in the legislation in order to avail itself of this benefit.

Partnerships

The assessment to VAT is always made in the name of the firm, which means that for VAT purposes changes in the partners are ignored. The firm is therefore treated as a separate entity apart from its members. As a result of this, if the same partners are carrying on two or more businesses they will only be entitled to one registration (*Commissioners v. Glassborrow* 1975). All the partners are jointly and severally liable for the VAT payable by the partnership incurred before the date on which a person informs the Commissioners that he has ceased to be a partner.

Agents

Where goods or services are supplied through an agent, the law (ss.32–4 Value Added Tax Act 1983) regards the supply as having been made by the principal to the third party. This is the usual approach of the Customs and Excise who would hold the principal liable for the VAT on the transaction. However, they have power where the true principal is not disclosed, or where the principal has insufficient funds to pay the tax due, to regard the supply as having been made to the agent by the principal, and by the agent to the third party.

Deregistration

Persons may voluntarily deregister if they can satisfy the Customs and Excise that their turnover of taxable supplies in the following year will not exceed the prescribed limit.

Disaggregation

It would seem an obvious move for a large business to divide itself up into smaller sections in order to avoid the necessity of registration for VAT. However, if the Customs and Excise are satisfied that the prime motive for the division of the business is the avoidance of registration, they will order that the businesses be deemed to be one venture and they will be assessed to VAT accordingly.

Accounting procedures

VAT records

Once a person has registered for VAT he or she is required to maintain comprehensive records of the transactions relating to taxable goods and services as well as all the exempt supplies made. Such records must be retained by the registered person for six years. Customs and Excise considers the following items to be the necessary business records:

- Purchase invoices and sales invoices.
- Records of daily cash intake.
- Bank statements and bank correspondence.

- Annual accounts.
- Cash and account books.
- Purchase and sales books.
- Records of orders.
- Credit and discount notes.

The tax return and the tax invoice

After registration, there exists a strict method of accounting procedure which requires all registered persons to submit VAT Returns on a quarterly basis. There are also regulations concerning bookkeeping arrangements centred around the use of *tax invoices* and the following essential matters must be included in the VAT invoice (the full form, and the shorter form of the invoice discussed later, are shown in Figure 9.1):

- Taxpayer's name and address (a).
- Taxpayer's VAT registration number (b).
- Taxpoint (c).
- Description of goods or services (including quantity) (d).
- Price of goods or services (e).
- Any discount allowed (f).
- VAT rate (g).
- Total charge *excluding* VAT (h).
- Total VAT payable (i).
- Total charge *including* VAT (j).
- Customer's name and address (k).
- Invoice number (l).

If a 'credit note' is issued to a customer who is able to reclaim input tax on the original supply, the party is not obliged to amend the original VAT charge provided that both parties agree. If they are not able to come to any such agreement, a credit note adjusting the VAT must be issued. The VAT Return (Form VAT100) shows the total of the taxable supplies made in the period together with the related VAT (see Figure 9.2). It also gives the total purchases, expenses and the amount of VAT borne on them. A VAT Return must be submitted within thirty

Full form of VAT invoice

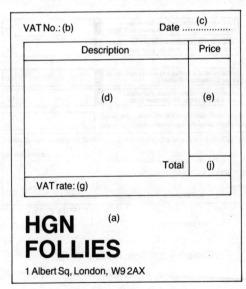

Customer details: (k)

HGN (a)   Date .... (c)

FOLLIES

1 Albert Sq London W9 2AX   VAT No.: (b)

Description	Quantity	Discount	VAT rate	Price	VAT
(d)	(d)	(f)	(g)	(e)	

Invoice No.: (l)

Delivery details:

Supplied subject to usual terms and conditions

	Totals	(h)	(i)
	Add VAT	(i)	
	Total due	(j)	

Payment due 14 days from date of invoice

Shorter form of VAT invoice (supplies under £100)

VAT No.: (b)   Date .... (c)

Description	Price
(d)	(e)
Total	(j)

VAT rate: (g)

HGN (a)

FOLLIES

1 Albert Sq, London, W9 2AX

Figure 9.1   VAT invoices

229

Value Added Tax Return

For the period

to

HM Customs and Excise

Registration number | Period

You could be liable to a financial penalty if your completed return and all the VAT payable are not received by the due date.

Due date:

For official use DOR only

Fold here

Before you fill in this form please read the notes on the back and the VAT Leaflet *"Filling in your VAT return"*. Complete all boxes clearly in ink, writing 'none' where necessary. Don't put a dash or leave any box blank. If there are no pence write "00" in the pence column. Do not enter more than one amount in any box.

£ p

For official use		
VAT due in this period on **sales** and other outputs	1	
VAT reclaimed in this period on **purchases** and other inputs	2	
Net VAT to be paid to Customs or reclaimed by you **(Difference between boxes 1 and 2)**	3	
Total value of **sales** and all other outputs excluding any VAT. **Include your box 6 figure**	4	00
Total value of **purchases** and all other inputs excluding any VAT. **Include your box 7 figure**	5	00
Total value of all **sales** and related services to other **EC Member States**	6	00
Total value of all **purchases** and related services from other **EC Member States**	7	00

Retail schemes. If you have used any of the schemes in the period covered by this return please enter the appropriate letter(s) in this box.

If you are enclosing a payment please tick this box.

DECLARATION by the signatory to be completed by or on behalf of the person named above. I, ...declare that the (Full name of signatory in BLOCK LETTERS) information given above is true and complete.

Signature ....Date ....19..........

A false declaration can result in prosecution.

VAT 100 CD 2850/N9(02/91) F 3790 (JANUARY 1992)

Figure 9.2 Specimen VAT100

230

days of the end of each return period accompanied by a cheque for the net VAT due. If the accounts reveal that the tax charged on outputs is greater than the tax paid on inputs, the balance must be paid to the Customs and Excise. If, however, the total of the output tax is less than the total of the input tax, there will be a reimbursement from the Department.

EXAMPLE

	1. Output tax exceeds input tax		2. Input tax exceeds output tax	
Total taxable turnover	£200,000		£200,000	
Total output tax @ 17.5%		£35,000		£35,000
Total taxable inputs	£160,000		£260,000	
Total input tax @ 17.5%		£28,000		£45,500
Balance payable to C & E		£7,000		
Balance repayable by C & E				£10,500

Cash accounting scheme

Where the annual value of taxable supplies, excluding VAT, does not exceed a given limit (for 1991/2 it is £300,000) a taxable person may elect for the *cash accounting scheme*. The VAT will then be charged on the amount of cash actually received and paid out, rather than on the tax invoices issued and received. Entry to the scheme is by application to the Customs and Excise, and the taxable person is obliged to remain within the scheme for a minimum of two years. The advantage of using this form of assessment is twofold: first, there is an automatic relief available for bad debts and secondly, the VAT will not have to be paid until the business has actually received the cash from the customer.

Annual accounting scheme

If a business has an annual turnover which does not exceed a prescribed limit (1991/2 it is £300,000) and it has been registered for at least one year, it may apply to submit one annual VAT Return within two months of the end of the year instead of the normal quarterly returns. Payments are initially made on account, on the basis of the previous year's liability to VAT, in ten monthly instalments commencing in the fourth month of the year. The tenth instalment is a balancing figure to make up the actual amount due based on the annual return. The advantage of this scheme is the saving made in terms of administration costs.

The taxable supply of goods and services

As was stated in the introduction to this chapter, a registered person is liable to pay VAT on any supply of goods or services made within the UK which are deemed to be taxable. This section will explore the application of this principle looking at the types of supplies envisaged by the legislation, exempt supplies, the rates of tax, the place of supply of goods and services, the time of supply, and finally the treatment of imports.

The supply of goods and services

In order to make a supply of goods, it is necessary for the ownership of the goods to pass from the supplier to the recipient. The Act covers 'all forms of supply, but not any thing done otherwise than for a consideration'. This legalistic phrase means that the goods must be paid for, either in money or in kind. As will be imagined, the scope of the supply of goods is extremely wide and includes everyday commercial transactions, sales by hire – purchase or credit, auction sales, the transfer of goods out of the business for the personal use of the registered person, or the production of goods by application of a treatment or process to another person's goods. So, for example, on the latter point, if a woman buys some cloth from a shop and then takes it to a dressmaker to have it made into an evening gown, then the dressmaker is said to have made a supply of goods. The principle is that, wherever a person is supplying a good in the furtherance of his or

232

her business or in the course of his or her business, provided it is not an exempt supply and the supply takes place within the UK, he or she will be liable to VAT.

The supply of services

The supply of services is 'anything which is not a supply of goods, but is done for a consideration'. Again, as with the supply of goods, the legislation (s.3 Value Added Tax Act 1983) mandates that the services supplied must be paid for either in money or money's worth. The scope is equally wide, and in addition to the normal interpretation of the term, includes the hiring of goods to another party, the lending of goods to another to be used outside the course of the taxable person's business, and the granting, assignment, or surrender of any right for money or money's worth.

An example of the latter situation arose in the case of *Neville Russell* 1987. Here, a lessee accepted a reverse premium, which was a sum of money paid by the landlord to induce him, as a potential tenant, to enter into a lease. This transaction was held liable to VAT because it was a supply of services given for a consideration. Services which are tangential to the supply of goods, for example the delivery of products, and their postage and packing costs are normally regarded as services, particularly when separately itemized on the invoice.

Certain rules concerning the supply of goods and services which derive directly from the European legislation, provide for specific cases where the transaction must be treated as either a service or a supply of goods. Some of these provisions are inconsistent with the manner in which the English law generally deals with such cases, but nevertheless they are the ones which must be followed when dealing with VAT. The significant provisions are as follows:

- The granting or assignment of a major interest (e.g. a tenancy agreement in excess of twenty-one years) is regarded as a supply of goods, whereas the supply of a shorter tenancy would be a supply of services.
- Supplying any type of power is deemed to be a supply of goods.
- Where a person applies a treatment or process to another's goods, the former will be regarded as having made a supply of goods.
- As was mentioned earlier, the transfer of the 'whole' ownership of goods is a supply of goods, but when only part of the ownership of

the goods is transferred, or only the possession of the goods is transferred, the transaction is deemed to be a supply of services.

Exempt supplies

The main categories of goods and services which are exempt from liability to VAT are listed in the legislation. There are eleven groups of exemptions which include the sale and leasing of used domestic and non-domestic buildings; insurance sales; educational services provided by schools, colleges and universities; services rendered by registered doctors, dentists, etc., in relation to health; sports competitions; and the provision of general banking services. Such supplies are outside the scope of the VAT system which means that input tax cannot be reclaimed (in a large number of situations the input tax which is related to exempt supplies will, however, be an allowable business expense for Income Tax and Corporation Tax purposes – where input tax can be claimed, it is the VAT exclusive cost which is deductible). These exempt supplies can be summarized as follows:

- Works of art.
- Welfare services.
- Trade union supplies to the membership.
- Some tenancy agreements (but not holiday lettings).
- Sports competitions.
- Postal services.
- Some land and building sales.
- Insurance.
- Health services.
- Funerals.
- Education and training by schools or universities.
- Credit.
- Betting.
- Bank and building society accounts.

It is worth noting that in relation to business entertainment expenses, input tax will only be allowable where it is incurred for staff entertainment for the purposes of the business.

Land and buildings

It should be noted that not all land transactions are exempt. For example, the freehold sales of new (that is less than three years old) buildings are taxable (except for those designated as dwelling houses or those certified for charitable use). The surrender of leases or other interests in land are also taxable events.

Where the business is concerned with the sale or letting of land and buildings not used for domestic purposes, it is possible to elect to charge VAT on supplies which would ordinarily be exempt, thus allowing the recovery of VAT on the costs of the business. The election is made in respect of individual properties or pieces of land, but once the election has been made it will apply to all the future sales or lettings of that property.

The VAT rates

There are two rates of VAT at present – known as the *standard rate* and the *zero rate*. As the name implies, no tax is payable on zero-rated transactions. However, such transactions still amount to 'taxable supplies' and this enables the taxpayer to reclaim input tax in exactly the same way as he would for standard rate supplies.

In order to ascertain which supplies are zero rated it is again, as with exempt transfers, a matter of looking at the legislation (Schedule 5 Value Added Tax Act 1983) which provides a complete list. The major items which appear on this list are summarized as follows:

- Water and sewerage services.
- Caravans and houseboats used for permanent residence.
- Supply, repair or maintenance of some ships.
- Some shipping services.
- Protective items of clothing sold to employees.
- Passenger transport.
- New houses and other residential buildings.
- Medicines.
- Gas for domestic purposes.
- Fuel oils (not petrol).

- Freight transport abroad.
- Food sold for human consumption (but note exceptions, e.g. confectionery and savoury snacks which are standard rated).
- Electricity.
- Drinks (but not alcohol, fruit juice, carbonated drinks).
- Construction and demolition work on houses (but excluding repairs or alterations).
- Coal.
- Children's clothing.
- Charity supplies.
- Books, newspapers, magazines.
- Some aircraft and air services.

There is a significant difference in the position of businesses making zero-rated taxable supplies and those making exempt and, therefore, non-taxable supplies. In neither of these situations is the business liable to charge VAT on its outputs. However, whereas the zero-rated supplier is entitled to claim back any related input tax, the exempt supplier is not able to reclaim related inputs because he is not entitled to register for VAT. If we look in greater depth at the possible results of this difference, it can be established that the exempt supplier would have to add onto the price of his goods an amount equal to the unclaimed input tax in order to achieve the same level of profit as the registered business.

Businesses with levels of supplies which fall below the prescribed minimum for registration may also fall within this trap. Here there is a possible solution: the small business or company may make an application for 'voluntary registration'. The decision as to whether or not to register relies on a careful scrutiny of the possible amount of input tax which may be claimed, balanced against the cost of administering VAT. In many cases, the small business will be able to pass on the benefit of reclaimed tax to the customer, thus making the business more competitive.

Partial exemption

Where a business has a mixture of outputs, in the sense that some of them are taxable at the standard or zero rate while the others are exempt, this is known as a *partially exempt business*. It follows that in this situation input tax will relate to both taxable and exempt supplies. Therefore, the input tax has to be apportioned in a way which is 'practical, accurate and fair', so that only the amount which is applicable to the taxable output is deducted.

In order to achieve this result, two methods may be used. The first is the 'standard method', which necessitates the identification of all supplies and imports received and then working out the extent to which they relate to taxable supplies. All the input tax will be reclaimable on supplies and imports which are wholly used in making taxable supplies whereas no input tax will be reclaimable on supplies and imports wholly used in making exempt supplies or in any other activity.

The second is the use of the 'special method' to apportion input tax, which has to be approved by Customs and Excise. This uses a formula which analyses the ratio of taxable output supplies to total supplies. It provides that the unattributed input tax is attributed to taxable supplies in the same proportion as the value of taxable supplies to total supplies:

$$\frac{\text{value of taxable outputs} \times 100}{\text{value of total outputs}} = \% \text{ input tax deductible}$$

The following supplies must be disregarded for the purposes of this calculation:

- Supplies of capital goods used in the business.
- Exempt or zero-rated supplies of land incidental to business activities.
- Exempt or zero-rated financial supplies incidental to the business (for example, the issue of shares to raise investment).
- The value of goods which are sold under a second-hand goods scheme.

The Customs and Excise operate a *de minimis* rule which dictates that the whole of the input tax will be recoverable where the exempt input tax falls into one of the following categories (at the time of writing):

- It is less than £100 per month on average.
- It is less than £250 per month on average and 50% of all the input tax.

- It is less than £500 per month on average and 25% of all the input tax.

The place of the supply of goods and services

The regulations state that only goods supplied in the UK are chargeable to VAT. To discover the place of the supply of goods, the location of the goods at the time they are allocated to the customer must be established. If the goods are in the UK at this stage, then they are liable to VAT even though they may be subsequently exported. Where the goods are found to be located abroad and are to remain overseas, transactions relating to those goods will not give rise to a liability to VAT. When the contract relates to the installation or assembly of goods, the deciding factor in terms of applicability of VAT is where the assembly or installation takes place.

In respect of the supply of services, the liability arises with regard to where the business 'belongs'. The primary test is to establish whether there is a business establishment in existence in the UK. If there is no such establishment, the next stage is to find out the place of residence. Where there is more than one establishment, the Customs and Excise will examine the location of the establishment which appears to be most closely related to the supply of the services in question. If this is found to be the UK, then a liability to tax will arise.

The time of supply

The time when the supply of goods or services takes place is known as the *tax point*. The VAT must be accounted for at the end of the VAT period in which the tax point falls. In relation to services, the basic tax point is the date on which the service is rendered. Where goods are the subject matter of the transaction, the basic tax point is the date on which the goods are sent to the client, the date on which he or she removes them, or the date on which they are made available to him or her. There are some important exceptions to this rule which are widely used by businesses.

The first exception relates to invoices which are issued within fourteen days of the time when the goods were taken away or made available to the client. Here, the date of the invoice becomes the 'actual tax point' and this allows the VAT Return to be completed using copy invoices. The second relates to payments in advance. Where this occurs, it is the date of either the invoice or the payment which will determine the 'actual tax point' of the supply.

Motoring expenses

VAT which is incurred as a result of purchasing a new car may not be recovered unless it is sold as unused, for example by a car dealer. However, if accessories are fitted at a later date and these are for the purpose of the business, a credit for input tax is given in the usual way. Equally, where a car is used for the business, input tax on any maintenance and repair to the vehicle can be credited without the need to apportion any private use of the car.

The VAT cost of fuel for vehicles used for business purposes is also treated as input tax. But where fuel is supplied for private use at an amount less than the cost of the fuel to the business, then, even though input tax on the fuel is allowed, the business is obliged to account for output tax using a mandatory scale charge. The charge depends on the power of the vehicle and the number of miles covered in a monthly or quarterly period. It is therefore essential to keep mileage records. The scale charge will not be applied if a business chooses not to reclaim input tax on fuel.

Where 'self-supply' arises in relation to car manufacturers and dealers, special considerations mitigate the general rule that VAT is not recoverable when the purchaser is the final consumer. The law states that the car dealer will be permitted to recover VAT on the cars which he or she sells during the course of trade, but he or she will be required to account for VAT on cars used in the business, for example as demonstration models, because in these circumstances the dealer will also be the final consumer.

Bad debt relief

The general rule is that no relief is given for bad debts. But this rule will be departed from provided the following points can be established:

• The debtor has become formally insolvent.

- The ownership of the goods has passed to the purchaser.
- The claim which has been made to the liquidator is for the amount of the debt excluding VAT.

In the Budget of 1991 it was announced that the relief 'waiting time' – that is, the age of the debt before bad debt relief can be given – is to be reduced from two years to one year.

The importation and exportation of goods and services

Exports of goods from the UK are currently zero-rated but discussions are taking place which may result in this being changed in relation to trade within the EC. It is important for the registered exporter to retain some evidence of export for his records. Where goods are supplied to visitors from overseas, these are also treated as zero-rated as long as they are removed from the UK, and the visitor has been in the UK for a period of less than one year in a two-year period. VAT is charged on the importation of most goods into the UK 'as if it were a duty of customs'. It is paid whether or not the person importing the goods is registered for VAT and in addition to any customs charge which may arise. Because VAT is regarded in the same light as a customs charge, it is paid at the time of entry into the country, rather than as a part of any accounting period. Relief is available where goods are brought into the UK on a temporary basis for the purposes of repair or processing.

Prior to 1984, where a person importing goods into the country was VAT-registered, there were special provisions which enabled postponement of VAT payments at the time of import. The VAT was included in the next quarterly return. This same principle also applied where a registered person removed goods from a bonded warehouse. However, the regulations have now changed with the result that an importer must pay the VAT one month after importation or the removal of goods from bonded warehouses. This means that the importer has to bear the cost of the VAT for a period before it is reclaimed.

To summarize the position on the taxing of imported goods, although VAT is not charged to the overseas supplier of goods, a charge is in fact levied in an alternative form, that is, as a customs duty.

The general rule concerning the supply of services is that there is no importation charge. However, services like banking and business consultancy from an overseas source may be treated as if the taxable person has made the supply him- or herself. In this situation, the taxpayer may have to account for the output tax as usual, but there would be an equivalent set-off of input tax for the imported services.

Transferring a business as a going concern

When a business or part of a business is sold as a going concern, this is not normally treated as a supply of goods or services for VAT purposes. This will be the case subject to the following two conditions:

- That the assets will be used by the purchaser to carry on the same type of business.
- Where the person selling the business is a registered person, the buyer must register forthwith if he or she is not already registered. In this situation, it is possible for the VAT registration number of the seller to be transferred to the buyer subject to the agreement of the Customs and Excise.

Where a sole trader decides to convert his business either into a partnership or into a limited company with one or more other people involved, the transfer provisions will apply and there will be no charge to VAT. In the same way, if a person sells only a part of his or her business, the transaction will not be subject to VAT provided that the portion sold is deemed capable of operating separately.

Retailers

Generally, the VAT system requires a business to maintain a record of each transaction as well as a record of all the tax invoices which have been issued. In the retail industry, in particular, this would involve an overwhelming amount of work given the large number of small transactions which take place. The legislation, therefore, takes a realistic approach to the problem by creating special regulations for this class of business.

There are two modifications to the rules. First, where a supply of goods or services is being tendered to the general public and the customer does not require a tax invoice, the business need not provide such an invoice (in the situation where an invoice is requested and the amount of the transaction, tax inclusive, is £100 or less, a short form of invoice may be given). Secondly, to address the problem concerning the number of transactions which retailers have to cope with, schemes have been designed to simplify the system of calculating output tax. Some of these schemes are only applicable to smaller businesses, and some of the schemes have conditions attached to them. This means that the retailer does not have a free choice from the schemes, but instead must pick the method most applicable to his or her trading position. In essence, the legislation allows for one of the following two basic methods to be used:

- The business may calculate the gross takings based on the payments received from customers, including credit customers.
- The business may calculate the takings again on payments received, but this time including credit sales when the customer is invoiced as opposed to when the credit account is paid.

Supply of second-hand goods

In general terms, the VAT legislation does not distinguish between the supply of new and second-hand goods. However, there are traders whose business is concerned almost exclusively with the supply of second-hand goods to customers who will almost certainly not be registered for VAT. This creates a problem, in that if the trader has to charge output tax on his or her transactions, there will be no input tax to balance this because his or her customers are not registered. Consequently, the tax payable to the Customs and Excise would always be greater than the amount appropriate to the value added. Again, in recognition of this situation, special regulations have been brought into force for this type of business. These schemes are known as the second-hand goods schemes and they enable the second-hand trader to calculate his or her VAT 'on the margin', which means the difference between the price at which he or she bought and sold the goods. The trader will therefore account for VAT at 7/47ths of the difference between his buying and selling price. No tax invoice is issued, which means that a customer cannot reclaim input tax if he or she is a taxable person.

10

Taxing inheritances

'In this world nothing can be said to be certain, except death and taxes.' These are the words of Benjamin Franklin, uttered in 1789 but they are equally applicable today. Inheritance Tax is a relatively new tax which was introduced by the Finance Act of 1986. However, its basis is the principles established by two former taxes, i.e. Estate Duty and Capital Transfer Tax. Inheritance Tax is a tax on wealth and is chargeable on the transfer of wealth from one individual to another. It is commonly thought that Inheritance Tax is only incurred upon the death of a person. However, this is not the case, and in this chapter we will demonstrate that the charge arises not only on death but also on certain lifetime transfers of wealth which are made between individuals, as well as transfers involving certain trusts.

Inheritance Tax is also payable at any time when gifts are made involving assets and holdings of shares in close companies. We will see that there are certain favoured transfers which are 'potentially exempt' and which will not attract Inheritance Tax at all, if the transferor survives for seven years after the transfer was made. It will be shown that special provisions exist when a business interest forms part of a transfer. For example, reliefs may be available where the subject of the transfer relates to business assets, shares, business property, agricultural property and woodlands.

In order to understand the significance of these forms of relief, it is first necessary to gain an understanding of how the system of Inheritance Tax works and especially to attain a firm grasp of the unwieldy terminology which is inherent in the system. Accordingly, the following issues will be discussed within the chapter: when the

243

charge to Inheritance Tax arises with particular reference to close companies; the meaning of transfers of value; transactions which are deemed not to be transfers of value; transfers which occur on death and during life; exempt transfers; potentially exempt transfers; reliefs; the rates of tax; trusts; Inheritance Tax and partnerships.

The charge to Inheritance Tax

The Inheritance Tax Act (1984) states that the tax will be charged 'on the value transferred by a chargeable transfer'. In outline, this means that the liability for Inheritance Tax arises when transfers of value are made on the death of an individual, or when 'potentially exempt transfers' (PETs) are made less than seven years before the transferor's death, or to lifetime transfers which do not qualify as exempt transfers, and finally, to transfers made into certain types of trust (see Figure 10.1).

Close companies

Inheritance Tax is charged on individuals, which includes trustees and executors, but it does not apply to transfers of value made by companies. However, there are special provisions which apply to close companies enabling the Inland Revenue to apportion a transfer of value between the company's participators (see p. 213 above for a definition of close companies and participators).

The apportionment will take place according to the rights and interests of the participators at the time when the transfer took place. A difficulty may arise if one of the participators is part of another close company. The legislation deals with this by further subapportioning the transfer of value.

EXAMPLE

A close company made up of five equal shareholders makes a transfer of value of £75,000. Here, each of the shareholders will be deemed to have made a transfer of value of £15,000.

If one of those shareholders is another close company which is made up of six

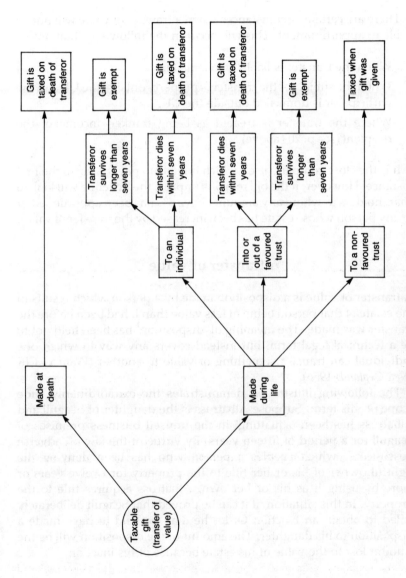

Figure 10.1 Introduction to the taxation of gifts under Inheritance Tax

equal shareholders, each of those six shareholders will be deemed to have made a transfer of £2,500.

There are certain circumstances when a transfer of value will not be liable to apportionment. This will occur in the following situations:

- When the transfer is liable to income tax.
- When the subject of the transfer is property outside the UK and the participator is domiciled outside the UK.
- Where the transfer is treated as being franked income of the recipient (see p. 209 above).

It is the close company itself which is liable to pay the tax in the first instance. However, if the bill remains unpaid, the Revenue will look to shareholders to whom any amount above 5% has been apportioned or to any person whose estate has been increased by the transfer of value.

A transfer of value

A transfer of value is a disposition made by a person which results in the estate of that person being of less value than it had been before the transfer was made. The meaning of 'disposition' has been held not to be a technical legal term, but instead covers any way in which one individual can transfer something of value to another (*Ward* v. *CIR (New Zealand)* 1956).

The following illustration demonstrates the extraordinarily wide scope of this term. Suppose Albatross is the daughter of Seagull and Albatross has been 'squatting' in the unused business premises of Seagull for a period of fifteen years. By virtue of the law of 'adverse possession', which enables a person who has been denying the rightful owner of his or her title to the property for twelve years or more by using it as his or her own, Albatross acquires title to the property. In this situation, if it can be proved that Seagull deliberately failed to obtain an Eviction Order he may be held to have made a disposition to his daughter. The amount of the disposition will be the amount lost to the value of his estate because of his inaction.

Associated operations

A very important part of understanding the significance of dispositions in Inheritance Tax is the notion of 'associated operations'.

These provisions widen the scope of Inheritance Tax to include a
series of activities which affect the same property and which taken
individually would not be regarded as a transfer of value, but when
they are looked at as a whole, enable the Revenue to treat them as a
transfer of value. In order to be chargeable, the associated operation
must form part of a scheme which confers a gratuitous benefit
(*MacPherson* v. *CIR* 1988). The provisions aim to dissuade people from
avoiding tax by attempting to disguise a diminution in the value of
their estate by splitting up the disposition into a number of seemingly
separate operations.

EXAMPLE

Whacky would like to transfer some property to Amiable. If Whacky were to make
a straight transfer this disposition would give rise to a liability to Inheritance Tax.

If Whacky were first to grant a lease to Amiable at the market rent this would not
give rise to a charge. Whacky could then transfer the reversion to Amiable which
would be worth considerably less than the property as it originally stood. Thus the
amount of tax he would pay would be much less than if he had made a straight
transfer. If the transfer of the reversion to Amiable took place less than three
years after the grant of the lease, the Revenue would be entitled to treat this as an
associated operation and charge Inheritance Tax on the original value of the
transfer.

The meaning of 'estate'

The essential feature in determining whether or not a disposition has
been made is to see if the estate of the person making the transfer has
become less valuable. For the purposes of Inheritance Tax, a person's
estate 'is the aggregate of all the property to which he or she is
beneficially entitled'. This refers to all the forms of property including
any right which is enforceable by law. For example, an option to
purchase a piece of land would be included, as would an interest held
by a beneficiary under a trust. The focus of Inheritance Tax is on the
amount by which the transferor's estate is reduced, rather than the
amount by which the recipient's estate is increased. Occasionally there
will be a significant difference between the two figures.

EXAMPLE

Lucky holds 70% of voting shares in Handy Ltd. He gives 30% of his shares to Fortunate who is then a minority shareholder. Fortunate's estate has increased by the value of the 30% shareholding he now has, but Lucky has lost more than just the value of the 30% shares, he has also lost control of the company. Therefore, the amount lost to his estate will be greater than the amount gained by Fortunate and the liability to Inheritance Tax will reflect this greater amount.

Transactions which are deemed not to be transfers of value

Certain types of dispositions are excluded from liability to Inheritance Tax. The first concession under the Act is a fairly obvious one. Inheritance Tax is aimed at taxing people who make a free transfer of property out of their estate into the estate of someone else. If the transferor receives consideration, in other words some form of payment for the transfer, then his or her estate may not have been reduced in value and therefore he or she should not be taxed. This is known as a 'non-gratuitous transfer'. However, it is necessary to establish that the transfer, although paid for, has not in fact been sold at an undervalued price (i.e. that the deal was done 'at arm's length'). In order for this provision to apply to the sale of unquoted shares or debentures there must have been a freely negotiated price at the time of sale. This may be a very difficult hurdle to cross where the shares are in a private company and the price of the shares in a sale is laid down in the articles of the company, and therefore is not open to negotiation.

A 'family maintenance' exemption applies to lifetime transfers which are made to family members, for example on divorce, or where provision is made for a dependent relative.

In relation to retirement benefit schemes, where a person is making contributions to an approved retirement scheme which provides benefits for services rendered by his or her employees, these may not be treated as transfers of value. However, there are strict rules which must be adhered to in order to ensure that a liability does not arise.

In the same way, where a person waives remuneration which is due to be paid to him or her this will not be regarded as a transfer of value if the remuneration waived would have been assessable under Income Tax Schedule E. Also a person who chooses to waive his or her right to a dividend within a period of twelve months before the right to the dividend accrues, will not be regarded as having made a transfer of value.

The grant of an agricultural tenancy in the UK, Channel Islands or the Isle of Man is excluded from being a transfer of value provided that it is made for full consideration in money or money's worth.

The legislation also allows for a certain amount of variation in the distribution of a person's estate after his or her death without incurring Inheritance Tax. These variations or disclaimers must be made within two years of death in order to be excluded.

If a disposition falls within any of the above definitions it will not be regarded as a transfer of value and, therefore, will not give rise to a charge to Inheritance Tax.

Lifetime transfers

Inheritance Tax will be charged on transfers made during the life of the taxpayer if they are deemed to be chargeable transfers and the amount of the charge will be related to how much the estate of the transferor has been reduced in value. A *chargeable transfer* is one that is not exempted by the legislation, whereas *potentially exempt transfers* are regarded as exempt unless the transferor dies within seven years of making the gift.

The existence of potentially exempt transfers has the effect of placing most lifetime transfers out of the reach of Inheritance Tax so that the main influence of Inheritance Tax is felt at the time of death, or shortly before.

Potentially exempt transfers (PETs)

Under the regulations (s.3A Inheritance Tax Act 1984) there are some transfers of value which, even though they do not fall under one of the exempted categories, may, nevertheless, be potentially exempt from liability. This occurs when a person has made one of the favoured transfers of value and then survives for seven years. The transfer will then be exempt from Inheritance Tax. If he or she does not survive for seven years the transfer becomes chargeable when the transferor dies.

The basic definition of a PET is a transfer of value which is made by an individual and which is one of the following:

- A gift to another individual.
- A gift into an accumulation and maintenance trust.

- A gift into a disabled persons trust.
- A gift into a trust in which a person other than the transferor has an interest in possession (the meaning of this term is explained later).

These transfers are treated for the purposes of Inheritance Tax as if they will eventually be completely exempt from liability. This means that PETs are not treated as affecting the transferor's cumulative lifetime chargeable transfers. They are also not taken into account when computing the annual exemption (see below). However, if the transferor dies before the seven-year period has expired, it is possible to use any annual exemption which was not applied in the year the PET was made in order to exempt part of the transfer which has now become chargeable. On death, the tax will be charged on the value of the asset at the time it was originally transferred. There are tapering relief provisions which apply to mitigate the amount of tax payable and which depend on how many years the transferor survived after making the transfer (see Table 10.1).

With the exception of the annual exemption it is obviously to the advantage of the taxpayer to make use of all the full exemptions before utilizing the potential exemptions.

Transfers on death

When an individual dies the Revenue regards him or her as having made a transfer of value of the whole of his or her estate immediately before he or she died. The recipients of the deceased's estate are deemed to be those who inherit his or her property by reason of the

Table 10.1 Tapering relief available for PETs

Percentage of full rate of tax payable	Years between the making of a PET and the transferor's death
20	6–7
40	5–6
60	4–5
80	3–4
100	0–3

deceased's will, or those who must inherit under the law when a person dies without leaving a will.

Occasionally a person may have attempted to 'give away' part of his or her property before death to the person who he or she intends should ultimately inherit it, while 'borrowing' the use and benefit of the property for him- or herself until he or she dies. For example, if a person owns a Ming vase then draws up a deed of gift transferring the ownership to his or her son, yet still continues to keep it on the fireplace in his or her drawing-room, this may be regarded as a 'gift subject to reservation'.

Where this is the case, the property is treated as continuing to form part of the estate of the transferor at the date of his or her death. If, however, the gift ceases to be subject to reservation before the transferor dies, the gift will be treated as a potentially exempt transfer, and if the transferor survives for longer than seven years after the gift ceased to be subject to reservation, it will avoid Inheritance Tax altogether.

Exempt transfers

In addition to the situations when certain dispositions are not regarded as transfers of value under the legislation, there are a number of exemptions which are applicable either during the lifetime of the taxpayer, or those which are available both during life and on death.

The result of a transfer coming under the ambit of one of the exemptions is that no Inheritance Tax will be payable on the part of the transfer which is considered to be exempt.

Lifetime transfer exemptions

Table 10.2 shows the exemptions which are available to a taxpayer during his or her life. These include an annual exemption below which Inheritance Tax is not applied, which in 1991/2 was transfers valued up to £3,000. It is possible to carry the allowance forward for one year where the exemption is not fully used in the current year.

The donation of 'small gifts' (in 1991/2 £250 maximum) equally does not give rise to a charge and normal expenditure out of income and

Table 10.2 General exemptions and reliefs available in respect of lifetime and death transfers

Exemptions and reliefs	Lifetime	Death
Transfers between spouses (no limit)	√	√
Transfers each year (up to a given limit)	√	
Small gifts to any one person (up to a given limit)	√	
Transfers by way of normal expenditure	√	
Gifts in consideration of marriage	√	
Gifts to charities (no limit)	√	√
Gifts to political parties	√	√
Gifts for national purposes or public benefit	√	√
Gifts made during lifetime for family maintenance including education	√	√
Business property relief	√	√
Agricultural property relief	√	√
Quick succession relief		√

gifts on the occasion of marriage (maximum £5,000) are further examples of lifetime exemptions.

Exemptions available during life and on death

Table 10.2 also shows the exemptions which are available both during the life of a person and on his or her death. It can be seen that transfers of value made to a spouse, gifts to charities and certain political parties, and gifts for national purposes and for the public benefit will not create a liability to pay Inheritance Tax.

Reliefs

There are a number of reliefs which are available to reduce the value of a chargeable transfer. This section will concentrate on those most applicable to managers as follows:

- Business property.
- Fall in value of quoted securities and interest in land.
- Agricultural property.

- Woodlands.
- Quick succession.
- Double taxation.

Business property

Business property can be divided into a number of categories each of which may allow for the reduction in the value of the transferor's estate. If the various conditions can be satisfied there will be a relief of either 30% or 50%. To obtain the relief the subject of the transfer must fall within the definition of 'a relevant business'. Basically, this includes professions and vocations but does not include any business carried on otherwise than for gain. It also excludes transfers of business property which are carried out for the purposes of dealing in land or buildings, making or holding investments, or dealing in stocks, shares and securities (but discount houses are eligible for the relief).

If the relief is available on the transfer, it will reduce the value of the transfer before any other exemptions are given.

Business property relief
The following is a summary of business property relief:

1. Property which comprises a business or an interest in a business, for example of a partnership or sole trader, can obtain relief of 50%.

2. Unquoted shares or securities which put the transferor in a position of control immediately before the transfer can also obtain relief of 50%.

3. The transfer of business assets (plant and machinery, buildings and land) which were owned by the transferor in his capacity as a partner, controlling director or sole trader and used for the purposes of the business, may obtain relief of 30%.

4. The transfer of a minority shareholding in an unquoted company may either attract 30% or 50% relief depending on whether the number of shares held exceeded a 25% holding.

5. The transfer of business assets which were used by the transferor for the purposes of a business and were held in trust and in which he or she had an interest in possession will attract relief of 30%.

To enable a claim to be made for the relief, it must be shown that the transferor owned the property for at least two years before the transfer took place. With regard to the assets of a business to be eligible for the relief it must be demonstrated that they were used wholly or mainly for the purposes of the business.

EXAMPLE

Bertie dies on 7 April 1991 leaving the following estate:

- 60% interest in Quack Ltd (an unquoted private company) worth £125,000.
- Freehold land used by Quack Ltd worth £35,000.
- Shares in Zany plc worth £15,000.
- Other property (net) worth £150,000.

Three years before his death, Bertie had transferred 35% of the shares in Quack Ltd to his son. Bertie has used all his annual exemptions. Bertie's son has retained his interest in Quack Ltd which at the date of the gift was valued at £40,000.

To calculate the Inheritance Tax arising on Bertie's death we must perform the following operations:

		£	£ balance
1.	1991 value of Bertie's estate 60% interest in Quack Ltd	125,000	
	Less business property relief (50% × 125,000)	62,500	62,500
2.	Freehold land used by Quack Ltd	35,000	
	Less business property relief (30% × 35,000)	10,500	24,500
3.	Shares in Zany plc		15,000
4.	Other property		150,000
			252,000
	Add transfer within 7 years gift of shares in Quack Ltd	40,000	
	Less business property relief (50% × 40,000)	20,000	20,000
			272,000

Summary: IHT payable 1991/2, first £140,000 = Nil.
Remaining £132,000 @ 40% = £52,800.
For details of the rate of tax, see below.

Table 10.3 compares the requirements and benefits of business property relief under Inheritance Tax (IHT) and retirement relief under Capital Gains Tax (CGT) – for details of retirement relief, see pp. 171–3.

Fall in value of quoted securities or interest in land

When the total value of all the deceased's securities quoted on a recognized stock exchange or dealt with on the unlisted securities market immediately before his or her death is more than the amount of money which could be raised on the sale of those securities within twelve months of the death, then the value that was transferred on death can be reduced by the difference in the original value at the time of death, and the sum actually raised.

The same principle applies to the valuation and sale of an interest in land. Here, the time limit on sale is three years from the date of death, and the difference in the value on death and the sale price must either exceed £1,000 or 5% of the value on death in order to qualify for the relief.

Agricultural property

There is relief where the whole or only a part of a transfer concerns agricultural property. Agricultural property is defined as 'agricultural land or pasture and includes woodland and any building used in connection with the intensive rearing of livestock or fish . . . and includes such cottages, farm buildings and farm houses, together with the land occupied with them'.

The agricultural property must be within the UK, the Channel Islands or the Isle of Man to qualify for relief and one of the two following conditions must be satisfied:

- The land must have been occupied by the transferor and used for agricultural purposes for two years before the date of transfer.
- The transferor must have owned the land for seven years before the date of transfer, and during that time it was occupied by him or her, or by someone else for agricultural purposes.

If a person is eligible for the relief, the value of the transfer is reduced by either 50% or 30%.

A relief of 50% will be given where the transferor has the right to

Table 10.3 Comparison between business property relief (IHT) and retirement relief (CGT) 1991/2

	Qualifying period of ownership	Age of owner	Availability to unincorporated businesses	Availability to companies	Qualifying shares	Relief
Business property relief	2 years	Not significant	Applies	Need not be a full-time working director	Majority holding in an unquoted company; or minority holding in unquoted company	50% or 30%
Retirement relief	1–10 years (minimum to maximum relief)	55 years (or under if retiring on grounds of ill health)	Applies	Must be a full-time working director	Must be in a family company	First £150,000 of gains and half of next £450,000 exempt

vacant possession of the property immediately before transfer, or has the right to obtain it within twelve months of the transfer. In all other cases the relief will be at a level of 30%.

The relief is now designed to cover both owner-occupied land and land which is let, but land subject to agricultural tenancies will only qualify for the lower rate of relief. This reflects the fact that land subject to agricultural tenancies is worth significantly less than land without such a tenancy.

Woodlands relief

The relief for woodlands situated in the UK, the Channel Islands or the Isle of Man is only available on transfers on death.

The relief will be available if some part of the deceased's estate is made up of land on which trees or underwood are growing. If this is the case an election can be made to leave the value of the trees and the underwood out of the total value of the estate on death. However, it must be established that the deceased was entitled to the land for a period of at least five years immediately prior to his or her death.

When the trees are eventually sold, Inheritance Tax will be levied on the person who is entitled to the proceeds of sale at the top rate applicable on the deceased's death. Usually, the value of the trees will have increased since the death, so although the relief allows postponement of payment, it may well mean that more tax will have to be paid than would otherwise have been the case. If it can be shown that the trees or underwood would have been eligible for business property relief at the time of the death, the amount on the subsequent sale which will be chargeable to Inheritance Tax will first be reduced by 50%.

Quick succession relief

If a person has been the recipient of a transfer and within five years of the transfer the recipient dies so that liability to Inheritance Tax arises for a second time, relief will be available. The amount of the relief is on a sliding scale of percentages which depend on the length of time which has passed since the original transfer was made.

Double taxation relief

If tax is incurred in a foreign jurisdiction in respect of either lifetime or death transfers some relief may be available to reduce the amount of

Inheritance Tax due on the foreign property. Its availability depends on establishing that the foreign tax paid is similar in nature to Inheritance Tax.

The rates of tax

Inheritance Tax is levied by reference to the value of the transfer. The rates at which the charge is made are set out in the Budget. In 1991/2 the 'nil band', that is, the value of the transfers which will attract no tax, is set at £140,000 – a figure which tends to be increased each year broadly in line with inflation. Transfers which are in excess of this figure incur a charge of 40%. However, as we have already established, most lifetime transfers are not considered to be chargeable transfers, but are instead treated as being potentially exempt. It will be recalled that no Inheritance Tax is payable in respect of these transfers as long as the transferor survives for seven years. If the transferor does die within the seven years, the potentially exempt transfer will 'prove chargeable' and the tax will then be levied, subject to the tapering relief referred to earlier.

There is a difference in terms of the rate of tax which is levied on lifetime transfers and those which occur on death. All transfers which are made on death or within three years of death are taxed at the full rate of 40%. Transfers which are made at other times, excluding PETs, are subject to a charge of half the death rate.

The rate of tax which becomes payable because of the death of an individual is the rate which is applicable at the time of death, rather than at the time the transfer was made.

The computation of Inheritance Tax

Inheritance Tax is a cumulative progressive tax which essentially means that the more a person gives away the more tax he or she will be liable to pay.

When Capital Transfer Tax was introduced, the original idea was that the value of gifts which a person made should be accumulated throughout his or her lifetime with the transfer at the time of death being the final gift. This proved to be unworkable, and under the Inheritance Tax regulations the period of cumulation has been reduced to seven years. Therefore, over a period of seven years each transfer must be added to the last one to find the amount of tax payable.

There are two situations as follows when the cumulative total may have to be altered:

- Transfers which are reported late to the Revenue.
- Potentially exempt transfers.

When transfers are reported late provisions exist for collecting any extra tax which may be payable as a result of an alteration in the cumulation figures.

In the case of potentially exempt transfers, no tax is payable immediately the transfer is made and the transfer is left out of the taxpayer's cumulative total. But if the taxpayer made a transfer, for example in 1988, and died in 1991, the potentially exempt transfer would become chargeable. In addition, the transfer would alter the cumulative total and the extra tax which results would have to be paid by the estate or by the person who received the transfer.

EXAMPLE

Ethel makes the following gifts to her three friends:

- £100,000 to Flo on 3 June 1987.
- £100,000 to Aggie on 31 July 1987.
- £100,000 to Gertie on 3 August 1987.

Ethel dies on 3 July 1994.

These gifts would be regarded as potentially exempt at the time of transfer. The first gift to Flo will be exempt from tax when Ethel dies because it was given more than seven years before her death. The gifts to Aggie and Gertie, however, will prove chargeable. The gift to Aggie will be her first chargeable transfer and will be calculated as a person who has no cumulative total. The gift to Gertie will be calculated on the basis of Ethel making a chargeable transfer of £100,000 while already having a cumulative total of £100,000.

Grossing up

When a person makes a lifetime transfer and the Inheritance Tax is paid by the transferor it is necessary to 'gross up' the net transfer so that tax is payable on the gross amount.

Grossing up is only relevant when the transferor pays the tax. This is because Inheritance Tax is levied on the amount by which the transferor's estate is reduced in value. This amount must, of course, include the amount of tax paid. In the situation where the person receiving the gift pays the tax, it is not necessary to gross up the figure because the value of the transferor's estates has only been reduced by the amount of the gift.

Liability to pay the tax

In respect of lifetime transfers it is the transferor who is primarily liable for the tax. Where transfers are made with regard to trusts, it is the trustees who must arrange for payment.

On death, the payment of tax is due from the personal representatives of the deceased, unless the property is 'settled', in which case, again, the primary liability lies with the trustees.

Accounting for Inheritance Tax

It is not necessary to make a return in respect of exempt or potentially exempt gifts. Chargeable transfers are required to be reported within twelve months of the end of the month in which the transfer was made.

Inheritance Tax becomes payable six months after the event which has given rise to the liability. However, there is an important exception to this rule in relation to lifetime chargeable transfers which are made between the 6 April and 30 September. Here, the tax is payable on the following 30 April. Where the tax is paid late, interest is charged from the date on which payment is due.

Where the donee agrees to pay the tax on lifetime chargeable transfers, he or she may elect to pay the bill by instalments. This is also true of liabilities arising on death. In order for this concesion to apply, the assets must fall into one of the following categories:

- Shares in a company in which the donor had a controlling interest.
- Some unquoted shares.
- Land.
- A business (or an interest in a business).

Table 10.4 is a summary of Inheritance Tax.

Table 10.4 Inheritance Tax at a glance!

	Disposals on death	Lifetime chargeable transfers	PETs	Gifts with reservation of benefit
Deemed value of transfer	Value of estate immediately prior to death	Value of gift at date of transfer	Value of gift at date of transfer	Value at date of death, or at date when transferor was finally excluded from using the gift
Date when IHT is charged	Date of death	Date of transfer	Only taxed when death occurs within seven years of gift	Date of death where gift was still reserved at this time, or where transferor was excluded from using gift within seven years of death
Previous transfers which affect the cumulative total	Chargeable transfers made within seven years of death	Chargeable transfers made within seven years of current transfer. Where death occurs within seven years PETs increase cumulative total	Chargeable transfers which occurred during the seven years before the current PET; PETs made within seven years of death	Chargeable transfers which occurred during the seven years before death
Rate at which IHT is charged	Full death rate	Half rate	Full rate (but tapering relief may apply)	Full rate (but tapering relief may apply)

Trusts and settlements

The area relating to the taxation of trusts and settlements is a complex one, yet it is important for people involved in business to be aware of the tax implications of placing some or all of their business interests into a trust. In order to gain a basic understanding of the subject, we will break the discussion up into a number of areas:

- The meaning of settlements and 'interest in possession'.
- How and when the settlements are taxed.
- Discretionary trusts.
- Accumulation and maintenance trusts.

Before we examine these areas it is useful to examine the types of situations where trusts might be set up.

Primarily, trusts are established to enable property to be used for the benefit of children, elderly people, disabled relatives, or employees and their relatives. They are also useful where family property might be placed in jeopardy by the extravagance of relatives. Trusts enable arrangements to be made for gifts to pass in the future, perhaps contingent on the recipient fulfilling certain requirements which may be laid down by the person setting up the trust. They allow land to be used for the benefit of people who are not allowed under the law to own it (for example, children) and are equally applicable to situations where a person wants to specify that his property will pass to a number of different individuals in succession. One of the main tax benefits of holding property on trust is that they can be used to minimize the tax which becomes payable on income, capital gains and, importantly, transfers from a person's estate.

Definition

The 'settlor' is the person who establishes the trust and provides the property which is the subject of the trust. In order to set up the trust, the settlor transfers the ownership of the property to 'trustees' who then have the legal duty of holding the property for the benefit of the 'beneficiaries' – that is, those parties who will receive some benefit from the trust. Trusts vary enormously in their composition and it is possible, for example, for the settlor to be one of the beneficiaries or one of the trustees.

To establish whether or not a settlement for Inheritance Tax purposes has been made we must see if the position of the parties and the manner in which the property is held come within the definition of the Inheritance Tax Act. Settlements are basically where property is held as follows:

1. For persons in succession (for example, property to Nigel for 30 years and then to Alf).
2. For any person subject to a contingency (for example, to Nigel if he marries).
3. To accumulate income.
4. So that the payment of income is at the discretion of a person.

It is only these particular types of trusts which are regarded as settlements for the purposes of Inheritance Tax.

For tax purposes settlements can be categorized into three particular types:

1. Settlements with an interest in possession.
2. Settlements without an interest in possession.
3. Favoured trusts (for example, accumulation and maintenance trusts).

The central feature in the treatment of all these is whether or not there is an 'interest in possession' in existence.

An interest in possession exists when a person has an immediate entitlement to the income of the trust, or to the use and enjoyment of the trust property. For example, if a beneficiary is entitled to the income from a trust for ten years he or she has an interest in possession during that time.

If, however, there is no beneficiary who has an immediate right to income there is no interest in possession. This may occur where the trustees have an obligation to accumulate the income, or where they have a discretion whether to pay out to the beneficiaries.

The last category is the so-called 'favoured trust'. The most common example of this is where income is used for the maintenance of infant beneficiaries or accumulated until they reach a certain age.

How settlements are taxed

The three types of settlements which have been mentioned are so different in their nature that the Revenue deals with them under separate tax regimes.

Since 17 March 1987 the establishment of a settlement with an interest in possession and an enlargement of that interest have been events potentially exempt (PETS) under Inheritance Tax. Settlements with no interest in possession suffer a charge on each 10th anniversary on the value of the property in the trust. The charge is at 30% of the half-rate normally charged on lifetime transfers. Favoured trusts, the most important example being accumulation and maintenance trusts, are quite different from the other two categories in that although they are a form of discretionary trust they are not subject to the same tax charges. This is discussed more fully below.

The manner in which the charge arises on the other main types of discretionary trust, i.e. settlements with an interest in possession and settlements with no interest in possession, depends when the settlement was created. If the transfer into a settlement is made on the death of the transferor then it will be a chargeable event unless there are exemptions which can be applied. If the transfer is made during life and the settlement is one which has an interest in possession then the transfer, as already mentioned, is potentially exempt so that the transferor will not be charged if he or she survives for seven years. Transfers involving accumulation and maintenance funds are also potentially exempt. Therefore, where property is settled on an accumulation and maintenance trust, and subsequently is made over to the beneficiaries on attaining the age specified under the trust, no charge to Inheritance Tax will arise. Quite clearly such trusts have major tax advantages!

The reliefs and exemptions which are available under the rules of Inheritance Tax also apply to settlements. For example, if a settlement provides that the settled property will pass to the registered charity or spouse on the death of the existing beneficiary, the reliefs will work in virtually the same way as if the property was not settled.

Discretionary trusts

A discretionary trust is one where there is no interest in possession and the trustees have discretion as to what to do with the income. Here, the Revenue focuses not on what happens to the income of the trust, but instead pays attention to the state of the capital within the trust. This means that tax is charged when the capital leaves the trust. However, it is commonly the situation that trustees might pay out the income to the beneficiaries while retaining the capital. This is circumvented by the imposition of the 'ten-year anniversary' charge, which raises a charge to tax on the value of the property immediately before the tenth anniversary.

There is also an 'exit charge' on discretionary trusts which applies when capital goes out of the trust. This could arise in a number of ways. The most obvious example is when the capital is distributed to the beneficiary. Inheritance Tax is imposed on the amount by which the capital leaving the trust has reduced the value of the trust property.

Accumulation and maintenance trusts

Accumulation and maintenance trusts exist when trustees hold property for a child until he reaches a maximum age of 25. There is no interest in possession, but nevertheless these trusts are not treated in the same way as discretionary trusts. Because these trusts have significant tax advantages, the Revenue is extremely particular as to who may reap these benefits. The following four conditions must be fulfilled:

1. There must be no interest in possession in existence.
2. The income not used for maintenance must be accumulated.
3. There must be an individual who will become beneficially entitled before the age of 25.
4. The duration of the trust is limited to a maximum of twenty-five years.

Inheritance Tax and partnerships

The final part of this chapter will concentrate on the way in which Inheritance Tax affects individuals who are in business as partnerships. It should be remembered that a partnership is not treated as a separate entity for the purposes of Capital Gains Tax and exactly the same applies to Inheritance Tax. Therefore, any disposition of a partnership asset or business which results in the reduction of the value of the partnership will be deemed to be a transfer of value subject to Inheritance Tax.

This section will deal with the following issues:

- Death of a partner.
- Availability of reliefs.
- Acquisition of a partnership interest.
- Alteration of a partnership interest.
- Retirement.

The death of a partner

Where a partner dies having leased property to the other members of the partnership during his or her life, the lease will terminate on his or her death. This will mean that the value of the property which had been leased prior to his or her death, will be increased. This increase will be taken into account when the deceased's estate is valued for Inheritance Tax purposes.

Where the death of the partner results in a reduction of the value of the goodwill of the partnership, this reduction will again be taken into account when computing the Inheritance Tax which is due.

Reliefs

In order to qualify for business property relief, it must be shown that the business property is subject to a binding contract for sale. This is particularly important where the partners have agreed that in the event of one of them dying before reaching the age of retirement, the deceased's personal representatives must sell the interest in the partnership to the surviving partners. The Revenue will treat this as a binding contract for sale and will allow business relief on this transaction. Agricultural property relief is available to farming partnerships providing they fulfil the usual conditions.

Acquisition of a partnership interest

If a new partner gives full consideration for entering into the partnership, either by giving money or assuming liabilities, there has not been a reduction in the value of his estate. Therefore, no liability to

Inheritance Tax arises. Where a new partner pays more into the partnership than his or her share is actually worth then it can be shown that a reduction in the value of his or her estate has occurred. However, provided he or she can establish that there was no intention to bestow a gratuitous benefit on the partnership, and that the transaction was made 'at arm's length', the transfer will avoid Inheritance Tax liability.

In terms of the existing partners, if their estate is reduced as a result of a new partner joining, they may be able to make use of the business property relief in order to reduce the value of the transfer by half.

Alteration of a partnership interest

The share of a partner is usually determined by the partnership agreement and that value will be taken into account for Inheritance Tax purposes. It would be possible for a partner to attempt to mitigate his or her liability to Inheritance Tax by rearranging the partnership interests. In order for this to be successful it would have to be shown that no gratuitous benefit was intended and it was a transaction which was such as might be expected to take place at arm's length between people not connected with each other. Where such a transaction does fall to be taxed, the transferor may make use of the business property relief.

Retirement

Provided that a retiring partner obtains full consideration for his or her interest, no liability to Inheritance Tax will arise.

Check-list

The following brief list shows how to make the best of Inheritance Tax and limit liability:

- The younger the transferor when he or she makes the gift the less likely that he or she will be caught by the seven-year rule.
- Give away assets which are rising in value.
- Make full use of exempted gifts.
- Consider an insurance policy to cover the potential IHT demand.
- Seek advice concerning the possible tax benefits of creating a trust.

11

Tax avoidance, pensions and tax payments

The previous chapters of this book have set out the principles and practice relating to the major taxes in the UK which impact on business: Income Tax, Corporation Tax, Capital Gains Tax and Inheritance Tax. In this final chapter we turn to the subject of tax avoidance. None of us likes to pay tax, so how might it best be avoided?

Tax avoidance schemes

The subject of tax avoidance is a controversial one which excites a variety of reactions from both taxpayers and the judges. In the case of *Ayrshire Pullman Motor Services* v. *CIR* (1929) it was held that a taxpayer is 'entitled to be astute to prevent, so far as he honestly can, the depletion of his means by the Revenue'.

The essence of this judgment is that there is a distinction which must be drawn between tax avoidance and tax evasion. The courts' approach to tax avoidance schemes has been to adopt a number of different techniques to cramp the style of the large tax-planning industry which has evolved in this country, and which comes up with ever more artificial schemes in its bid to minimize the tax liabilities of its clients.

The leading case of *CIR* v. *Duke of Westminster* (1935) established the doctrine of *form and substance*. Here, the Duke had entered into a covenant so that his gardener was paid an annual sum of money. It was set up in such a way that the payment was, in theory, without prejudice to the gardener being entitled to claim for remuneration. However, it was clearly understood by the gardener that, in fact, the Duke did not expect him to claim wages while the covenant was in force. The use of the covenant allowed the Duke to pay a lower rate of tax than he otherwise would have done had he classed the payments as wages. The Revenue sought to establish that the payments were 'in substance' wage payments and that the Duke should pay the higher rate.

In the House of Lords, they found in favour of the Duke and the principle was established that where a transaction is *in form* one sort of transaction but *in substance* another, the courts will look primarily at the form, as long as the transactions are not 'shams'.

The result of this case was that people started to divide up their transactions into a series of activities, supposing that the court would look at the form of each of the individual transactions rather than the substance of the complete activity. The schemes were sometimes taken to extreme lengths so that transactions were entered into with the sole aim of avoiding tax.

A change of direction was indicated in the case of *Floor* v. *Davis* (1978) when one of the judges in the Court of Appeal said, 'I see this case as one in which the court is not required to take each step in isolation.' This approach was subsequently followed in *W. T. Ramsay Ltd* v. *CIR* (1982) where a company carried out a series of prearranged steps in order to create an allowable loss to set off against its chargeable gains. Lord Wilberforce said here:

> If it can be seen that a document or transaction was intended to have effect as part of a nexus or series of transactions, or as an ingredient of a wider transaction intended as a whole, there is nothing . . . to prevent it being so regarded. It is the task of the court to ascertain the legal nature of any transaction to which it is sought to attach a tax or a tax consequence and if that emerges from a series or combination of transactions, intended to operate as such, it is that series or combination which may be looked at.

The result was that the *self-cancelling transactions* which Ramsay had set up to offset a Capital Gains Tax liability failed in their objective.

This principle was extended in *CIR* v. *Burmah Oil Co. Ltd* (1982) where the taxpayer had entered into genuine transactions to obtain an allowable loss. The circumstances were different from Ramsay in three important respects: there was no preconceived plan; in *Burmah Oil* the plan could have been abandoned at any time, whereas in *Ramsay* the scheme had to proceed to its natural conclusion; the money to finance the scheme did not emanate from loans, whereas in Ramsay the loans involved raised doubts as to whether any 'real money' existed at all. Despite the fact that these differences emerged, the court still found against the company in that it had suffered no real loss.

As a result of these cases the principle was established that the court can look at substance rather than form provided the following two matters can be shown:

- There is either a preordained series of transactions or one single composite transaction.

- There are steps inserted into the process which have no commercial or business justification save the avoidance of tax.

The wide-ranging nature of this approach was felt in *Furniss* v. *Dawson* (1984) when the Dawson family wanted to sell some shares in their companies to Wood Barstow. They attempted to avoid immediate liability to Capital Gains Tax by forming an investment company in the Isle of Man to which they sold shares on a share-for-share basis. There were legal consequences of this transaction in that the Dawsons did not end up with money for the sale of their shares, but instead had shares in the investment company. However, a further and preordained step had been introduced into the transactions. The introduction of the investment company as a buyer from the Dawsons and as a seller to Wood Barstow was deemed to have no other commercial purpose than the avoidance of tax. Therefore, the scheme failed.

This remained the approach of the courts until a group of three cases went to the House of Lords. The facts in *Craven* v. *White* (1988) were similar to those of *Furniss* v. *Dawson*. Basically, the argument from the Revenue was that where disposals of assets were made by taxpayers to companies, followed by the disposal of the same assets by those companies to ultimate purchasers, the transaction should be treated as a direct disposal from the taxpayer to the ultimate purchaser. The Court of Appeal had refused to apply the Ramsay approach so that the insertion of the companies could be disregarded. It was held that the successive transactions should not be treated as a preordained series of transactions unless at the time of the first step all the remaining steps in the transaction had been determined by people who had both the intention and the capacity to carry them through. In *Craven* v. *White*, when the initial sales to the company were first made, there was no firm intention established regarding the sales to the ultimate purchasers. This being the case, the first condition of the *Ramsay* principle could not be met and so the Revenue's argument failed.

The House of Lords agreed with this analysis and laid down a number of criteria which had to be present before the Ramsay principle could be applied, as follows:

- The series of transactions was preordained at the time when the intermediate transaction was inserted.
- The only purpose for the existence of the intermediate transaction was to avoid tax.
- It was never considered that the intermediate transaction would survive independently of the preconceived chain of events.
- The preordained results did ultimately take place.

This is where the law stands today in relation to tax avoidance. If the Revenue can establish the above criteria, they will be able to connect the start of the series of transactions with the final result. For example, if there were a transfer from Agatha Ltd to Bell Ltd to Chapel Ltd, it could instead be treated as a straight transfer from Agatha Ltd to Chapel Ltd.

The game of tax avoidance is one that is constantly being played between the Revenue and tax experts in the private sector. It is undoubtedly a problem which would be alleviated by the introduction of general 'anti-avoidance' legislation giving firmer guidelines for all the parties involved as to what type of tax mitigation is acceptable.

Pensions

Pension premiums are tax deductible and are a most obvious means of reducing the amount individuals pay in tax. Making provision for old age is also, of course, prudent in other ways. The self-employed, including partners, and those employees in otherwise non-pensionable employment, up until 30 June 1988 were able to buy *retirement annuity policies* from insurance companies. Since that date relief is given for payments under qualifying *personal pension schemes*. At the same time, scope exists for those in pensionable employment to make *additional voluntary contributions*.

Retirement annuity policies

Tax relief continues for premiums paid under these policies taken out on or before 30 June 1988. For those aged up to 50, payments of up to 17.5% of 'net relevant earnings' obtain relief (including contributions by the employer where relevant). The ceiling rises for those over 50, to a maximum of 27.5% of net relevant earnings for those aged 60 or over. There is scope to do the following:

- Carry forward unused relief where the premiums paid in any year are less than the maximum allowable.

- Carry back premiums to the preceding tax year so that they can be relieved against earnings in that year (subject to the normal contributions ceiling) or the year before that if there were no net relevant earnings in the preceding year.

When the policy matures, the policyholder receives a taxable annuity and an option to receive part of the benefits as a lump-sum payment. The lump-sum payment cannot be more than three times the reduced pension provided by the policy, with an overall limit of £150,000.

Net relevant earnings are as follows:

- Profits of a trade, profession or vocation, less capital allowances and loss relief.
- Net emoluments taxable under Schedule E.

Personal pensions

Since 1 July 1988, the self-employed and those not in pensionable employment have been able to invest in a personal pension scheme. Contributions to the scheme are paid net of basic rate Income Tax and employers may contribute on behalf of their employees. On retirement a lump sum of up to 25% of the total value of the benefits under the scheme may be taken, up to a maximum of £150,000. There is a maximum premium on which tax relief may be given on payments into a scheme; for more details see p. 63. Personal pensions are marketed by unit trusts, banks and building societies, as well as insurance companies.

Additional voluntary contributions

Where the business provides a pension to a director or employee, the pension contributions paid by the business are treated as a business expense. At the same time, individuals in pensioned employment under an approved scheme obtain tax relief for contributions up to 15% of salary. There is an upper earnings limit on which tax-deductible contributions can be made (£71,400 of salary in 1991/2 – the figure is indexed annually) for individuals joining pension schemes from 1 June 1989. Few schemes maximize the 15% limit and employees may make additional voluntary contributions (AVCs) into an employer's or an independent AVC scheme.

Due and payable dates

To avoid unnecessary interest and penalty charges, it is important that tax is paid on time. The date on which tax is due and payable to the Revenue varies depending upon the tax, the Case and the Schedule, as summarized in Table 11.1.

Where an assessment is issued within thirty days before these dates, or after these dates, the due and payable date is thirty days after the date of the assessment. Where the taxpayer appeals against an assessment, the above dates still apply unless a *postponement application* is also made. An application to postpone the payment of some or all of the tax (and Class IV NIC when applicable) shown on the assessment should be made where it appears excessive. The Inspector will agree the postponement or, where he disagrees, refer the application to the General Commissioners. Once the postponement application is accepted, the normal due and payable dates are modified.

In the case of the tax which is postponed, the due date is now the *later* of the following:

- Thirty days after the appeal is finally determined and the tax due is notified.
- The normal due date as set out above.

Table 11.1 Due and payable dates: a summary

Tax, Schedule or Case	Normal due date
Income Tax:	
Schedule A	1 January in the year of assessment
Schedule D Cases I and II	Two equal instalments on 1 January in the year of assessment and the following 1 July
Schedule D Cases III to VI	1 January in the year of assessment
Schedule E	Employer deducts tax on payment and pays it over to the Collector by the 19th of the following tax month or quarterly if the average monthly amount is less than £400
Schedule F	Employer pays ACT on payment of a dividend and pays the tax over to the Collector at the end of each quarter
Taxed Income	1 December following the end of the tax year
Capital Gains Tax	1 December following the end of the tax year
Corporation Tax	9 months after the end of the company's accounting period
Inheritance Tax	Normally 6 months after the end of the month in which death or the chargeable transfer occurs. Tax on non-exempt lifetime gifts made 6 April to 30 September is due on 30 April in the following year

In the case of the tax which is not postponed, the due date is now the *later* of the following:

• Thirty days after the postponement application is agreed with the Revenue or determined by the Commissioners.
• The normal due date as set out above.

Interest due on tax paid late

If the taxpayer pays the tax after the due and payable date, the Revenue will charge interest (known as 'Section 86 interest') on the amount outstanding, though it is normally waived when it does not exceed a *de minimis* limit (currently £30). The interest is calculated from the 'reckonable date' to the date of payment. The 'reckonable date' is normally the due date, but for Income Tax is 1 July following the end of the relevant tax year where payment occurs later because of a

274

postponement application or determination of an appeal. The interest rate varies with movements in national interest rates (and differs for Inheritance Tax). The current rate can be obtained from a local tax office.

EXAMPLE

Sue is a self-employed textile designer, who received an estimated 1990/1 Case I tax assessment dated 6 November 1990 for £30,000. She appealed against the assessment on 27 November and asked to postpone payment of tax on £10,000 of the estimated profit. The Inspector agreed the postponement on 8 January 1991. The appeal was finally settled on 6 September 1991 in the figure of Profits £24,000.

Sue paid the tax as follows (all in 1991):

		£
9 February	(1st instalment of tax not postponed)	10,000
1 July	(2nd instalment of tax not postponed)	10,000
6 October	(Balance)	4,000

The interest charged by the Revenue would be calculated as follows (using the official rate in March 1991 of 11.5%):

	Amount involved £	Normal due date	Due date allowing agreement of postponement application	Reckonable date	Date payment made	Interest due £
1st instalment	10,000	1.1.91	7.2.91	7.2.91	9.2.91	2/365 × 10,000 × 11.5% = 6.30
2nd instalment	10,000	1.7.91	1.7.91	1.7.91	1.7.91	Nil
Balance	4,000	1.1.91/ 1.7.91	6.10.91	1.7.91	6.10.91	97/365 × 4,000 × 11.5% = 122.25
Total interest payable						128.55

The interest charged is *not* an allowable deduction for tax purposes. From 20 April 1988, interest is also charged on PAYE tax paid late to the Collector where liability is determined by an Inspector.

Certificates of tax deposit

Individuals and companies can purchase certificates from the Collector of Taxes in return for deposits to meet future tax liabilities. In this way they can protect themselves from a potential liability to interest on overdue tax. Interest on the certificates is paid gross by the Revenue and is taxable in the year of receipt. At the time of writing the minimum initial deposit is £2,000.

The deposit can be used to pay tax at any time, in which case the tax is treated as having been paid on the later of the normal due date or the date the deposit was made. The deposit can also be withdrawn at any time, but a higher interest rate applies to deposits used to pay tax.

Official error

Occasionally the Revenue may fail to assess or collect tax due. For example, a taxpayer submits a Tax Return showing rental earnings, but the tax office overlooks the entry and no assessment is issued. In law it is the *taxpayers' responsibility* to see to it that their tax affairs are in order and should the Revenue realize its error, it can recover the tax. It may be of some consolation to know that the Revenue will normally not pursue tax lost through official error back further than six years.

The Revenue recognizes that in certain cases recovering tax from earlier years following official error could cause hardship. The department may, therefore, write off tax lost. The write-off is geared to the taxpayer's current income or ability to pay and guidelines are occasionally published.

Repayment supplements

The Revenue pays interest where tax is repaid more than twelve months after the end of the tax year to which it relates to a UK resident individual or company, provided the tax repayment is more than £25. Known as a 'repayment supplement', it is calculated from the 'relevant time' to the end of the tax month in which the repayment is made. The 'relevant time' for Income Tax is the *later* of the following:

- The end of the tax year following the year to which the tax repayment relates.
- Where the tax payment was made by the taxpayer more than twelve months after the tax year to which it relates, the end of the tax year in which the payment was originally made.

Similar rules apply to companies. The interest rate is the same as that used for tax paid late, and the supplement is tax-free.

Value Added Tax

The Customs and Excise issue estimated VAT assessments where a VAT Return is not made on time. The taxpayer may then appeal against the assessment, the appeal being heard by the local VAT tribunal. VAT should be paid one month after the end of the tax period and interest and penalties are charged by the Customs and Excise for VAT paid late.

In the past, statutory payments of interest to taxpayers were limited to specific instances, for example on a successful appeal to a VAT tribunal, following a court order, or where VAT was wrongly paid on imported goods. However, in the interests of equity the Commissioners frequently made *ex gratia* payments representing interest where the taxpayer had suffered loss through departmental error.

In the 1991 Budget, the Chancellor announced the introduction of a statutory right to interest where as a result of departmental error too much VAT was paid, or underclaimed, or where the taxpayer was prevented from recovering VAT at the proper time.

Concluding comment

The purpose of this book has been to outline the essence of the UK tax system. Since taxation is exceedingly complex it should be appreciated, however, that this kind of book can be no more than an introduction to the subject. It is important to seek professional advice before embarking on any business venture which may have tax implications.

Mark Twain once distinguished the taxidermist and the tax collector by observing that 'the taxidermist takes only your skin'. It is easy to sympathize with Mark Twain. However, it is possible to preserve a little flesh through judicious tax planning. At the same time, it is easy for businesses to fall foul of the tax regulations resulting in a tax investigation. Tax investigations are expensive in managerial time, accountancy and legal fees, and in terms of the interest and penalties levied by the tax authorities. The best way of avoiding them is to stay within the law.

Index